INVENTIVE WEAVING *on a Little Loom*

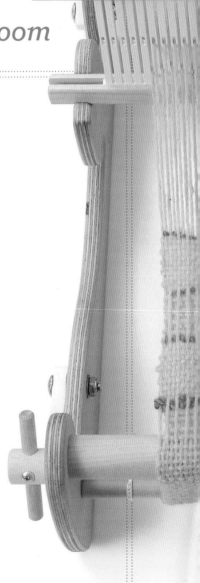

INVENTIVE WEAVING

on a *Little Loom*

Discover the Full Potential of the Rigid-Heddle Loom

FOR BEGINNERS AND BEYOND

Syne Mitchell

Storey Publishing

The mission of Storey Publishing is to serve our customers by
publishing practical information that encourages
personal independence in harmony with the environment.

Edited by Gwen Steege
Art direction and book design by Jessica Armstrong
Technical advice by Elisabeth Hill
Indexed by Nancy D. Wood

Cover photography by © John Polak
Interior photography by John Polak, except for © Ashford Handicrafts, Ltd., 18 (bottom left);
    Backstrap loom, Solola, Guatemala, 2005 (wood, cotton & dye), Guatemalan School,
    (20th century) / Collection of the Lowe Art Museum, University of Miami / Museum
    Purchase / Bridgeman Images, 15 (top); Courtesy of Craft in America, Jennifer Gerardi,
    115 (bottom); © DEA/G. DAGLI-ORTI/Getty Images, 11; © Harrisville Designs, 18 (top);
    © Ingetje Tadros/Getty Images, 14 (top right); © John Polak, 273; © Kromski N.A., 19
    (bottom); © magpiejst/iStockphoto.com, 14 (top left); Mars Vilaubi, 109 (top), 126, 199,
    211; © McClatchy DC/Getty Images, 14 (bottom right); © Michael Lichter, 15 (middle
    & bottom); © Ruth McLaughlin, 23; © Sami Sarkis/Getty Images, 14 (middle right);
    © Smithsonian American Art Museum, Washington, DC / Art Resource, NY, 115 (top);
    © Soren Lauridsen, 14 (bottom left); © Syne Mitchell, 242 (left)
Illustrations by Allegra Lockstadt
Charts and diagrams by Ilona Sherratt

© 2015 by Syne Mitchell

Storey Publishing
210 MASS MoCA Way
North Adams, MA 01247
www.storey.com

Printed in China by R.R. Donnelley
10 9 8 7 6 5 4

Library of Congress Cataloging-in-Publication Data
Mitchell, Syne, 1970–
  Inventive weaving on a little loom : discover the full potential of the Rigid-Heddle loom,
    for beginners and beyond / by Syne Mitchell.
    pages cm
  ISBN 978-1-60342-972-6 (pbk. : alk. paper)
  ISBN 978-1-60342-851-4 (ebook) 1. Hand weaving. 2. Handlooms. I. Title.
TT848.M587 2015
746.1'4—dc23
                            2015019702

DEDICATION

*For everyone whose heart beats a little
faster when they play with yarn.*

CONTENTS

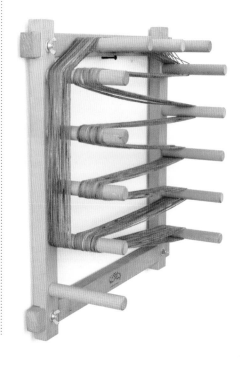

CHAPTER 1

Welcome to the WARP SIDE

WEAVING IS ONE OF THE OLDEST FIBER TECHNOLOGIES, with a history that stretches back to the dawn of civilization. Woven cloth is fragile and doesn't last as long as stone arrowheads, so samples of ancient weavings are rare, but tools and images of weavers crop up in archeological finds, and on rare occasions, a precious fragment of fabric surfaces. In 2009, a team led by two Harvard professors working in the Republic of Georgia uncovered the oldest remnant of woven cloth found thus far: a 34,000-year-old piece of linen.

Whether spinning predates weaving is a mystery. Did ancient peoples twist plant leaves into cordage first, or did they begin by weaving baskets out of flexible branches? My guess is that spinning and weaving grew up together: one village learned to weave baskets, another to spin, and groups exchanged skills with each other through trade and intermarriage. In any event, you are about to embark on a textile adventure that has kept humanity warm and protected for endless generations, one that provided baskets for carrying food and clothing to protect against the elements, and that created houses to live in and burial shrouds for the grave.

Fabric for a funeral cloak from pre-Inca culture in the sixth century B.C.E.

The Magic and Mystery of Weaving

THERE ARE TWO COMPONENTS IN WEAVING: warp threads and weft threads. The warp threads run lengthwise through the cloth, and the weft threads run side to side. During weaving, the warp threads are held on the loom under tension, and the weft is inserted ("thrown") by the weaver.

Cloth is created where warp and weft interlace. The mother of all weave structures is plain weave, also known as "over one, under one." This is the weave structure that many of us learned when we wove strips of colored paper together in kindergarten. But there are countless other ways to combine warp and weft. For example, by floating the weft over two threads in the warp you can create half basketweave. Or you can shift the threads so the floats move over by one each time you throw the shuttle and create a twill.

Now that you've got an idea of how cloth is made, you are only beginning to touch what I call the magic and mystery of weaving. Be careful! Many folks who try weaving get bitten by the weaving bug and soon find themselves weaving off warp after warp. I know because I'm one of them. What started as a class taken on a whim soon became an obsession that has guided and enriched my life in unexpected ways.

Why, in this age of big-box stores and cheap clothing do so many people weave? It's a question I ask myself regularly, and that I've asked other people who've made weaving their life's work or avocation. Answers vary, but it also comes down to the simple fact: weaving is fascinating.

My own reason for weaving is this: it makes my whole brain happy. There is analytical puzzle solving to delight my left hemisphere, and colors and textures galore to tickle my right. It's an art that can be as simple or as complex as you like. Three-year-olds can weave, but it's also an art form that's so rich and full of possibilities that you couldn't possibly learn it all in one lifetime.

Weaving is full of surprises, the way colors interact on the loom, for example. The tiny dots of warp and weft combine to create new, unanticipated colors. Even weavers with decades of experience can make new discoveries. The cloth changes when you take it off the loom's tension, and again after it's washed (known as wet-finishing). Something flat and lifeless on the loom might suddenly pucker into a deep waffle weave. It's this challenge and sense of discovery that keep me coming back to the loom. There's a profound sense of "what'll happen if...?"

On the other side of the spectrum, weaving can be therapeutic. Studies with stroke patients at the University of Maryland in Baltimore have shown that rhythmic, repetitive actions that alternate using your left and right hands improve how the two sides of your brain work together. I wove a simple plain-weave fabric while recovering from jaw surgery, and found it a soothing release from pain and worry. During World Wars I and II, army hospitals used weaving as occupational therapy to help injured soldiers recover. Many of those men went on to weave avocationally, spurring the weaving boom of the 1950s. From cloth woven in the dawn of civilization, to the woven T-164 Teflon fabric that protected Apollo astronauts on the moon, to the unimaginable future, weaving is an integral part of human civilization.

a) plain weave, b) Danish medallions, c) weft-dominant plain weave, d) point twill, e) log cabin, f) half basketweave, g) pile loop, h) shadow weave

Old and New Looms:
from Simple to Complex

THE FIRST QUESTION STUDENTS ASK ME in beginning classes is "Why is it called a rigid-heddle loom?" To answer it, you first need to understand what a heddle does. On any loom, heddles select the threads the loom raises or lowers to make an opening, or shed, for the shuttle to pass through. On a backstrap loom, heddles are usually created by string wrapped around a stick. In a shaft loom, heddles are usually either metal, string, or wire and are placed on shafts to make it easier to pick up complex patterns. On a rigid-heddle loom, the heddles have holes drilled in a rigid material (traditionally wood or bone, now more commonly plastic) that also acts as a warp spacer and beater. This, then, is the rigid heddle of a rigid-heddle loom. That the heddles (the patterning devices) are combined with the beater and reed (the spacing device) is the defining characteristic of a rigid-heddle loom.

Rigid-heddle looms have been found in archeological digs dating back to Roman times. The Museum of Antiquities of Newcastle University and Society of Antiquaries of Newcastle upon Tyne has in its collection a Roman rigid heddle that was made of bone slats bound together at the top and bottom with sheet bronze. One of the simpler looms to build (you can create one with wooden craft sticks and a bit of creativity), they have been, and continue to be, used all over the world.

← **OPPOSITE PAGE.** *Since weaving is so ancient and diverse, humankind has developed many types of looms to interlace threads: backstrap looms, rigid-heddle looms, multishaft looms, frame looms, tapestry looms, inkle looms, and more. Each one fills a particular need and is specialized to certain types of weaving. In this section, we'll take a closer look at the features of the rigid-heddle loom.*

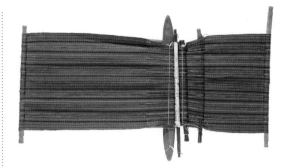

BACKSTRAP LOOM. *Warp threads are raised and lowered by heddles created with string wrapped around a stick or a pickup stick.*

SHAFT LOOM. *Schacht's Baby Wolf has metal heddles arranged in wooden frames (shafts) when raised or lowered by the attached treadles.*

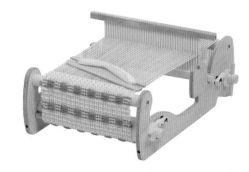

RIGID-HEDDLE LOOM. *The Schacht Cricket is a rigid-heddle loom, in which warp threads run through holes and slots in the heddle, which also serves as a beater.*

A QUICK TOUR OF THE RIGID-HEDDLE LOOM

▶ *Rigid-heddle looms come in all shapes and sizes, but there are features common to all.*

▶ **WARP BEAM.** The warp yarn is wound onto the warp beam to store it compactly during weaving.

▶ **BACK ROD.** This is how the warp is attached to the warp beam, usually by either looping it over the rod or tying it onto the rod. The strings that run from the warp beam to the warp rod should allow it to come close to the back of the heddle; this enables you to weave off more of the back of your warp.

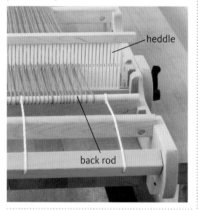

heddle

back rod

▶ **CLOTH BEAM.** As you weave, the cloth is rolled forward onto this beam for storage.

▶ **HEDDLE.** This is where the magic happens. The heddle raises or lowers to create a shed, or opening, for the shuttle to pass through. In this type of loom, it also acts as the beater, pressing the weft into place. The heddle has two components: slots and holes. You thread the warp through both the slots and holes, creating passive and active threads. When the heddle is raised, the hole (active) threads raise and the slot (passive) threads don't move. This creates an up shed for the shuttle to pass through. When the heddle is lowered the hole (active) threads lower and the slot (passive) threads don't move. This creates a down shed for the shuttle to pass through. In addition, the rigid heddle controls how closely the threads are spaced in the warp by how closely the holes and slots are positioned on the heddle. One heddle might have 12 threads per inch, another 8 threads per inch.

▶ **HEDDLE BLOCK.** The heddle block shape varies between loom manufacturers, but they all work the same way. There is an up position, which raises the heddle, and a down position, which lowers the heddle. Modern rigid-heddle looms typically also have a neutral position where the heddle is neither raised nor lowered.

▶ **BRAKE.** The brake is used to stop the warp from unrolling from the warp beam and to apply tension to the warp threads. Typically this is done with a dog-and-pawl gear system on both the warp beam and the cloth beam. Some older rigid-heddle looms, however, have other brake systems, such as tightening down a wing nut.

▶ **FRONT ROD.** This is how the warp is attached to the cloth beam, usually by tying on. The strings that run from the cloth beam to the front rod should allow it to come close to the front of the heddle; this enables you to weave off more of the front of your warp.

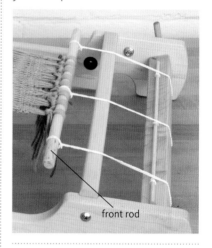

front rod

▶ **TABLE BRACE.** Most rigid-heddle looms have a way to brace the loom against a table to hold it steady during weaving. This can be either a cutaway or notch at the bottom back of the loom or extra feet on the back of the loom.

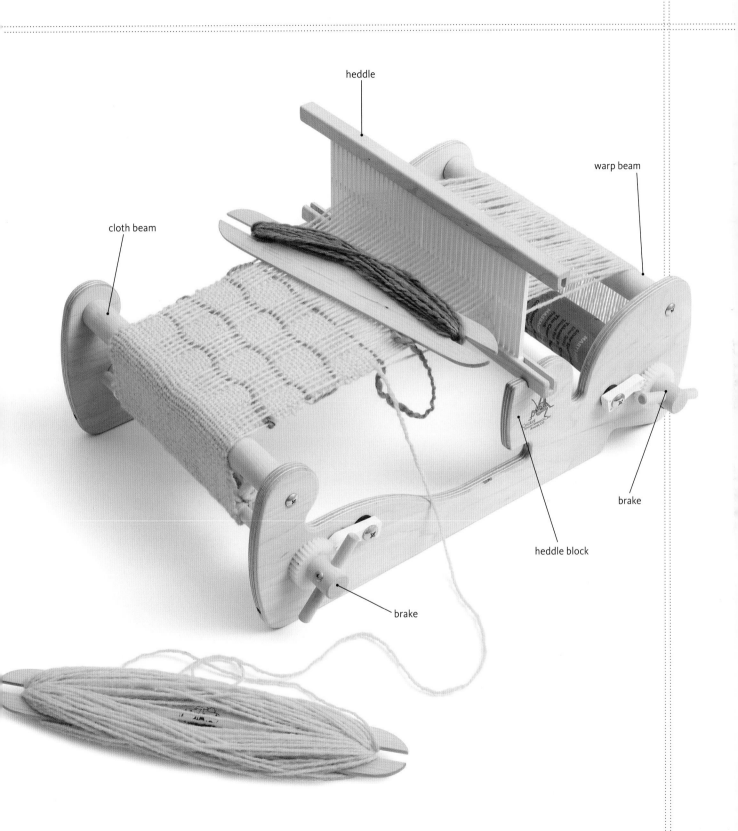

heddle

warp beam

cloth beam

brake

heddle block

brake

What Kind of Rigid-Heddle Loom Should I Buy?

THIS IS A QUESTION THAT I GET ASKED ALL THE TIME. The answer is: it depends. I've used several models of rigid-heddle looms in my classes, and they all have their pros and cons. People come in all shapes and sizes, and they weave in different ways, so the model of loom that's best for me might not be the model that's best for you. My advice is to test-drive a few looms and see what feels right. It's worth noting that although the Schacht Flip is the only rigid-heddle loom with a second heddle block built in, other companies offer second heddle blocks as add ons.

ASHFORD KNITTER'S LOOM. This was the first rigid-heddle loom to revitalize rigid-heddle weaving. It's a great lightweight travel loom. The plastic gears are surprisingly strong, and it holds good tension. The 12" model fits under the seat in front of you on an airplane. The downside to this loom is that the lightweight wood does have a tendency to dent. It's the trade-off for being lightweight, and doesn't affect the weaving at all. (Ashford also carries a wider loom.)

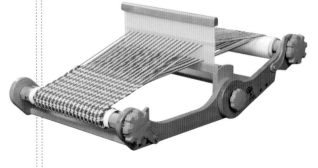

HARRISVILLE EASY WEAVER. Sold as kids' looms, pre-warped and ready for weaving, these are actually quite functional rigid-heddle looms. Their main limitation is their narrow weaving width.

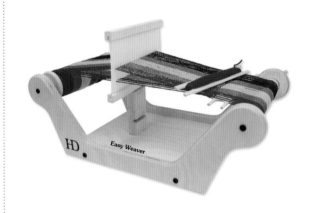

SCHACHT FLIP. This is my favorite loom for using multiple heddles during weaving because it's the only rigid-heddle loom with a second threading slot, which makes it easy to thread multiple heddles. I use the Flip as my teaching loom because they are bulletproof. I have four teaching looms that I've tossed in my car for years, banging them together, and they look as good as the day I first took them out of the box. They hold good tension, and the frames are sturdy and won't flex. The downside to the Flip? They're heavy compared to other looms.

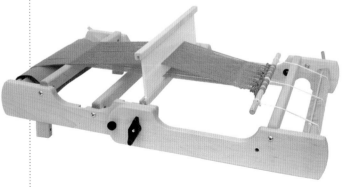

SCHACHT CRICKET. The Cricket is a tiny, nonfolding rigid-heddle loom. I believe it was first marketed to kids, but grownups found it sturdy and a low-cost way to get into weaving, and they snapped them up. The benefit of the Cricket is that it is small. You can weave during car trips (passenger side only!). I've fit one in my roll-on suitcase by putting it in first and packing clothes around it. The downside of the Cricket is that because of its small size, there's not much room behind the heddle for patterned pickup work.

GLIMAKRA EMILIA. The metal gears on this loom from the Swedish manufacturer Glimakra enable you to get a firm tension. Early versions had a pin placement that would cause the loom to fold during weaving if the tension was firm. The location of the pin was moved in subsequent versions.

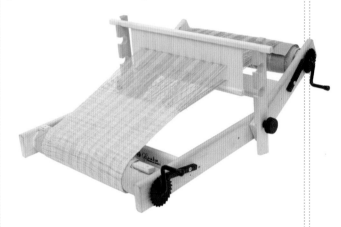

KROMSKI HARP FORTÉ. This loom incorporates a warping board into the back of the loom, which is nice to have but not as essential as when the loom first appeared, due to the popularity of the single-peg method of warping (see page 51). It's a beautiful rigid-heddle loom, with turned-wood components and a curved frame. On the downside, I find it a bit lightweight for the strong tension I like to weave with; the frame can flex. Older versions of this loom had issues with the brakes slipping during weaving, but this has been fixed in newer versions.

USED LOOMS

Rigid-heddle technology hasn't changed much over the years, so buying a used rigid-heddle loom can be a great deal. If you do, however, make sure that the frame is square (measure from the top left corner to the bottom right corner and compare that number to the measurement from the top right corner to the bottom left; they should be the same). In addition, check that the braking system works and will stand up to firm tension. The best situation, of course, is if you can weave a bit on the loom before purchasing it.

OTHER STUFF YOU NEED

▶ *In addition to the rigid-heddle loom, you'll need other tools before you can start weaving.*

▶ **SHUTTLES.** A shuttle contains and protects your weft during weaving. It is possible to weave without a shuttle by using yarn butterflies (page 63) or pushing balls of yarn through the shed, but you'll soon discover that the weaving process is hard on informal yarn packages, and that a shuttle of some sort is worth having. There are several types, and each has its strengths and weaknesses. Two of the most useful for rigid-heddle weaving are stick shuttles and boat shuttles, which are described, along with how to use them, on pages 65–67. Ski shuttles are another option, especially if you're using bulky yarn or fabric strips, but because of their size, they may be tricky to get through the narrow shed created during rigid-heddle weaving.

▶ **WARPING PEG OR WARPING BOARD.** Before you can put a warp on your loom, you need a way to measure out the warp yarn while keeping it under control. For this you can either use a warping peg (and the direct-peg method of warping, page 51) or a warping board (and the traditional method of warping, page 40) There are other tools that you can use, such as a warping reel and warping wheel, but since these would cost more than your loom, they're beyond the scope of this book. If you don't have a warping peg or a warping board, you can improvise. For example, an Irwin Quick-Grip clamp (readily available online and in hardware stores) turned upside down and affixed to a table makes an excellent warping peg, and, in a pinch, an overturned table can become a warping board.

▶ **FRINGE TWISTER.** Twisted fringe (page 91) is a decorative way to finish and protect the warp ends of a finished piece of cloth. You can create twisted fringe completely by hand, or use a mechanical or electric device to make the work go faster. My favorite fringe twister is electric-powered, sold as a hair braider (though it actually plies hair instead of braiding it). Lacis offers a similar electric fringe twister.

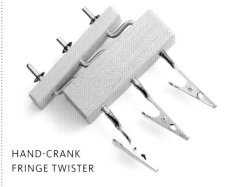

HAND-CRANK
FRINGE TWISTER

▶ **SCISSORS.** Scissors are handy to have in your weaving kit. I use a small pair of embroidery scissors to trim threads and a pair of sewing shears to cut the warp off the loom at the end of weaving. If you are cutting up paper bags to use as warp separators, use a third inexpensive pair, as paper quickly dulls the blades.

STICK SHUTTLE

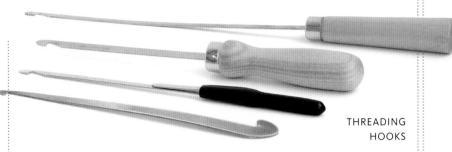

THREADING HOOKS

▶ **WARP SEPARATOR.** When you wind the warp onto the back beam, you need a way to keep each successive layer separate from the previous layers. This needs to be something rigid, such as heavyweight paper from a cut-open grocery bag, slats (one per turn of the back beam, staggered), or, my personal favorite, reed blinds or place mats cut to fit your warp beam. (For information on how to use warp separators, see page 56.)

▶ **NOTEBOOK AND PEN.** You'll want to keep notes of your weaving: things you've tried that worked, things you tried that didn't, things you'd like to try next as soon as you've woven off the warp on your loom. (You'd be surprised how many great ideas for the next warp come up while you're weaving.) Recordkeeping is one of the best ways to learn from your weaving experiences, and it comes in handy when your best friend says, "That scarf you wove me eight years ago, kinda blue and bumpy, it became my wooby-comfort scarf, I wore it every waking moment. . . . The new puppy just ate it, and I'm heartbroken. Can I please have another one exactly like it?"

▶ **TEXSOLV** is a useful cord that comes in many sizes and styles and can be used by weavers in many ways: fine weight for tapestry and inkle-loom heddles, medium to create string heddles, and heavy for tie-on cord.

▶ **THREADING HOOK.** This tool is used to pull the warp yarn through the slots and holes of the heddle. Modern rigid-heddle looms include a threading hook, but you can buy them from weaving supply stores or even make one out of a paper clip in a pinch. They come in different sizes and shapes, but most are fashioned out of flat metal with a hook cut in the end. Some have a large hook at one end (for the slots) and a small hook at the other end (for holes). Other types of hooks are actually flexible loops of wire that you push through and use like a giant needle threader.

The important thing to look for in a threading hook is whether it will fit through the holes on your smallest heddle; also make sure the hook is not so sharp that it will cut the warp threads as you pull them through the holes.

▶ **TAPESTRY NEEDLE.** Tapestry needles serve several purposes in weaving. You can use them to repair errors and skipped threads after the cloth is off the loom, for hemstitching (an edge-finish technique; see page 95), to darn in loose ends, to sew up seams, and even to embellish the finished cloth. The size you need depends on the yarn: you want a tapestry needle that you can easily thread with the yarn you're using, but one that won't leave holes in your cloth. A good guideline is a needle that is as wide (or thereabouts) as your yarn doubled. The following table lists some recommended needle sizes for some popular yarn weights.

RECOMMENDED NEEDLE SIZES

TAPESTRY NEEDLE SIZE	YARN WEIGHT
13	Worsted (1,000 yards per pound)
18	Sock yarn (2,000 yards per pound)
20	10/2 cotton (4,200 yards per pound)

NEEDLES

INTUITIVE VS. ANALYTICAL WEAVING

All weavers have a brain with a right half and a left half. This means that all weavers are both intuitive and analytical, though the art of an individual weaver often expresses one side more than the other.

ANALYTIC WEAVERS are the scientists of the weaving world, approaching each project as a chance to learn more about how threads fit together. They research and plan; often you'll find them gleefully playing with weaving software, coming up with intricate patterns or color combinations. Often their early projects are successful, and they keep notes of what they liked or didn't like about each one. If they persist, they are the ones who weave projects that make you ask, "How did you *do* that?" And they'll smile, because they know.

Neither intuitive nor analytic weaving is better than the other, because science and art are two sides of the same coin — both are creative, both seek to explore the world around them and define it in new ways. Every weaver uses a bit of both.

INTUITIVE WEAVERS approach weaving as a grand adventure, playing with projects, throwing things together on a whim, and weaving them up just to see what will happen. Intuitive weavers tend to have more absolute disasters early in their career. If they persist, however, they're often the weavers whose work seems absolutely magical, though often they can't express exactly why or how they chose that color combination or knew that weave structure would wet-finish in exactly that wonderful way.

As you go through this book, you'll see that some strategies are intuitive and others are analytic. Try the one that resonates most with you. And then, I'd encourage you to try things the other way around as well. Play in both sides of your brain.

Get Set to
WEAVE

ONE OF THE WONDERFUL THINGS ABOUT WEAVING is how easy it is to create your own designs. With just a few simple techniques, you can pull yarns from your stash to make custom creations, or wander a yarn store confident that selections in your basket will be enough yardage of the right kind of yarn for your next project.

The first thing you'll need is some idea of what you want to weave. Do you want a soft, drapey scarf? An absorbent dish towel? Gauzy curtains? Super-sturdy fabric for a bag or upholstery? The materials and methods for each one of these differ; you have to know your final destination before you can map your way there.

Most often, what you'll weave on a rigid-heddle loom is yarn: thick yarn, skinny yarn, fuzzy yarn, smooth yarn. But we'll see in later chapters that you can also weave nontraditional materials such as fabric strips, paper, metal wire, and even plants from your garden. For the moment, however, let's talk about yarn. It's good to know the basics before you experiment with the wild stuff.

Choosing Yarn

WARP AND WEFT ARE THE MOST IMPORTANT PART OF THE WEAVING PROCESS. You can weave without a loom, but you can't weave without yarn (or other suitable materials). The warp is what you put onto the loom. The weft is what you put on a shuttle and throw through the weaving shed. When you look at cloth with the selvedges on the right and left, the warp threads run vertically and the weft threads horizontally.

Because the warp and weft yarns are what cloth is made of, it follows that you have to select yarns that have the same properties as the cloth you want to weave. There is no technique or weave structure that will let you make a next-to-the-skin soft scarf out of a wiry rug yarn. Pick yarns that already embody the qualities you want in your cloth. Want a soft and cushy scarf? Worsted-spun Merino wool is a great choice. A hard-wearing and absorbent dish towel? Put down the Merino and embrace cotton or linen. Become a fabric detective, and look at the cloth around you. You can learn much from the fiber choices of industry.

Planning and Weaving a Sample Scarf

In the pages that follow, I describe what you need to consider for your first weaving project, as well as instruction on how to wind a warp, thread the loom, and get started weaving. So that you can practice as you read, I suggest that you obtain a skein of worsted-weight yarn similar to what we used for this beginning project, with approximately 110 yards in 50 grams, and warp your loom and weave along as you read, section by section. By the time you get to the end of the chapter, you'll have woven a scarf, with a final measurement of 8" × 72".

Warp yarns (from left to right): Tencel, 10/2 pearl cotton, 3/2 pearl cotton, worsted-weight wool, silk

What Makes a Good Warp Yarn?

There are urban legends floating around about what you can use to warp a loom. You'll hear people say you can't warp with handspun, or singles yarn (yarn with only one ply), or fuzzy yarns, or yarns that stretch, or yarns that are completely inelastic, or yarns that snap if you tug them hard between your hands, which is frankly damn nonsense — I've woven with all those yarns as warp. If you can get it on your loom and open a shed, you can weave it. What is true is this: an easy and reliable warp yarn is strong and smooth, and has some give and a balanced twist. Read on for what all of this means.

» **STRONG.** Strong warp threads will not break during the abuse that is weaving. You can put them under too-tight tension, abrade them with the heddle, hit them accidentally with your shuttle, and they hold together. The stronger your warp yarns, the easier your weaving will be.

One common test of a potential warp yarn's strength is the snap test. Grab either end of a section of yarn and snap your hands apart sharply. If the warp yarn survives, it'll be strong enough to weave easily. An even more important test is the drift test. Take one end of the proposed warp in each hand and apply even, slow, tension. If the yarn stretches and then stops, it's a good warp yarn. If it stretches and keeps stretching to the point that it pulls apart, use it as weft. Do not wind a warp with a yarn that drifts apart: heartache and madness will ensue.

» **SMOOTH.** Smooth warp yarns, such as cotton, silk, or worsted-spun wool, slip past each other easily when you open the shed. This makes them more forgiving if you thread them too close together on the loom.

» **SOME GIVE.** Getting even tension over the warp threads is one of the most important things to accomplish when you're setting up your loom. A warp thread that has some give will self-tension to a certain degree and make up for small tension irregularities you've introduced. Too much give, on the other hand, can make for a fabric that seems to weave well on the loom but shortens dramatically when you take it off tension and the warp relaxes. If it shortens too much, there may not be room for the weft in the cloth and it will ripple and wave. (Of course, this can be a lot of fun if it's the effect you're striving for.)

» **BALANCED TWIST.** To be a knowledgeable weaver, you have to understand yarn construction. Yarn is the stuff cloth is made of, after all. Nearly all yarn is created by taking short fibers, staggering their lengths, and twisting them together to make a long, continuous yarn. (The exceptions to this yarn structure are extruded yarns, such as synthetic polymer yarns, and reeled silk.) This creates a singles yarn that, because all the fibers are twisted in the same direction, has a certain amount of potential energy. If you took it into space and let it go in midair, it would untwist until it was again a poof of fluff. Back on earth, if you tried to wind a warp with it and let go for an instant, it would kink and knot back on itself in a nearly insoluble tangle. To take away the pent-up energy of the singles yarn, spinners ply two singles together in the direction opposite from the way the singles were spun. This balances the twist to create a yarn that can safely be left alone on a table without snarling.

A demonstration of stretch. *To figure out how much stretch is ideal for an easy warp, I performed a stretch test on some common warp yarns. I measured out a yard of four different warp yarns, tied them together in an overhand knot at one end, slid the knot over a hook, then applied a standard warp tension as evenly as possible to all four to see how much they stretched. I threw the linen into the test to show you what to expect from an inelastic warp. Linen is commonly considered a tricky warp yarn because of its unforgiving inelasticity. Fibers (from left to right): linen, silk, cotton, wool*

Examples of twist. *The yarn on the left is a singles; two strands of it plied together were used to make the 2-ply yarn at the right.*

What Makes a Good Weft Yarn?

Weft yarns live a pretty soft life. The requirements for them are much more forgiving than for warp yarns because they're not under tension, so they don't have to be as strong or as smooth as warp yarns. Unabused by the weaving process, they just hang out on the shuttle until it's their turn to go into the shed: all they need to do is fit through it and hold together long enough to be locked into place by the warp. If they're a bit weak and fragile, the strong warp is there to hold them together. In addition to fitting through the shed, however, an easy and reliable weft yarn is also flexible enough to turn easily at the selvedges.

Although the weft is playing a lesser role in the strength of the fabric, it still lends its qualities to the finished cloth, so pick a weft that complements your warp. Crossing a silk warp with wiry wool yarn will not make the lusciously soft fabric you're wishing for. (That scarf would likely outlive you, however, not only because of its strength, but also because no one would ever wear it.)

Flexible wefts are the norm, but as you will see in chapter 7, you can even weave with completely inflexible wefts.

CONSIDERATIONS FOR BOTH WARP AND WEFT YARNS

SOFTNESS. Is it important that the finished cloth be soft? If you're planning to wear the garment next to your skin, the answer is likely to be yes. If you're weaving cloth for a purse or a rug, this is less important.

SIZE OR THICKNESS. Do you want to weave a fine cloth? Then you'll need to select thin yarns. Want a thick, lofty fabric? Select thick yarns.

STRENGTH. Usually softness and strength are a trade-off: the softer the yarn, the weaker it is. Silk and many synthetic fibers are an exception to this.

DRAPE. Is the yarn flexible? If so, it'll contribute to the flexible hand of the finished fabric. Silk has a lot of drape, whereas linen (until it's been used a lot) does not.

ABSORBENCY. Does the finished textile need to absorb water (as in a towel) or should it be water repellent (if you are weaving outerwear)?

THERMAL INSULATION. Are you weaving winter clothing? If so, then how well a yarn holds heat is important. Silk and lofty woolen yarns provide great insulation. Cotton and rayons do not.

CONDUCTIVITY. This is typically important only if you are weaving eTextile applications.

Planning Your Width and Length

Things on the loom are not as large as they appear! Aspects of weaving such as loom waste, draw-in, and take-up each affect the finished size of your project. If you don't take them into account when planning a project, your finished cloth will be smaller than you intended.

Loom Waste

Loom waste is the simplest to understand. This is the section of warp at the beginning and end that you can't weave, either because it's used to knot the warp onto the loom or because it stays behind the heddle. The amount of loom waste is dependent on the type of loom and the technique you use to attach the warp to the loom. One of the benefits of weaving on a rigid-heddle loom is it generates very little loom waste. Whereas a standard floor loom might have a loom waste of a yard or more, the loom waste on a rigid-heddle loom is typically less than 12".

There are ways to minimize loom waste, such as tying on with shoelaces. In fact it can be a fun weaver's game to see how little loom waste you can produce. Minimizing loom waste is also useful when you're weaving with yarn that is precious (your son's first handspun) or expensive (qiviut).

To calculate loom waste, weave a sample project — one where length isn't critical. Use your favorite method for attaching the warp to the loom. When you are done, cut the cloth off the loom

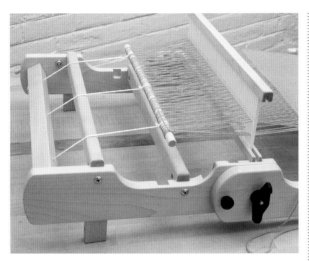

Loom waste. *The warp left unwoven at the end of your project, both in front of and behind the heddle, is the loom waste.*

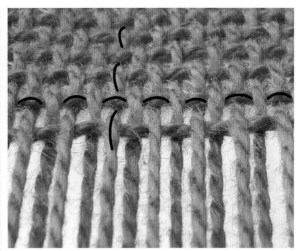

Deflection. *This close-up of a weaving in progress shows how both warp and weft threads bend over and under one another.*

and measure the amount of unwoven warp. That is your loom waste.

For projects such as a scarf or table runner, the loom waste may become part of the project as fringe and not be wasted at all. For other projects, such as garment fabric, you may choose to add extra length to your warp to counteract the length lost to loom waste.

Take-Up

Cloth isn't two-dimensional. If you look closely at the structure of woven cloth, you'll see the warp threads don't lie straight. They bend over and under the weft threads. This up-and-down deflection uses up some of the length of the warp, causing the length of the finished object to be shorter than the original warp. This quality is called take-up.

The take-up of the cloth is affected by several things. The bigger your weft threads, the farther the warp has to travel to climb over and under them and the bigger the resulting take-up. Structure also affects take-up. Plain weave, having the most intersections, produces the largest amount of take-up.

What can you do about take-up? Nothing. It's part of the physics of weaving. The only solutions are to estimate or sample what the take-up will be, and

then add additional length to the warp to cover it. (Or, if you're a happy-go-lucky weaver, put more warp on than you need, or promote the short scarf as the coming thing.)

Draw-In

As you weave, you'll likely notice that the sides of your cloth are narrower than the width of the warp in the heddle. This is draw-in. Like take-up, it is caused by the fact that the weft doesn't lie straight in the cloth. It has to bend over and under the warp threads. If you look closely at cloth, you'll see it's an interlocking mesh of undulating yarns, not a grid of rigid rods. This deflection uses up some of the length of the weft and causes the fabric to draw closer together in the cloth than it is in the heddle. Too much draw-in can strain the selvedge threads and cause them to break.

You can work against draw-in by either putting more weft into the shed when weaving (page 36) or using a temple (page 83). Moderate draw-in isn't a problem for most projects, however, and in fact if you work to have no draw-in at all, you may create another problem for yourself. If the warp threads on the selvedge don't weave up and down like the rest of the warp, the majority of the warp is experiencing take-up, while the selvedge threads are not. Since the selvedge threads aren't being used up as fast as the warp threads in the body of the fabric, they will become loose compared to the rest of the warp, and the weft at the edges will creep down and begin to "frown" in those low-tension areas. (For more about frowning warps and how to fix them, see page 79.)

So, what to do about draw-in? Make sure that you're adding enough additional weft when you weave so there is minimal draw-in. The amount of draw-in that's acceptable in a project depends on the yarn and weave structure. The best way to counteract it is to weave a sample, figure out the percentage of width lost to draw-in, and then make your warp wider by that percentage. (For a photo and more advice about how to avoid draw-in, see page 75.)

Wet-Finishing and Shrinkage

Another factor that can cause your fabric to be smaller when taken off the loom is wet-finishing (washing, see page 101) and shrinkage. When your fabric is on the loom, it's under tension. This means that it's being stretched out longer and skinnier than it would be if it was just fabric lying on a table. When you take it off tension, the fabric "schlurps" together.

You will be able to picture this effect if you've ever knit lace. You know how knitted lace looks like a random pile of yarn until you stretch it out and the pattern suddenly appears? Taking a project off the loom is like the opposite of blocking lace. In weaving, the fabric is effectively blocked while it's on the loom and then collapses a bit when you take it off. When removed from tension, the cloth draws together, causing it to shorten and often grow narrower (though in some cases it can grow wider off the loom, depending on the physics of the warp and weft).

The fabric relaxes even further once it's washed. The water fluffs up the fibers and makes it possible for them to move around in the fabric, reducing the dimensions more and sometimes even creating special effects.

In addition, there can be additional shrinkage from the fiber itself. Some yarns shrink when washed, especially if washed in hot water: wool in particular is known for this. If you wash a non-superwash wool in hot water with soap and agitation, it will shrink dramatically due to fulling and felting (see page 134).

Getting It Right

Given that there are several factors working against your cloth to make it smaller once it's off the loom, how on earth can you weave a perfect 20" by 28" tea towel? The answer is you have to know how much your project is going to shrink and add back in that much more width and length in the warp.

For example, if you know that a given cotton fabric will shrink 10 percent in length and 5 percent in width after it's off the loom and washed, then you'd have to weave a cloth that is 110 percent as long as you want, and 105 percent as wide. So, to end up with a 20" wide by 28" long tea towel, you'd need to weave a cloth 21" wide and 30.8" long. If you're planning a double-fold hem (see page 100), you'll have to add extra length for that as well.

That's all well and good, but how can you know precisely what the shrinkage will be of a cloth you haven't woven yet? The short answer: you can't. The only way to be absolutely certain what the shrinkage will be is to weave the cloth, take it off the loom, and wet-finish it. Then compare the measurements of the cloth on the loom with those after washing. Of course, few folks are willing to weave a set of under-size dish towels just so they can then weave a set of full-size ones. So what's a weaver to do? Cheat. See Guesstimating Shrinkage on the facing page for some strategies.

GUESSTIMATING SHRINKAGE

▶ **STRATEGY 1: DECIDE YOU DON'T CARE.** Many projects will work even if the size is slightly off. Does it matter whether that scarf is 9" or 8½" wide? Probably not. If you can stand losing a bit of the dimension and still have the item work, you can choose not to care about shrinkage.

▶ **STRATEGY 2: FIND A PUBLISHED PROJECT** where someone has already woven the item and measured the shrinkage. Weave exactly the same thing, with exactly the same yarn. The first limitation here is obvious: What if you can't find a pattern that's exactly what you want to weave? And what if you can't find that exact same yarn? If you only weave following someone else's strict recipe, you'll miss out on a lot of the adventure and artistry of weaving. Not only that, but even if you are happy following in another's footsteps, you might still find that your shrinkage is different from theirs. Factors such as the amount of tension on the warp, how tightly the weaver packed the weft into place, whether the weaver used a temple (page 83), and local humidity can all affect shrinkage. So even if you follow the directions exactly you may still end up with a different result.

▶ **STRATEGY 3: ADD 10 PERCENT TO EVERYTHING.** This is an amalgamation of strategies 1 and 2. If you look at a lot of rigid-heddle projects (such as the ones in this book), you'll see that the average shrinkage is around 10 percent most of the time. If you don't care too much about the final size, adding 10 percent is not a bad first guess. (One caveat: some weave structures and some yarns will shrink a lot more than 10 percent, so this method can lead to . . . surprises.)

▶ **STRATEGY 4: MAKE A SMALL SAMPLE.** Many weavers who want accurate information about the fabric they're going to end up with put a small sample warp on to test-drive the project without committing a lot of yarn. The problem is that a 2" wide warp weaves differently than a 12" wide warp, even if the yarn, loom, weaver, and weave structure are the same. The reason is two-fold. First, in a narrow warp the selvedge (edges) form a greater percentage of the cloth. Selvedges draw together tighter than the center of the warp, so when they form a larger percentage of the cloth, the overall cloth is more tightly packed, which means a denser feel and less shrinkage. The second factor is that a narrow fabric interacts with the beater differently than a wider fabric. There's less friction. So, weaving a small sample is good, but know that small samples can lie.

▶ **STRATEGY 5: MAKE A FULL-SIZE SAMPLE.** Hey wait! Isn't this what we were trying to avoid? Well, yes — and no. We want the accuracy of the full-size sample without having to weave the project twice. Here's how to do that: make your best guess as to what shrinkage is going to be (option 3), plan your project accordingly, and then add 1 to 2 extra yards to the warp. You'll use this extra yardage to weave a sample, cut it off, and then wash that sample to determine the actual shrinkage. Then you can add or remove warp threads from the project, until you get just the right amount to counteract your shrinkage. Not only do you get a full-size sample without having to weave it twice, you even saved having to wrap it twice, as in strategy 4.

▶ **IN MY OWN WEAVING, I TEND TO BOUNCE AROUND** between strategies 1, 3, and 5, depending on how precisely I need to hit the project's desired size.

How Structure Affects Outcomes

The structure you choose to weave has a big impact on the finished fabric. The way threads interlace and interact affects the fabric's drape, loft, and shrinkage. It may also change the way the fabric needs to be sett. Like the scarf we're planning here, many projects woven on a rigid-heddle loom are woven in plain weave, but that's not the only option. For more structural choices, see chapters 5–7. When planning a project, you should understand how the structure will affect the fabric.

The best way to learn about a structure is to play with it. Weave samples without any goal other than learning how the structure works. If you weave samples in the yarn you intend to use for your project, you will also get information about the fabric's draw-in and shrinkage after washing.

WAFFLE WEAVE

Structure and width. If you choose to weave your woolen shawl in waffle weave without understanding that waffle weave can have a draw-in of 30 percent, you might be disappointed to discover that your finished "shawl" is only 7" wide!

OH, WHERE SHALL I PUT MY FACE?

"Face" is a weaverly term that refers to whether the warp or weft dominates the fabric.

A warp-dominant fabric is one where you see more of the warp threads than the weft threads on the surface of the fabric. In a completely warp-faced fabric, the warp threads entirely cover the weft threads, and you see the weft only at the selvedges.

Similarly, a weft-dominant fabric is one where you see more of the weft than the warp as you look at the fabric. An example of a completely weft-faced fabric is tapestry, in which the beautiful designs created by the weft threads completely cover the warp.

A balanced fabric is one in which you see equal amounts of the warp and weft on the surface of the fabric. A fabric with more warp ends per inch (epi) than weft picks per inch (ppi) is likely to be warp-faced, and a fabric with fewer warp epi than weft ppi is likely to be weft-faced, though weave structure also plays a part. (See also Say What?, page 34.)

The three fabric examples here illustrate weft-faced, warp-faced, and balanced weave structures. In tapestry weaving (top left), the weft completely covers the warp. In the pick-up patterning seen in traditional Andean weaving, such as this narrow band (bottom left), the warp completely covers the weft. (Warp-faced fabric is difficult to weave on a rigid-heddle loom, but you can use the loom as a frame to hold the warp, without threading it through a heddle.) In a balanced weave, warp and weft are equally visible (above).

Sett for Success

Sett describes the number of warp threads in an inch when the loom is warped. If you count the number of holes and slots in an inch on a rigid-heddle, this gives you the default sett for that heddle. (Most modern heddles have this number printed somewhere on the plastic.) The more threads per inch that you have in your warp, the denser the finished fabric will be. Fabric density is one of the tools you have to build the fabric of your dreams. For a thicker, more durable fabric, set your warp tighter (more threads per inch). For a more flexible, thinner fabric, set it looser (fewer threads per inch). Because the heddle we're using here has 4 holes and 4 slots per inch, our sett is 8 ends per inch.

Sett can also affect how easily a warp weaves up. If you set the warp too close together, the warp threads will rub against each other and abrade until tiny little fibers stick out from the warp threads and stick to each other when you try to open a shed. Even if you are able to weave off a too closely sett warp, you might find yourself creating the first Merino-silk trivet, instead of weaving a soft scarf. On the other hand, if you set the warp too open, it's easy to accidentally create skips and floats in your cloth. The finished cloth might not hold together well enough for your intended purpose; warp and weft threads may slide out of position.

It's interesting to note that some projects use setts outside the so-called normal range. Some examples of when you might encounter this are if you're felting (page 134), playing with differential shrinkage, cramming or spacing a group of warp threads, or using both thick and thin

Top: The thin cotton warp threads are completely covered by the rayon chenille weft, creating a velvety, weft-dominant fabric.
Bottom: The use of both thick and thin warp threads brings textural interest to this plain-weave fabric.
Below: An 8-dent heddle is warped with a sett of 8 ends per inch.

SETT CHART

The following setts are guidelines for weaving plain-weave fabric of a moderate density. If you want a fabric that is dense or airy, you'll need to adjust the sett up or down, accordingly. If you are weaving a twill fabric, you'll want to use a sett that is approximately 20 percent denser than the plain-weave sett. Other variables that might make you want to try a different sett for your fabric include the weft you use, irregularities in the thickness of the warp, or a fuzzy warp. When in doubt, weave a sample.

KNITTING YARNS

Super Bulky	5 ends per inch
Bulky	6 ends per inch
Worsted	8 ends per inch
DK	10 ends per inch
Sport	12 ends per inch
Fingering	12 ends per inch
Lace	20 ends per inch (two 10-dent heddles)

WEAVING YARNS

3/2 cotton	12 ends per inch
10/2 linen	20 ends per inch (two 10-dent heddles)
10/2 cotton	24 ends per inch (two 12-dent heddles)
20/2 linen	24 ends per inch (two 12-dent heddles)
20/2 cotton or silk	36 ends per inch (three 12-dent heddles)
120/2 silk	144 ends per inch (6 threads in each hole and space of two 12-dent heddles)

threads in the same warp. This is why sampling is so fun; you can discover intriguing fabrics when you push the envelope.

So, if sett can be too close, and sett can be too open, how do you know what sett to use for a given yarn? This is the question that weavers ask themselves at the beginning of every project, and there are several ways to get the answer.

SAY WHAT?

Weaving has its own terminology, which can be confusing until you learn what things mean. In this section, some terms to know are epi (ends per inch), which is the number of warp threads in one inch of warp width when the warp is on the loom, and ppi (picks per inch), which is the number of weft threads per inch of cloth length when the cloth is on the loom.

Together the epi and ppi define how densely woven the fabric is, and these factors vary depending on the thickness of the threads you're using for warp and weft. You'll see these terms used in the projects you'll find later in the book.

If you see a sentence about *sleying* fear not: it simply means the act of pulling a thread through the rigid heddle; no humans (or vampires) will be harmed.

WRAPS PER INCH. One method for estimating an initial sett is to wrap the yarn around a ruler until you've covered an inch or two of its length. Then count the wraps per inch, divide that number by two, and use that as a starting plain-weave sett. It's not a bad strategy, and I've used it with some success. The thing to be aware of when using wraps per inch to estimate sett is that you can vary the wraps per inch depending on how tightly you pull and pack the yarn. It's a simple method, but not very precise.

ASK SOMEONE. This method is the fastest way to get started weaving when you have to weave a project right now and don't have the extra yarn or time to bother with experimenting. Simply find someone who's woven with the yarn and weave structure you intend to use and ask them their sett and how it turned out. This is one reason that belonging to a guild of fellow weavers is valuable: you can share the work of experimenting with new yarns.

If you don't have weaving buddies to ask about sett, refer to the chart on the opposite page for guidelines for some commonly used yarns, or go to one of the following resources for further information.

» Most introductory weaving books have a sett chart reference for common yarns.

» Published projects in sources like *WeaveZine*, *Weaver's Craft*, and *Handwoven* magazines include sett information.

» Online references, including *Handwoven* magazine's Master Yarn Chart, All Fiber Arts, and the New York Guild of Handweavers, provide sett information.

» Online retailers, such as WEBS, Halcyon Yarn, and Yarn Barn of Kansas, often list suggested setts for the weaving yarns they sell.

» Ask fellow weavers online through websites such as weaving Yahoo groups, Weavolution, and Warped Weavers on Ravelry.

(For web addresses for all of the above, see the appendix, pages 283-85.)

The downside is that if you consult an outside resource (such as a book or fellow weaver) you may find that your results differ from theirs because the yarn, your loom, the way you weave, your weave structure, or the humidity in your house, differs from theirs. When looking up sett, I often consult several sources and take the most common suggestion. Even then, I consider that only a starting point. If the cloth is not turning out how I'd like, I change the sett in the middle of a project. (For more about that, see Fabric That's Too Dense or Too Loose, page 83.)

EXPERIMENT. There is no better teacher than the loom. If you keep records of your experiments, soon you'll have your own custom weaving reference, completely accurate for you and your loom. I keep records of everything I weave in a notebook beside my loom where I jot details about what I'm doing, changes to my original plan, and ideas for future exploration. Often I learn the most from my disasters, and sometimes they pave the way to innovation. (For a sample of the form I use for recordkeeping, see Yarn Requirements, page 39.)

A fun way to try out several alternate setts is to weave a sample, cut it off the loom, and re-thread the yarn onto a new heddle with a different sett to weave another sample. In this manner you can try out several setts and only wind the warp onto the loom once.

How Much Warp?

Once you know your finished dimensions, shrinkage, loom waste, and sett, you are ready to precisely calculate the length of warp to wind for your scarf. We want the scarf we're using as an example here to be 8" wide and 72" long, with 8" long fringes at either end that we'll twist into a shorter plied fringe later. The yarn we're using is a worsted-weight yarn set at 8 ends per inch. We've sampled and know that we'll have 12" of loom waste, 10 percent draw-in, and 15 percent take-up after the cloth is washed. I'll walk you through a series of equations as an example of how this works.

» **ALLOW FOR DRAW-IN.** The first step is to figure out the width you need to weave so that, after draw-in and shrinkage, your textile will be the correct size. You know that the yarn you're using for your 8" wide scarf shrinks 10 percent (0.1 as a decimal), so you learn that you need to make your warp 8.9" wide to have the finished fabric end up 8" wide. To make threading easier, I rounded this up to 9".

(finished width) ÷ (1–[draw-in as a decimal])
= (width in the heddle)

8" ÷ (1 − 0.10) = 8.9"

» **ALLOW FOR TAKE-UP.** A similar equation works when applied to the length. Say that our sampling had shown a 15 percent take-up in length, and we want a finished length of 72". You learn that you need to weave 84.7" on the loom to end up with a textile 72" long.

(finished length) ÷ (1–[take-up as a decimal])
= (length to weave)

72" ÷ (1 − 0.15) = 84.7"

» **ALLOW FOR FRINGE (OR HEMS).** Because we want an 8" fringe at each end, we add this to the length without accounting for take-up because the fringe isn't woven and thus doesn't experience take-up. (If your project will have fringe at both ends, remember to add twice the length of the fringe to the length of the fabric on the loom; the same goes for fabric needed to turn a hem.)

(dimension to weave) + (2 × [fringe length])
= (length of fabric on the loom)

84.7" + (2 × 8") = 100.7"

» **HOW LONG A WARP TO WIND.** Keeping in mind how long your fabric needs to be on the loom and your loom-waste length, you're ready to calculate the warp length. Divide this value by 36 (the number of inches in a yard) to get the minimum length in yards.

(length of fabric on the loom) + (loom waste)
= (minimum warp length)

100.7" + 12" = 112.7"

112.7" ÷ 36"/1 yard = 3.13 yards

» **IF YOU'RE USING A WARPING BOARD** (page 40). Warping boards are usually calibrated in yards. In this case, you have three options: round down to 3 yards (and make the project 4.68" shorter, either in the cloth or the fringe), play around with a measuring tape and different paths around the pegs until you find something close to 3.13 yards, or round up to 4 yards and use the extra warp for experimenting and sampling.

» **IF YOU'RE USING THE DIRECT-PEG METHOD** (page 51). With a warping peg, you can be precise about the length of your warp by simply setting the peg at the right distance from the loom. When you do this, however, make sure you measure from the back rod to the peg, as this is the path the warp will travel. Even with a warping peg, however, you might want to give yourself a bit of extra warp to experiment with. I often audition different wefts to see if there's anything better than the one I had planned. One of the fun things about weaving is discovering surprises at the loom.

» **AND NOW, THE GRAND TOTAL.** Now that we have the sett, length, and width of our warp, we are ready to calculate the total amount of warp yarn needed for the project. First, find the number of warp threads by multiplying the width by the sett. Then, multiply the number of threads by the length of each thread. This gives you the total amount of warp yarn required for the project. The example below shows the result with the length of the warp rounded down to 3 yards. For the sample scarf, you'll need about two 50-gram skeins of yarn (110 yards per 50-gram skein) for the warp.

(width in heddle) × (sett) = (number of warp ends)

9" × (8 warp ends/inch) = 72 warp ends

(number of warp ends) × (warp length)
= (total amount of warp)

(72 ends) × (3 yards) = 216 yards of warp required

OTHER CONSIDERATIONS

▶ **A LESS WASTEFUL LOOM.** If you are finishing your project with fringe, your loom waste (see page 28) can become fringe. So in this example, since you have loom waste of 12", we probably needed to add only 4" for the fringe in the preceding step instead of 16". This, however, assumes that your loom waste is evenly split between the front and back of the loom. The safer option is to proceed as we have here, adding both the amount needed for loom waste and fringe.

▶ **STRIPES AND OTHER REPEATS.** If you are winding a warp with a stripe or structural repeat every so many threads, you may have to make the warp width a little wider or a little narrower to adjust to the weave patterning and avoid having partial repeats in your fabric.

Note that in this symmetrical design the stripe pattern is centered on the scarf.

How Much Weft?

Calculating the weft works in much the same way as the warp calculation. Instead of sett, you use the ppi (picks of weft per inch of woven fabric). Sampling will give you the exact ppi, or, if you are working with a balanced-weave structure, you can approximate ppi using the same number that you used for sett.

» **TOTAL WEFT PICKS.** The woven length multiplied by ppi gives you the number of weft picks, which is the number of weft threads in the cloth. (Since we are weaving a balanced plain weave for the scarf, we will approximate the ppi by using the sett figure. Note that you use the woven length, not the warp length, for this calculation.)

(woven length) × (ppi) = (number of weft picks)

(84.7") × (8 weft picks/inch) = 677.6 weft picks

» **TOTAL WEFT AMOUNT.** The number of weft picks multiplied by the length to be woven is the total amount of weft needed. Note that neither the amount of loom waste nor fringe is included, because no weft is used in them. Since you don't weave partial picks, round the number of picks up.

(number of weft picks) × (width in heddle) = (total amount of weft)

(678 weft picks) × 9" = 6,102"

Convert the number of inches to yards by dividing by 36:

(6,102" of weft) ÷ 36 = 169.5 yards of weft required

You'll need three 50-yard skeins of yarn for the weft. You'll notice that you use more warp than weft in a project. That's because some of the warp becomes fringe and loom waste.

All this calculation and sampling might seem like a lot of effort, but the reward is the freedom to design any textile you can imagine. The payoff comes when you take something from the loom that is wholly yours, something unique and special. And really, isn't that what handweaving is all about?

DOING THE MATH THE QUICK WAY

This simple formula is another, though less precise, way to calculate how much yarn you'll need for a project, or you can use weaving software to calculate your yarn requirements.

▶ **WARP.** To calculate how much warp you need for a project, multiply the length of each warp thread by how many you have in the project. (This is the sett of the project times the width of the project in the heddle.)

(project length + loom waste) × (sett) × (width in heddle) = total warp needed

▶ **WEFT.** The total number of weft picks is the picks per inch times the length of the cloth. Each time you throw the shuttle through the shed you create one pick, or shot, of weft. If your project has a balanced-weave structure, such as plain weave, the number of picks per inch (ppi) of cloth will be the same as the sett.

(project length) × (ppi) × (width in heddle) = total weft needed

Add an extra 10–20 percent of the total yardage of both warp and weft to allow for shrinkage, draw-in, and take-up.

YARN REQUIREMENTS

Name of project: _____   Date: _____

Gift (optional): _____

Yarn used: _____
     (brand)   *(line)*   *(fiber content)*   *(weight)*   *(yardage)*   *(weight symbol)*

Finished project dimensions: _____   Warp sett (epi): _____   Weft (ppi): _____

CALCULATING WARP

Allowing for draw-in

finished width ÷ [1 – (draw-in as a decimal) = width in heddle]

Allowing for take-up

finished length ÷ [1 – (take-up as a decimal) = length to weave]

Allowing for fringe/hem

dimension to weave + [2 × (fringe or hem length)] = length of fabric on loom

Total warp length

length of fabric on loom + loom waste = minimum warp length ÷ 36 = warp length in yards

Total amount of warp yarn needed

width in heddle × sett = number of warp ends

number of warp ends × warp length in yards = total amount of warp yarn

CALCULATING WEFT

Total weft picks

woven length × ppi = number of weft picks

Total weft amount

number of weft picks × width in heddle = total amount of weft ÷ 36 = total yards of weft needed

MEASURING THE WARP

THERE ARE SEVERAL WAYS TO GET WARP ONTO A RIGID-HEDDLE LOOM. It doesn't matter which technique you use, as long as the final outcome is evenly tensioned warp threads that are not tangled and which correctly weave the pattern. I'll first describe using a warping board, the more traditional method of measuring a warp. Starting on page 51, I describe how to use the direct-peg method, which is faster, easier, and requires less equipment than using a warping board. I recommend the latter for anyone new to rigid-heddle weaving. Whichever method you use, after you measure the warp, the rest of the process (winding the warp on, threading the heddle, and tying on to the front) is the same.

Using the Warping Board Method

The older method of warping a rigid-heddle loom involves winding the warp on a tool called a warping board (or a similar tool called a warping mill) and then transferring that warp to the loom, using a strategy known as "the cross" to keep the threads in order. Warping boards are a rectangular frame with pegs along the top and sides. You wind the threads between the pegs to measure out a specific yardage. Why use a warping board? Because it lets you measure yards and yards of warp without having to run all the way down the hall and back.

Pros

» It allows you to wind a bunch of warps ahead of time.

» It's good if you get a great idea for a warp while your loom is occupied or otherwise unavailable.

» It's a compact way to wind long warps.

Cons

» A warping board can be large and is not easily portable.

» The threads lose tension between the warping board and the loom, which gives them an opportunity to tangle.

» Depending on how you apply the warp to the loom, it may result in extra loom waste (more about that later).

» It takes longer than the direct-peg method.

The Crosses

Before we begin winding a warp, there are two important concepts you need to understand: one is a thread-by-thread cross, and the other is a counting cross (also called a raddle cross).

THREAD-BY-THREAD CROSS. When you're winding a warp, you need a way to keep the threads in order, so you can put them on the loom in the same order that you put them on the warping board. This keeps the threads aligned and prevents tangles. How do you achieve this feat? By crisscrossing threads as you wind the warp. The cross keeps them from slipping past each other and getting out of order. To create a thread-by-thread cross, you alternate the path around a set of pegs at the beginning of the warp as shown below. The first thread goes over peg 1 and under peg 2. The second thread travels the opposite path: over peg 2 and under peg 1. By changing the path of each subsequent thread you build up a thread-by-thread cross that protects the order of your threads, which is especially important when you take them off the warping board and they lose tension.

COUNTING CROSS. This is similar to a thread-by-thread cross in that you alter the path of threads to keep them in order, but this time you wind a set of threads in one path and then change the path for the next set of threads at the end of the warp. You can see this in the photo below.

I use the counting cross to keep track of how many threads I've measured out. There may be people in the world who can count from 1 to 120 without daydreaming and losing their place, but I am not one of them. I put ½" worth of thread into each section, so if my mind wanders and I need to check how many threads I've wound, I can simply count off the sections and see.

Why put ½" into each segment? Because with the setts I generally use for projects, this gives me a small enough number to keep track of before it's time to change to the next segment. If you are weaving with a coarse sett, say 6 threads per inch, you may want to put 1" worth of warp into each counting cross segment. If you are weaving fine, say 24 threads per inch, you may want to put ¼" worth of threads into each segment. Play with this and see what works for you.

Above: *Thread-by-thread cross at the beginning of the warp*
Right: *Counting (or raddle) cross at the end of the warp.*

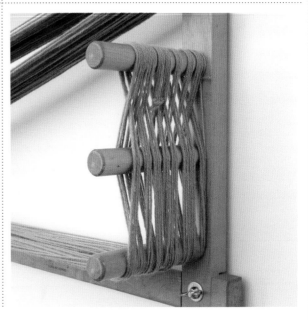

THE WARPING-BOARD METHOD

STEP 1: *Pick a Path to Adventure*

Before we start putting warp on the warping board, we need to pick a path between the pegs that gives us the length we want the warp to be. (See page 36 for how to calculate warp length.) I do this by measuring the warp length in a non-stretchy yarn that contrasts wildly with the yarn I intend to use for warp. I then tie loops in either end of the string using half-hitch knots (because they are simple and don't move) and then use this string to find a path on the loom. I place the threading cross at the top of the warp, and the counting cross at the bottom. There's no reason you couldn't do it another way, this is just what I'm used to.

Since I wind a lot of warps, I keep a set of color-coded measuring strings on hand in various lengths: red for 3 yards, yellow for 5 yards, and green for 7 yards. This serves two purposes: it saves me from having to cut and measure a new string for every warp, and it lets me wind multiple warps that are exactly the same length. This is important if you are weaving a wide project and have to wind the warp in several chains because the whole warp won't fit on the warping board's pegs, or if you are a person (like me) who gets in a mood to wind lots of pretty warp chains and then decide later how to combine them.

With your warp length decided and laid out on the warping board, you are now ready to wind the warp.

7 yards

5 yards

3 yards

Color-coded warp measuring strings

NOTHING WRONG WITH RUNNING!

Running all the way down the hall and back is a perfectly valid warping method. In traditional cultures, where equipment is at a premium and space is plentiful, warping often occurs by running a warp between two pegs set into the ground. Active small children who have been convinced that running back and forth is a grand game are especially helpful if you're winding a warp in this way, but in my experience, the kids catch on after a warp thread or ten.

CHAPTER 2: Get Set to Weave

WINDING THE WARP

① Tie a half-hitch loop in the end of the warp and slip it over the first peg.

② Follow the path of the measuring string on the path out.

measuring string

③ When you get to the end of the measuring string, turn around and follow the path back, alternating pegs when you get to the thread-by-thread cross.

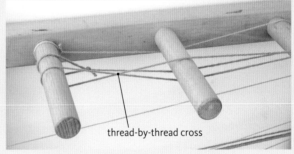

thread-by-thread cross

→ *Repeat steps 2 and 3 until the whole warp is wound, changing the order of pegs at the counting cross after every ½" of warp.*

④ Leaving an 8" tail, cut the warp and tie a second half-hitch loop on the loose end. Slip the loop over the last peg.

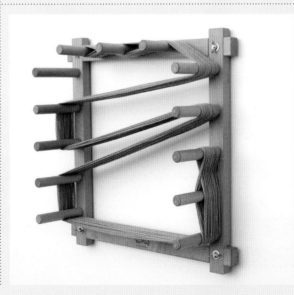

Continued on next page ▷

STEP 1: Pick a Path to Adventure, *continued*

TYING THE CHOKES

The next step in the warping process is to make choke ties and chain the warp (both things that prevent it from tangling when you take it off the warping board).

① Cut several 8" lengths from a strong, non-stretchy yarn. I use 8/2 carpet warp.

② Tie the first half of a surgeon's knot (see facing page) around one leg of warp threads near the starting/ending peg, wrapping the yarn around twice (see the illustration on the facing page), and pull as tight as you can. The warp threads should be tied so tightly that they cannot slip past each other. (Take care not to catch the counting thread when you wrap the warp threads.)

③ Finish the surgeon's knot with a bow. (The reason you use a bow instead of finishing the surgeon's knot in the conventional manner is that you need to be able to easily take off the choke tie while warping the loom.)

④ Tie choke ties on all four legs of the thread-by-thread cross and the counting cross. Tie a choke tie once every yard of warp. Tie two choke ties at each end loop so it's easy to reopen the loops later.

OH, WHAT A TANGLED WEB . . .

Weaving author and teacher Peggy Osterkamp has a saying that "a thread under tension cannot tangle." Time and time again, weaving has taught me that this and its corollary — a loose thread will tangle the first instant it can — are true.

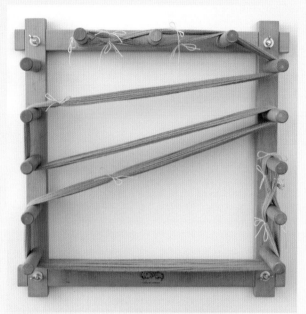

CHAPTER 2: Get Set to Weave

WARP-WINDING TIPS

▶ **No pile ups.** Don't let the threads pile up on each other when you're winding the warp. This will cause them to be different lengths, leading to tension irregularities. The threads should lie side by side on the warping-board pegs.

▶ **Paths all straight and true.** Ideally, all the warp threads should be exactly the same length and exactly the same tension when you measure them. This means that each thread follows the same path around the pegs. Stop every once in a while to make sure no single threads are creating their own path around the board. If you find one and it's only a few threads back, unwind the warp, put the thread on the correct path, and continue warping. If you find one when it's 150 threads back, cut it in the middle, tie the loose ends off to the front and end pegs of your winding, and replace it with a new warp thread. Depending on the pattern of the warp you're winding, you can either replace the thread with a new one in the exact location of the old one or just add an extra to the working end of the warp.

▶ **Firm, even tension.** You don't need to wind the threads onto the board with super-tight tension. This can make the warp hard to get off the warping board later. It's best to wind the warp with a firm, even tension. A too-tight tension can even cause the warping pegs to bend in at the top, making one side of the warp shorter that the other when you go to put it on the loom. You want the threads taut so they're not drooping, but not so tight that the warp is hard to get off the board later. Even tension is more important than whether it's tight or loose.

▶ **Keep count.** For an easy way to tell if it's time to change to the next group in the counting cross, look at the end peg of your warp. Count those threads. Because this is where the threads turn around, each wrap represents two warp threads: you have to count only half as many threads. So if I'm winding a counting cross where I'm putting 8 threads in each section, I'll look at the end peg and change to the next section of the counting cross when I see 4 wraps on the end of that peg.

▶ **Comfortable position.** Mount the warping board at the right height for your body. You should be able to wind the top row without straining your shoulder and reach the bottom row without leaning down. I mount my warping board on the wall using rubber-coated forked hooks that hold it snugly in place. I've attached rubber bumpers to the back of my warping board to protect the wall.

▶ **Eliminate knots.** If you come to a knot in the yarn while you're winding a warp, cut the yarn at that point and unwind the thread back to the end peg. Trim the warp thread at the peg so that you can re-join the yarn with a knot at the peg, rather than in the middle of the warp.

SURGEON'S KNOT

Begin by tying a knot in the same way you tie your shoes, taking the left thread (or bundle of threads) over the right, but wrap the left thread over the right twice, instead of just once (a). To complete the knot, take the right thread (or bundle of threads) over the left (b), or, for a knot that's easier to release, finish it with a bow instead of a knot.

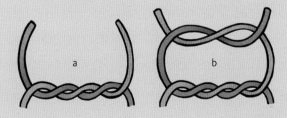

Using the Warping Board Method

STEP 2: *Controlling Your Warp by Chaining*

Now that your warp is secured at the critical points, you can remove it from the warping board. The instant you take it off tension, however, entropy will try to have its way with your warp and tangle it. There are several mechanisms you can use to combat this: chaining the warp, using a kite stick, or being gentle with the warp. (This last method works best in the absence of children, pets, and strong breezes.)

Chaining is a traditional method of compacting and securing a warp for storage, whether you intend to store it for the hour or so it takes to get it on the loom, or the months or years it will take you to get to this project. Essentially, you crochet the warp, turning it into a tight chain that resists tangling. The only downside to this method is one of technique. If you chain the warp correctly, you can simply pull on one end to release it. If you chain the warp improperly, it won't unfurl, and you'll be a frustrated weaver, laboriously undoing the warp chain one link at a time.

HOW TO MAKE A CHAIN

① Start from the counting-cross end of the warp (a). Create a loop and reach through with your hand and grab the next segment of warp (b & c).

② Continue pulling loops through until you reach the other end of the warp. To prevent the warp from twisting, some weavers alternate hands when pulling the loops through.

③ Pull the tail through. You can hang the warp chain up by this last loop.

A set of warp chain waiting to be woven is a pretty and inspiring thing to look at while you weave.

ALTERNATIVES TO CHAINING

▶ **KITE STICKS.** Peggy Osterkamp recommends the use of a kite stick in her book *Weaving for Beginners*. A kite stick is simply a stick that you wind the warp onto figure-8 style. The purpose of the kite stick is to keep the warp bundled in a tight package under tension, which prevents the warp threads from tangling. Weavers who have trouble chaining a warp often have success with a kite stick. The only downside I've found with the kite stick method is a minor one: the warp can become twisted when you wind it off the kite stick, but this is easily fixed by untwisting it.

▶ **GENTLE HANDLING.** You may find that neither a warp chain nor a kite stick is necessary. Simply lift the warp from the warping board and drape it over a hook or rack until you're ready to weave it. The benefit of this method is speed; there's nothing to do or undo. The downside is risk. Because nothing is preventing the warp from tangling, you may one day find your tidy warp collapsed in a heap. If you've tied choke ties, you can usually straighten out the warp by looping one end of the warp over a post, unfurling the warp to its full length, and then putting your hand in the loop at the other end of the warp and snapping it briskly.

a

Lay the stick under the loop at the counting cross end of the warp, then draw the length of the warp through the loop, and pull firmly to the left.

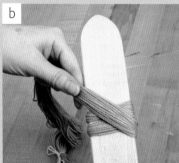

b

Bring the warp under the stick and then cross it over the warp at an angle from bottom to top to wrap it around the stick.

c

Continue to wrap the warp around the stick, criss-crossing it from bottom to top and then from top to bottom with each wrap.

d

When you have wrapped on the entire warp, fasten the end under the last wrap.

STEP 3: *Capturing the Cross with Lease Sticks*

When you are ready to put the warp onto the loom, the first thing to do is put the cross onto lease sticks. These are a pair of sticks that hold the cross during the warping process. Usually they are flat sticks with a hole drilled in each end, but round dowels work just as well. You can make a pair of lease sticks from ¼" × ¾" wooden screen moulding, found at a hardware store. Slide one stick through each of the openings formed by the choke ties at the cross. Tie or tape the ends of the lease sticks together so the warp threads can't slide off them. The photo at right shows the cross secure on a pair of lease sticks.

At this point, with the lease sticks secure, you can remove the choke ties from the cross. As you wind onto the back beam, you'll undo the choke ties from the length of the warp as they come up.

Leaving choke ties on right up until the point they become a hindrance keeps the warp in order, as the choke ties prevent the warp threads from shifting position and tangling.

Tip: Do not use scissors to cut choke ties off your warp. It's too easy to accidentally cut warp threads when you cut off the choke ties and this is not a fun moment. My first weaving teacher, Judith MacKenzie, recommends keeping scissors far from your loom during the entire warping process.

STEP 4: *Threading the Heddle from the Cross*

I describe this process a bit differently from what you'll see in other rigid-heddle books. Traditionally, at this point you'd be told to cut the loops open and begin threading individual threads through the slots and holes. This method is called front-to-back warping; it comes from shaft-loom weaving, and weavers adapted it to the rigid-heddle loom. It works, but I prefer to leave the warp uncut so that I can thread loops through the slots, and wait to thread the holes after the warp is wound onto the back beam. Here are my reasons: First, it saves warp otherwise lost to tying the cut ends on to the back beam. Second, and even more important, holes and slots exert different levels of friction during the winding-on process. In shaft looms, all the threads run through both a hole (metal or string heddle) and a slot (reed), so this

tension difference doesn't arise. This friction difference between rigid-heddle slots and holes isn't a problem for many warps, but it can bite you on those warps where the difference is enough to matter, so why not play it safe and use this method on all your warps? Third, and equally important, it ensures all threads remain the same length, which helps you wind your warps on smoothly and without any tangles. If you tie onto the back instead, your knots will make some warp threads slightly shorter and others slightly longer, and you'll have to pull those differences all the way through the warp to get even tension at the front, leading to tangles. For a short warp this isn't a big deal, but as you wind on longer warps, it becomes more of an issue.

Continued on next page ▷

Threading the Heddle from the Cross, *continued*

HOW TO THREAD THE HEDDLE

① Put the cross, safe in the lease sticks, on the loom in front of the heddle, with the threading cross toward the heddle and the front of the loom. (If you haven't already done so, you can remove the chokes at the cross, once you've captured it on the lease sticks.) You may find it helpful to tie the lease sticks to the loom as shown. This keeps the lease sticks in place and prevents them from slipping off the loom during the warping process. I often use shoelaces for this, since they are cheap, flat, and have enough grip to hold the sticks in place.

② Pull the first loop from the cross. This loop and the last loop in the cross have only one thread attached. Subsequent loops bring forth one thread from the top and one thread from the bottom of the lease stick closest to the heddle. *Note:* I work right to left because I am right-handed. If you are left-handed, you may find it more convenient to work left to right.

③ Thread the loop through a slot, then slide it onto

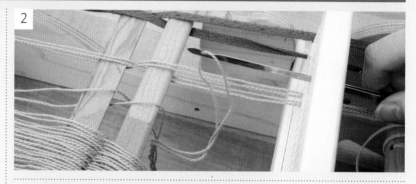

the back rod. (For how to identify the correct slot to begin with, see page 52.) On many looms you can push the back rod out of its ties to make it easy to slide the warp loops over. If you have a loom where the back rod is fixed in place, such as an Ashford Knitter's Loom, you can slide the loops onto a dowel and then lash the dowel into place along the rod after all the loops have been threaded onto it.

④ Continue until all the warp-thread loops are attached to the back rod. Make sure that you pick up the warp loops in the order they appear in the cross. Their position in front and behind the cross doesn't matter: it is the cross that preserves the order in which they were wound. When you are done threading all the loops, you can remove the lease sticks. Note that the first and last slot contains only one warp thread, not loops.

→ *The next step is winding the warp onto the back beam. To learn how to do that, skip ahead to How to Wind onto the Back Beam, page 57.*

Warping with the Direct-Peg Method

The direct-peg method of warping a rigid-heddle loom is fairly new, and was published by weaving teacher Rowena Hart in her book *The Ashford Book of Rigid Heddle Weaving*. Since that time, it has become the more popular warping method because of its simplicity and speed. With this method, you measure and spread the warp in a single step. The threads are never off tension, so the warp has no opportunity to tangle. It's a wonderful way to warp a rigid-heddle loom.

Unlike when you use a warping board, with the direct-peg method you don't have to worry about making sure the threads take the correct path: there's only one path to take. The thing to watch for in this case is that each thread is wound with the same tension. You don't have to obsess about this for most yarns (linen and metal wire being exceptions), but you shouldn't see any too-tight threads or any danglers. Don't wind the warp tightly or loosely; the goal is a nice even tension.

Pros

» The method is faster than the warping board method: measuring and threading happens simultaneously.

» There's less chance for the warp threads to tangle because they are always under tension.

» It uses a small, easy-to-pack peg instead of a big warping board.

Cons

» You cannot prepare warps ahead of time. Your loom will be tied up until the warp is completely on the loom.

» You need a place to attach the peg. Since you'll be stretching the entire length of the warp out at once, this might need to be at a long distance from the loom.

» This method is inefficient for long warps, since you'll have to run back and forth between the loom and the peg.

THE DIRECT-PEG METHOD

How to Use a Warping Peg

① Attach the loom to a stable surface such as a table. Most looms come with clamps to facilitate this.

3a

② Attach the peg to a stable surface at a distance from your loom. The front of your loom should be the side nearest the peg. The distance between the peg and the back rod of the loom will be your warp length. Make sure there is a clear walking path between the loom and the peg. (To determine which side of your loom is the front, put the heddle in place and examine the loom. The front side of any rigid-heddle loom is the side with more space. This is because the weaver needs room to make the shed and throw the shuttle.)

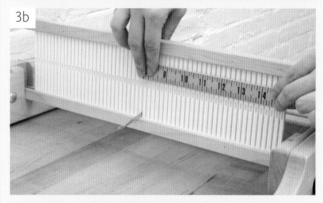

3b

③ Figure out the width of the warp on the loom. Center this width in the heddle. To find the center of the heddle, use a tape measure to measure its width (a), fold the tape measure in half, and hold it so that the fold indicates the midpoint (b). Mark the center with your threading hook. To determine which slot you should start threading in, measure from the center half the width of your project (c). (Here, for a 9" wide warp, you start 4½" from the center. You can start on either the left or right, depending on your preference and whether you're right- or left-handed. *Tip:* Permanently mark the center of your heddle by looping a string through the center slot and tying it tightly to the top bar of the heddle.

3c

center

④ Put the warp source (cone, ball of yarn, etc.) on the floor behind the loom.

⑤ Tie the free end of the warp onto the back rod of the rigid-heddle loom. You can tie it on using any knot that does not slip and tighten. I like to tie this first warp end onto the back rod in such a way that I leave a loop that I can slip my scissors through when I'm cutting the finished project off.

⑥ Using a threading hook, pull a loop through the first slot you identified in step 3 (on either the right- or left-hand side of the warp). It is important to note that you are pulling loops through slots in this step, not individual threads. You are also ignoring the holes in this step. Pull the loops taut but not tight. It is more important for the tension of each loop to be even than tight.

⑦ Walk the loop you just pulled through the slot over to the peg and slip it over the peg.

⑧ Wrap the warp over the back rod and through the next slot. (See Ensuring the Warp Goes Over the Back Rod, page 55.)

→ *Repeat steps 7 and 8 running the loops alternately over and under the back rod, until you have threaded all the slots needed for your project.*

⑨ Run the warp back to the back rod of the loom, leaving enough extra yarn to tie onto the back rod, and cut the warp source off.

Continued on next page ▷

6

7

8

9

⑩ Tie the last warp thread onto the back rod of the loom in the same manner that you did in step 5. Make sure that the knot will not slip; this would cause the tension in the last warp thread to be too loose.

⑪ Slip the warp threads off of the peg and onto your wrist. Do *not* cut the threads at this point. *Tip:* When the threads are on the peg, they're all the same length and tension. If you preserve the loop as you wind on, you can return the threads to the same length and tension at any time by pulling on the loop until the threads are taut. This makes it much easier to get even tension across your warp.

⑫ To prepare for tensioning the threads while you wind on, have an assistant hold onto the loop, or use a lark's head knot to fasten the loop to a 4-pound dumbbell. I use the kind that is coated in neoprene or rubber. You are now ready for the next step, winding on.

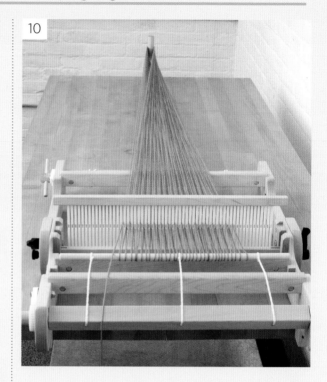

10

CORRECTING WARPING ERRORS

ENSURING THE WARP GOES OVER THE BACK ROD

In step 8 (page 53), check that you have run the warp behind the back rod. If you see "stitches" on the back of the heddle (as shown at right), this means you forgot to run the warp behind the back rod. You have two options for fixing this:

▶ **IF YOU HAVEN'T CUT THE WARP FROM THE YARN SOURCE,** you can pull the loops between the stitch and the yarn source to get enough slack to slip the stitch over the back rod or tie it onto the back rod with a short piece of yarn. Make sure all the the loops are the same tension as the rest of the warp at the end.

▶ **IF YOU HAVE CUT THE YARN SOURCE OFF,** cut the stitch.

▶ **IF YOU FIND DOUBLED THREADS NEXT TO AN EMPTY SLOT,** pull one of the loops off the peg and put it into the emply slot.

stitch

CORRECTING DOUBLED THREADS

▶ **IF YOU FIND AN EMPTY SLOT,** take a length of warp yarn long enough to go the peg and back with a little extra for knots. Tie one end to the rod, run it over to the peg, and tie the other end to the rod.

▶ **IF THERE ISN'T AN EMPTY SLOT,** pull one of the loops off the peg and to the back of your loom. Tie an overhand knot in the loop so it snugs up to the back rod and cut extra yarn away.

WINDING THE WARP ON AND THREADING

WITH YOUR WARP ALL MEASURED, you're now ready wind it onto the back beam, thread the heddles, and tie the warp threads to the front beam. Let's take it a step at a time.

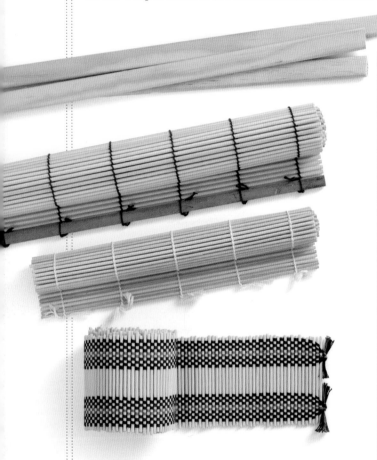

Warp separators (top to bottom). *Wood slats, reed blind, sushi mat, handwoven separator*

Warping the Loom

Whether you used a warping board or the direct-peg method to measure your warp, the next step is winding it onto the back beam. This stores the warp compactly until it is ready to be woven, and makes it possible to move the loom with the weaving in progress. To prevent tangles and tension irregularities, the goal is to wind on each thread evenly at the same rate.

WARP SEPARATORS. To ensure that the threads are evenly wound, they must be wound on flat, so they all travel the same length and end up the same tension at the end. If you don't have anything between the layers as you wind on, some warp threads may fall down between other threads and follow a shorter path, causing tension differences. The solution is to add a warp separator between the layers. Corrugated cardboard is often sold as a warp separator, but it can be problematic. As it ages, some of the ridges on the back flatten and others don't, turning your once-consistently flat cardboard into something that introduces tension problems into your warp. For a long-lived warp separator that gives great tension, master weaver Laura Fry uses reed mats. When purchasing one, make sure that the reeds are even and that the mat is as flat as possible. The warp separator should either fill your back beam entirely or extend at least 1" beyond each side of your warp. This prevents threads from falling off the ends of your warp separator. *Tip:* I buy reed blinds from the hardware store and cut them to be exactly the same width as my back beam.

THE WARPING PROCESS

How to Wind onto the Back Beam

① Check to make sure that you have two, and only two, threads in each slot. If you've made an error and put two loops (four threads) in one slot, now is the easiest time to cut one loop off the loom. It's also the easiest time to add in a loop if you missed a slot. In either case, don't forget to tie the new ends onto the back rod. (If you are winding on from a warp measured on a warping board, the first and last slots will have only one thread.)

② Find the loop that was on the peg, or at the end of your warp chain, and stick your hand inside to keep it open. To tension the threads while you wind on, have an assistant hold onto the loop or use a lark's head knot to fasten the loop to a 4-pound dumbbell. I use the kind that is coated in neoprene or rubber. *Tip:* When the threads are on the peg, they're all the same length and tension. If you preserve the loop as you wind on, you can return the threads to the same length and

tension at any time by pulling on the loop until the threads are taut. This makes it much easier to get even tension across your warp.

③ Make sure the brake foot is properly engaged at the top of the brake, and then begin to wind on.

④ Insert the warp separator, and wind on the warp. The warp separator should be wide enough to fill the back beam, or at least 1" wider than the warp on both sides.

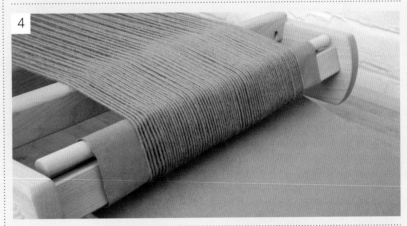

⑤ Wind (adding additional warp separators as needed) until the loop reaches the front beam.

⑥ Cut the loop open at the pivot point, so all threads are the same length.

The next step is to thread the holes. If you are not going to thread the holes immediately, loosely tie the warp threads in one big overhand knot in front of the heddle. This protects the threads from falling out of the slots until you come back to the loom.

Continued on next page ▷

How to Wind onto the Back Beam, *continued*

CIGAR-SHAPED WARPS

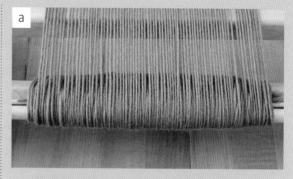

When the majority of the warp has scrunched together in the center of the warp and threads have piled on top of threads without a separator to keep them apart, the warp becomes cigar shaped (a). This causes tension problems because the threads will be different lengths.

Another problem is caused when new weavers use their hands to turn the warp beam. When you do this, your hands may slide in toward the warp and inadvertently crowd the threads together (b). On a narrow warp, where there is plenty of room for your hands on the beam, this might not be an issue, but it's good to get into the habit of always using the crank handle on the outside of the loom instead.

Threading the Holes

It doesn't matter whether the first hole you thread is to the right or the left of the slot. What does matter is that, if you go to the left, you continue to thread each hole to the left of its slot, and if you go to the right, you continue to thread each hole to the right of its slot. What you want at the end is a warp that's threaded hole-slot-hole-slot, and so on, with one thread in each hole and each slot all the way across.

Most first-time weavers start threading the holes of a rigid-heddle loom by leaning over the heddle so they can watch the hook grab the thread and pull it through. This is hard on your back. I encourage you to trust your sense of touch and find the threads by feel.

How to Thread the Holes

(1) Pull both threads in a slot to put them under tension. This makes it easy to separate them.

(2) Pick one thread; for most projects it doesn't matter which one. (If you are working on a project where it does matter, such as a pattern with a distinct color or texture sequence, pick the thread that is next in the pattern.) Lift that thread and, reaching behind the heddle (at the right in this photo), use your fingers to spread it horizontally for about an inch behind the hole you're threading and remove it from the slot. Drop the other thread, and leave it in the slot.

(3) Without leaning over the heddle, use the hook to reach through the hole and grab the yarn you've tensioned with your fingers. Pull the yarn through the hole.

Continued on next page ▷

How to Thread the Holes, *continued*

④ Take the threads that are finished — both slot and hole — and flip them out of the way so you can tell where to start threading the next hole. You may want to secure threaded sections every inch or so by tying the group of threads into bundles with a slip knot.

⑤ Continue threading in this way until all the holes are filled, Then take a moment to check that there's one (and only one) thread in each hole and slot. The exception, of course, is if you're deliberately leaving some holes empty, as in crammed-and-spaced threading or like multiple-heddle work (starting on page 202).

→ *To check the threading, I raise the threads to isolate the slots (a) and then lower them to isolate the holes (b). If you find any discrepancies, now is a great time to fix them.*

A WORD ABOUT TENSION

One of the most important things in weaving is getting even tension across all of your warp threads. Many things in weaving you can fudge, or get partly wrong, and still end up with a successful project. Tension is not one of them. Even tension is the one thing that can make or break a project. It's so important that if I discover my tension is uneven when I finish warping a loom, I stop and fix the tension problems before I go any further. Experience has taught me that tension problems only get worse as a warp progresses. Having proper tension can make the difference between weaving happily or cursing at your loom. At the end of warping your loom, you should be able to close your eyes, slide your hands across the warp, and feel that each thread has the same tension.

a

b

CHAPTER 2: Get Set to Weave

PROBLEM-SOLVING THREADING ERRORS

Even experienced weavers make threading errors from time to time. Here's a rundown of the most common and how to fix them.

▶ **DOUBLED THREADS IN HOLES OR SLOTS.** If you determine that there are extra threads, you can dispose of them by pulling them out of the hole or slot and throwing them off the back of your loom. This works best if the project is one where the number and order of the warp threads isn't crucial. If you are doing a color-and-weave project where a missing thread would cause a flaw in the pattern, you'll have to move threads over in the heddle to make a space for one of the doubled threads. You'll have to keep pulling the extra threads back as you advance the warp while weaving. As you do, watch for a loose warp thread when you get to the end of your warp. This loose thread is the "partner" of the dangler. When you notice it, trim the thread, and tie it to the back rod. The upside of this approach is that if you break a warp thread, the loose thread can stand as a replacement, ready to fill in.

▶ **THREADING ERRORS IN COMPLEX WEAVES.** Even if you check your threading before you begin to weave, you may miss a subtle threading error, especially in a complex weave structure or pattern. It's worthwhile to look at your weaving after the first 2 or 3 inches to see if you notice any anomalies, such as doubled warp threads or gaps in the fabric or pattern. The sooner you identify a threading error, the easier it is to fix it. If you notice a threading error after the first few inches of weaving, for instance, you can often fix it without having to unweave or cut out your fabric. Simply loosen the knot with the affected thread, slide the thread out, rethread it, and then tie it back into the bundle, allowing the moved thread to float on top of the fabric.

▶ **SKIPPED HOLES OR SLOTS.** The most common threading error on a rigid-heddle loom is to miss a hole or a slot. Before you tie on, it pays to pause for a moment and examine your threading. Are all the holes and slots filled? Are the right colors and threads in the right places? If a thread is missing near the side of your project, and you don't mind a project that's one or two threads narrower than you'd originally intended, you can simply move over threads to fill in the gap. Before you do that though, check that the missing threads haven't simply fallen down behind your heddle. It's annoying to finish moving everything over and then find the threads and have to move everything back to its original place. If the missing thread is in the middle of the warp, it may be easier to simply add in a new thread. The quick way is to measure off a new thread the length of the warp and hang it off the back of the loom the same way as you would a repair thread for a warp thread that breaks during the weaving process (see page 87). If you have many threads to insert or simply don't like things dangling off the back of your loom, you can fix the thread completely by measuring out a new length of thread, unwinding the warp from the back beam, and tying the new thread onto the back of the loom, then winding things back up. If you decide to take this approach, I suggest you knot the cut ends of the warp together in front of the heddle, pulling that knot *and* the heddle forward together. This avoids dragging the warp through the heddle and introducing small tension irregularities between the slots and the holes.

Tying onto the Front

There are two goals when you're tying the warp onto the front rod. One is to attach the loose ends of the warp to the loom, and the other is to evenly tension all of the warp threads. The key to both is learning how to tie a surgeon's knot, which can be tightened down snugly and won't slip free, but that also can be easily loosened if it's too tight. (For surgeon's knot, see page 45.)

The size of the bundles you tie depends on the thickness of the threads. For most warps, I tie bundles about an inch thick. For finer threads, such as a 10/2 cotton or Tencel, I use bundles about ½ inch thick. The angle of the threads on the edges of each bundle shouldn't be more than 45 degrees, The number of threads in each bundle doesn't need to be exactly the same, but it should be close. Knot all the warp threads in the same way, alternating sides as you work. It can help you maintain even tension if you tighten the front brake by one click before the next one or two knots.

How to Tie On

① Starting at the center of the warp, divide a bundle in half, and take each half over the front rod and up on each side ready to tie a surgeon's knot.

② For the first half of a surgeon's knot, wrap the left bundle of threads over the right, then over it again. The extra friction of this second wrap secures the knot until you complete the knot (step 3). If you get a knot too tight and need to undo it, you can capsize it by pulling down on one leg of the knot, which will loosen and fall apart.

③ When the entire warp is tied onto the front rod and the tension is even across all of the warp threads, wrap the right half over the left, as you would finish tying a square knot.

PREPARING THE WEFT AND BEGINNING TO WEAVE

WITH THE WARP ALL SET TO GO, you now can turn your attention to packaging up the weft so it's easy to slip into and out of the shed.

Winding Weft Yarns

You have several choices of how to "throw" your yarn through the warp shed. These include yarn butterflies and stick and boat shuttles. Your choice depends on the tools you have at hand, but also on the yarns you are using for the warp and weft.

Yarn Butterflies

The simplest way to package yarn is without any shuttle at all, but instead to create a butterfly-shaped bundle that spools the yarn easily from one end. This method is best used when you have relatively short amounts of weft and/or many different wefts, and it's especially useful for tapestry weaving, where a single row might involve weaving 30 or more different-colored wefts. As mentioned earlier, weft packaged this way isn't protected as well as when it's used with a shuttle, and it may therefore become abraded more when you weave with it. This is a problem especially with long wefts, and it may even fall apart on you as the cumulative damage from being pushed back and forth through the shed finally rips it apart. (An alternative to a yarn butterfly is a netting shuttle; see photo at right.)

Top to bottom: *Boat shuttle, stick shuttle, netting shuttle, yarn butterflies, bobbin*

How to Wind a Yarn Butterfly

1. Put the yarn in the crook between your thumb and palm.

2. Wind the weft back and forth around your fingers.

1 & 2

3. Finish the butterfly by folding the last bit of weft over to form a loop and passing the tail end through. Cinch down to secure the butterfly package.

3

4. When you're ready to use the yarn butterfly, pull from the end that was tucked under your thumb at the beginning. If all is right, the weft will spool off effortlessly.

4

Stick: The Simplest Shuttle

The most basic form of a shuttle is the stick shuttle. Essentially it's a flat stick with notches cut out of each end. Most often these are made of wood, but you can create them out of any relatively stiff medium, even cardboard.

Most rigid-heddle looms come with one or two stick shuttles, for two reasons: the stick shuttles are inexpensive for the manufacturer to produce, and they're thin enough to fit nicely through the narrow sheds that rigid-heddle looms tend to produce. When I first started weaving, I moved quickly from stick shuttles to boat shuttles and felt that I'd "outgrown" stick shuttles. Now that I'm a more experienced weaver, I've realized that stick shuttles have a lot going for them. They take more skill to weave with efficiently, but they can hold three times as much yarn as a boat shuttle of the same size. That means fewer joins in your finished cloth. There are downsides to stick shuttles: they are slow, and, because the yarn rides on the outside of the shuttle, it's subject to more abrasion than shuttles where the yarn rides on the inside.

Pros

» A stick shuttle can hold more yarn than any other type of shuttle, an advantage if you want to weave for as long as possible without having to join in a new weft because your shuttle runs out of yarn.

» Stick shuttles are cheap; you can even make your own out of wood or cardboard. (For template, see page 275.)

» Being thin, a stick shuttle can fit easily through a narrow weaving shed.

Cons

» Yarn does not flow automatically off the stick shuttle; the weaver has to manipulate the stick shuttle to release the thread. It takes practice to do this smoothly and efficiently.

» Because of the above manipulation, weaving with a stick shuttle is often slower than weaving with other types of shuttles.

Stick shuttle and netting shuttle

How to Wind onto a Stick Shuttle

The obvious way to wind weft onto a stick shuttle is to wind it around the center. This isn't wrong, but because the yarn increases the thickness of the shuttle, it's harder to fit through the shed. Here's a better way.

① Attach the yarn to the shuttle. Either tie a loop in one end and hook it over one of the forks of the stick shuttle, or, if your stick shuttle has a slot for starting the yarn, tie a knot in the yarn to secure it in there. Both methods require you to undo a knot or cut it off when you have used up all the weft on the shuttle. I don't like waste, so I simply hold the yarn with my thumb and give it a couple of good wraps to begin. After you've wound yarn onto the center for a while, do figure 8s on one side of the shuttle.

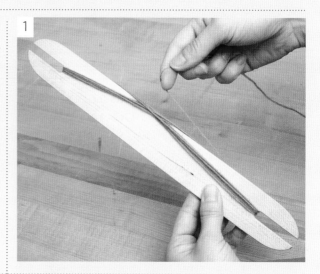

② Wind figure 8s on the other side of the shuttle as well. If you are using a belt shuttle (a type of stick shuttle where one side is sharpened or beveled so it can be used to pack in weft during weaving), you may not want to wind weft on that side, not because it would hurt the weft, but because you might want to use the sharpened edge to beat in the weft. If you know that you won't be using the belt shuttle as a beater, you can wind figure-8s weft on both sides.

→ *Repeat these steps until you've either run out of weft, or the shuttle is about 1" thick with yarn.*

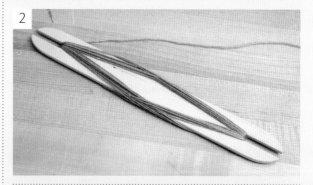

MAKING YOUR OWN STICK SHUTTLE

Creating your own weaving tools is economical and rewarding, and a stick shuttle is one of the easiest to fabricate at home. Photocopy the pattern on page 275 and trace it onto a rigid material such as wood or cardboard. Then use a jigsaw (for wood) or scissors (for cardboard) to carefully cut out the shuttle. Trim or sand off any rough edges that might catch the yarn. That's all there is to it!

Boat Shuttle: A Faster Weave

In shaft looms, boat shuttles are ubiquitous. Their speed of spooling off the weft yarn matches the pace of a shaft loom, but there's no reason you can't use their speed to increase the pace on your rigid-heddle loom as well. The fact that it can't hold as much yarn as a stick shuttle of the same size isn't a problem when you are weaving with finer yarns, such as 8/2 and 10/2 cottons, but for bulky yarns it could mean a lot more joins in your fabric. Whether you're willing to have more joins in exchange for speed is up to you.

Boat shuttles come in a variety of shapes, colors, and sizes. They all have two features in common: a vaguely canoe-like shape (hence the name) and a removable bobbin or quill that holds the weft and can be quickly exchanged to refill the shuttle. The way a boat shuttle works is that you wind the weft onto the bobbin, using a technique that ensures it unwinds without tangling, and feed it through the eye in the front of the shuttle. As you throw the shuttle back and forth (without turning it) the yarn unspools smoothly, which makes for faster weaving.

Boat shuttles designed for shaft looms are tall (one inch or greater) and can be too thick to comfortably fit in the smaller shed of a rigid-heddle loom. Modern shuttle makers have realized this and are now coming out with mini-shuttles less than an inch high. Damask shuttles (designed for weaving in the very narrow sheds created by draw looms) also work well.

Pros

» Yarn feeds automatically from the bobbin; you don't have to turn or otherwise manipulate the shuttle to release the weft. This makes your weaving smoother and faster.

» You can wind several bobbins ahead of time and swap new ones in quickly when your current bobbin runs out.

» The bottom of a boat shuttle slides easily over the bottom warp yarns in the shed, which makes for easier weaving and protects delicate weft threads from abrasion during weaving.

Cons

» You cannot wind as much weft onto a bobbin as on a stick shuttle; this is especially true for bulky yarns. Boat shuttles work best for weaving with thin wefts.

» Depending on the model, some boat shuttles are too high or tall to comfortably fit in the smaller shed of a rigid-heddle loom.

» Boat shuttles are typically more expensive than stick shuttles.

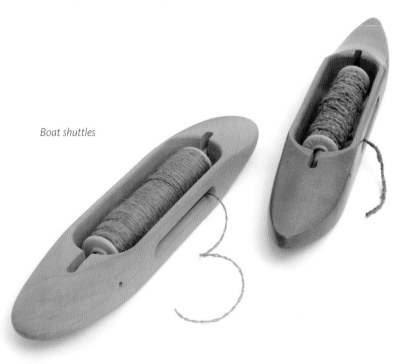

Boat shuttles

How to Wind a Bobbin

Boat shuttles hold bobbins, which carry the yarn. These bobbins have flanges on each end to keep the yarn from falling off the edge and getting tangled around the central shaft of the boat shuttle. (Bobbins without these flanges are called quills and are wound a bit differently, and are not covered here.) If you're going to be using a boat shuttle on a regular basis, you'll want a bobbin winder. You can wind bobbins by hand, but it's a tedious process. You can buy hand-cranked or electric bobbin winders, or you can devise your own by inserting a dowel in a drill. If you're improvising your own bobbin winder, be sure to mount the drill to a table or press (for safety) and use a slow speed setting. Take care to wind your bobbins carefully, so that there are no "mushy" spots in it. A well-wound bobbin will help you maintain an even selvedge when you're weaving.

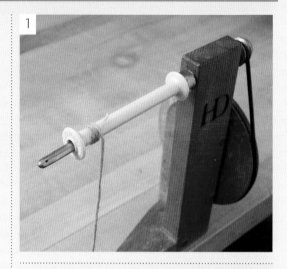

① Attach the yarn to the bobbin. This can be done by winding a few wraps of yarn on top of each other and tightening them down, or simply by tucking the loose end of the yarn into the hole of the bobbin before you put it on the bobbin winder.

② Wind back and forth across the bobbin, never stopping, with a smooth motion. The yarn will build up at the ends where you turn around. When the pooled ends of the yarn are nearly as high as the flanges on your bobbin, start making shorter paths across the bobbin, working your way toward the center. The goal is a smoothly wound yarn package that is not higher than the flanges at the end of the bobbin.

③ When you are winding only the center of the bobbin, you can cheat a bit and create a bit of a bulge. Make sure, however, that the bulge isn't so big that it will catch on the inside of your boat shuttle. You want it to be able to turn freely.

Spreading the Header

Look down at the warp you've just tied on. You'll see that the knots are pulling the warp threads into bundles where they attach to the front bar. If you started weaving without spreading the warp out, there'd be holes in your cloth. Many weaving books have you close that gap by weaving with a heavy thread, or weaving in strips of plastic garbage bags or even lengths of toilet paper. But there's a simpler way, a neat little trick that I learned from my first weaving teacher, Judith MacKenzie, a master spinner and author of *The Intentional Spinner*. In addition to being fast and saving you from needing a header weft, this method spreads the warp in a shorter distance, resulting in less loom waste. This method is not how you weave the rest of the cloth; it's just a step that you do once or twice at the beginning to spread the warp.

How to Spread the Header

1. Raise the heddle to open the up shed in the warp threads. Pass the shuttle containing the weft from one side of the open shed to the other, leaving behind a line of thread (a weft pick) in the shed. Do not use the heddle to beat the thread into place.

2. Lower the heddle to open the down shed and throw a pick of weft across. Do not beat the thread into place.

3. Open the up shed again and throw a pick of weft across.

4. Beat hard to smack all three weft picks into place together (a). With most projects, your warp will now be spaced just like it is in the heddle. With some projects, especially those with slick yarns or a loose sett, you'll need to repeat steps 1 through 3 one or two times more (b).

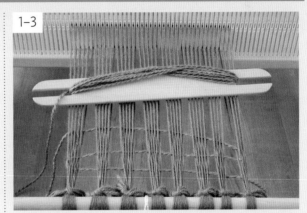

1–3

4a

4b

CHAPTER 3

Get Your Weave Thing Going

Now that you've got warp on your loom and weft on a shuttle, and the header is spread, you are ready to get down to weaving.

Making the Shed

The first step is to make the shed. Don't worry, this doesn't involve hammer and nails. In weaving, the shed is the opening in the warp threads that the shuttle passes through. On a rigid-heddle loom, you create the shed by putting the heddle in either the up or down position. The rigid-heddle is able to create a shed because the hole threads and the slot threads act differently when you move the heddle. When you raise the heddle, you move only the hole threads: these are the active threads. The slot threads are passive and keep going straight. So how do you get the passive threads on top for the other half of plain weave? By moving the active (hole) threads down and out of the way.

The shed on a rigid-heddle loom is always an unbalanced shed. This means that the hole threads stretch when you create a shed, but the slot threads do not. The fact that hole threads are active and slot threads are passive is a simple but important concept that will come into play later when we are weaving patterns, and for dealing with tricky warps.

When the heddle is raised, the warp that's threaded in the holes rises while the warp in the slots remains neutral, thus creating the shed.

Finding Your Beat

To lay in your first weft thread, open a shed, insert your shuttle, and draw the thread all the way across the warp, leaving a tail of about 1 inch extending beyond the warp. Keeping the same shed open, wrap the tail around the first warp thread on the edge and lay in the tail parallel to the first weft thread. Beat and then close the shed. You are now weaving!

Happy weavers make happy cloth. It's important to establish a rhythm in weaving, because rhythm breeds consistency. In my opinion, the peaceful state when the warp and weft flow together is the best reason to weave. Cloth is a bonus.

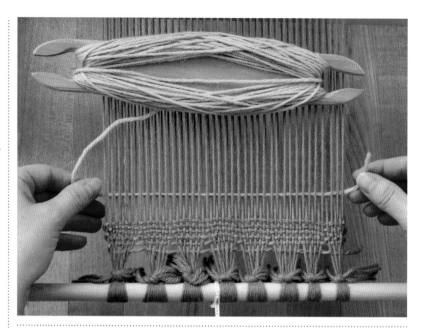

Weaving the first pick. *Insert the shuttle, leaving a 1-inch tail. Without changing the shed, wrap the tail around the first warp thread and tuck it into the shed next to the first warp pick (detail at left).*

INSPIRATION

Throughout our history, humans have used music and song to keep a rhythm, whether it was rowing a Roman boat or harvesting crops. Similarly, many weavers use music to keep an even pace at the loom. Music not only lifts your spirits, but by encouraging you to move in an even and consistent way it can improve the consistency of your cloth. Production weaver Laura Fry uses music to inspire her work and keep her weaving lively; Nadine Sanders, the "Singing Weaver," brings music into her work through song as well as inspiration.

If you prefer spoken word, you can enjoy audiobooks or podcasts. Podcasts are programs that you download from the Internet and can listen to on your computer or a device that plays digital audio. Most are free, and there are many with a fiber-arts twist. You can subscribe to most podcasts either through iTunes (free, and you don't need an iPod to use it) or a standard RSS feed. For more information on how to access podcasts, search on the Internet for "how podcasting works."

How to Use a Stick Shuttle

The simplest tools demand the most skill from the weaver, and stick shuttles are no exception. When you weave with a stick shuttle, you manually remove the weft from the shuttle, either by turning the shuttle or by popping the weft off the end. An easy mistake to make is either to take too much off the shuttle, and have extra weft getting in your way (a), or to take too little, and have the shuttle not make it across the warp (b). Here are tips for using a stick shuttle efficiently.

→   Choose a stick shuttle that is a couple of inches wider than your warp. This ensures that when you take one wrap of weft off the stick shuttle, it's enough to cross the entire warp, without being so much that you get tangled up.

→   Use the stick shuttle to tension the yarn (c).

→   Keep the shuttle in your hand as you beat and change sheds. The more time it spends in your hand, the less time you'll lose to putting the stick shuttle down and then picking it back up again. Seconds here and there add up surprisingly over the course of a long warp.

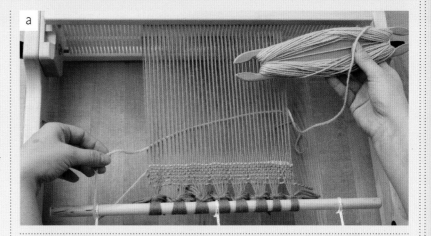

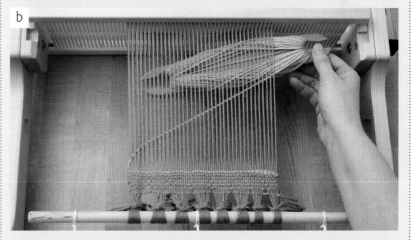

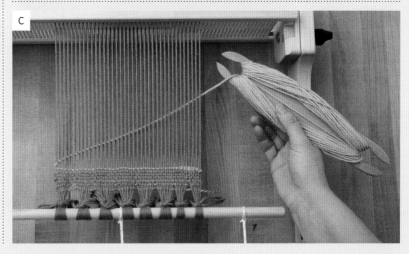

How to Use a Boat Shuttle

The length of the boat shuttle compared to the warp isn't an issue as it is with stick shuttles. But the height of the boat shuttle should be small enough to fit through the shed, which is narrower on a rigid heddle loom than on a shaft loom. Look for boat shuttles that are 1" tall or less. Damask shuttles, designed for draw looms, which also have a narrow shed, are a good option.

Different boat shuttles have different mechanisms to open up the central shaft: in some there's a spring or magnet holding the rod in place; in others there's a hinge, or the rod may simply lift free. When you load the bobbin onto the shaft, make sure the yarn is coming from beneath the bobbin when it spools off.

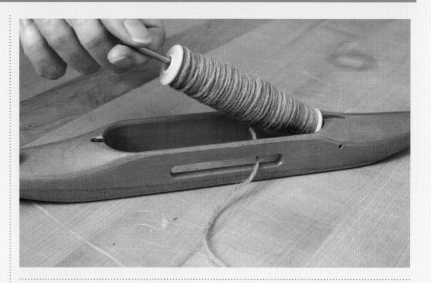

Feed the free end of the yarn through the eye or hole at the front of the boat shuttle. To ensure that the yarn spools off freely while you're weaving, this eye should always face you. You do not rotate a boat shuttle the way you do a stick shuttle; you simply slide it back and forth across the warp.

Tip: The expression "throwing the shuttle" comes from the fact that the shed is often wider than the shuttle, and so you have to toss it from one side to the other. You should throw the shuttle as efficiently as possible; I throw with my palms facing upward.

Example of why deflection matters. This cross-section view of felted fabric provides an inside view of the path the warp and weft takes to create fabric.

Finessing the Throw

When you are weaving, you can't just throw the weft straight across the warp. If you do, the sides of the weaving will draw in strongly. The reason for this is that in weaving, the warp and weft threads deflect across each other, nestling together. In order to make sure that you have enough weft to gracefully bend around the warps, you need to leave extra in each weft pick. You can do this in two ways: by bubbling the weft or angling the weft.

Which technique should you use? Try both and see which gives you the best results on your project. As for me, most of the time I bubble (since that's what I learned first), but there are projects when angling the weft gives me a better selvedge.

BUBBLING THE WEFT. In this strategy, you insert the weft in an arc or bubble, catching the weft at the selvedge on either side. It may take a bit of experimentation to find the right-size bubble for a given project. The bubble size you should use depends on several factors: the tension on the warp, the stretchiness and size of the yarn, the width of the warp, humidity, and more. The best way to figure out the proper size of the bubble is to look at the selvedges. You want to have the selvedge threads weaving and deflecting with the rest of the warp, but with minimal draw-in. For faster, more consistent weaving, create the bubble by pulling on the shuttle, not by hand-manipulating the threads.

ANGLING THE WEFT. With this technique, you insert the weft at an angle in the shed. One end is tucked into the selvedge, but the other remains free and can pull in additional yarn if necessary. The amount of weft is determined by the angle: a shallower angle provides less weft, a wider angle provides more. As with the bubbling technique above, you will have to experiment with different angles at the beginning of a warp before you find the one that is right for that project. When you find the proper angle, use that throughout the project. You don't need to pull out a protractor (unless that seems like fun or you're weaving a completely inelastic yarn); just eyeballing the angle will be fine. As with bubbling, strive to create the angle with the motion of the shuttle instead of extra hand manipulation.

BUBBLING

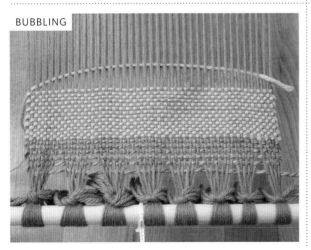

ANGLING

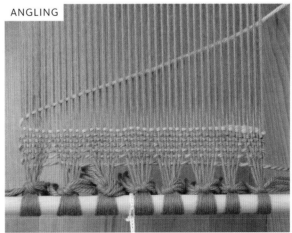

Starting New Weft

When you use up the yarn you've wound onto your bobbin or shuttle (or when you want to start a new color), you will need to neatly and securely end the old yarn and lay in the new.

For most weft yarns, simply overlap the new yarn for about an inch in the shed. Bring the tail ends of both the old and the new weft to the front of the cloth. Do this join at the edge of the cloth, instead of the center, to make it less conspicuous.

For fine and slippery yarns, such as 10/2 Tencel, use the denser fabric at the selvedges to lock the old and new weft into place. Weave with the old weft until you have enough to get across the last shot with 2 or 3 inches left over. Change the shed. Tuck the loose end of the old weft back around and into the new shed for an inch. On the other side of the fabric, start the new weft, leaving 2 or 3 inches hanging off the side. Change the shed. Tuck the loose end of the new weft in for about an inch.

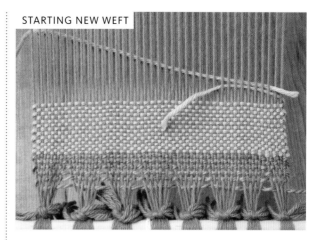

STARTING NEW WEFT

If you are weaving with a weft that felts, you can create a nearly invisible join using spit splicing. Pull the cut end off the old weft, leaving a wispy tail behind. Pull the cut end off the new weft, leaving another wispy tail. Overlap the two tails. Lick your palms and roll the tails togeher in your palms until they felt together.

Advancing the Warp

As you weave, the fabric will grow toward the heddle. If you do nothing, you'll eventually run out of room to weave. To avoid this, advance the warp every 2 or 3 inches that you weave. To do so, loosen the back brake enough to allow several inches of warp to come forward, then tighten the brake on the cloth beam to the same tension you were weaving with.

By frequently advancing the warp, you create better cloth because you are weaving in the same place on the loom throughout the warp. The shed and beating angle change as you move from the cloth beam to the heddle, so weaving in the same location on your loom (the "sweet spot") increases the consistency of your cloth.

Removing Your Woven Fabric from the Loom

As you near the end of the warp, you'll notice that the shed gets smaller until it's difficult to get a good opening (a).

To remove the project from the loom, loosen the tension, and either cut the loops along the back rod (b) or slide them off the rod. Unwind the fabric from the cloth beam, and untie the warp at that end. Secure the ends before washing your woven fabric. (For advice on various options for securing the ends, see Getting the Perfect Finish, starting on page 90.)

TECH SUPPORT:
When Things Go Wrong

I TELL MY STUDENTS THAT THE DIFFERENCE BETWEEN A MASTER WEAVER AND A NEW WEAVER is that the master weaver has made more mistakes. Mistakes aren't the end of a project; they're the beginning of learning something new about weaving. If you've been paying attention, hopefully each mistake teaches you something new. (Though to be fair, I've had my share of remedial lessons.) So if you want to be a better weaver, grab a loom and get on with the mistake-making! Of course, once you've made a mistake, it's good to know how to get out of it as well. In this section, I'll take you on a whirlwind tour of some of the problems weavers run into, and how to fix them.

Tension Problems

Most of the things that go wrong in weaving relate to uneven tension. Weaving fabric is literally creating a web of yarns, each pulling in a specific direction, either warpwise or weftwise. If one yarn is pulling harder or softer than the others, the web shifts, often in a way that doesn't make things easier for the weaver. In this section, we'll see all the woes that uneven tension can create, and how to address them.

Having even tension across your warp threads makes the difference between weaving that is fun and weaving that . . . isn't. Warps with even tension make for better selvedges, prevent broken warp threads, and avoid rippling in the finished fabric.

After you've tied on to the front and before you begin to weave, check your tension by closing your eyes and running your hand across the warp threads at the back of the loom. The tension should feel the same across all warp threads with no hard or soft spots. Once you've begun weaving, look to your fell line, the line created by the latest weft pick you've beaten into place. If this line ripples instead of lying straight, that shows where the tension is uneven. The peaks in your fell line are areas of high tension; the valleys are areas of low tension. At the beginning of a project, you can often fix a wavering fell line without having to undo any of your weaving. Simply tighten the knots that are too loose, and loosen the knots that are too tight.

WHEN NOT TO WORRY

There is one time in your weaving when a rippling fell line shouldn't worry you. That's at the beginning of the warp, when you first wind the finished cloth over the knots that attach the warp to the front rod of your loom. You'll notice that your fell line creates peaks where the knots are. This is because the height of the knots has temporarily increased the tension in that area.

As you continue to weave and wind on, the subsequent layers of cloth will pad the knots and even out the tension across your warp. For 90 percent of warps, this temporary tension issue will have no effect on the finished cloth. For the other 10 percent — inelastic warps such as linen and wire — you can roll a warp separator over the knots to prevent them from affecting the warp tension.

Frowning Warps

As you continue weaving, you may find that the tension in your selvedges becomes tighter or looser than that of the rest of the warp. Too-tight selvedge tension makes your warp look like it's frowning at you. This can be caused by excessive draw-in. Compare the width of your woven fabric to the width of the warp in the heddle. If it's drawing in more than ¼ inch on each side, try bubbling more weft as described on page 75.

What happens when you have excessive draw-in is that the warp on the edges of the fabric is used up faster than that in the middle of the fabric, causing these threads to tighten relative to the rest of the warp.

You may also get a frowning warp if you beamed on your warp in a cigar shape (for explanation, see page 58). In that case, the edge threads are shorter than the center threads, leading to tightening tension on the edges as you weave.

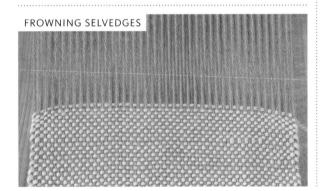

FROWNING SELVEDGES

Smiling Selvedges

By comparison, smiling selvedges indicate loose tension at the edges. The first thing I check here is how the warp is wound on to the back beam. Is it bow-shaped? Are there any threads that have slipped out of their warp separator layers? If so, they aren't traveling as far as the other warps around the back beam, something that will show up as loose selvedges.

Another thing that can cause smiling selvedges is bubbling too much weft when weaving. (See page 75.) Doing so causes the edges of the fabric to become slightly weft-faced (the weft threads cover, or nearly cover, the warp threads). Because weft-faced cloth takes up warp at a slower pace than balanced cloth, the edges will eventually become looser and start smiling.

SMILING SELVEDGES

Poorly Measured Warps

The first place tension played a role is when you measured the warp. As you saw earlier (page 45), the reason that you want to wind a warp with an even tension is to ensure that all the warp threads are the same length. If they are different lengths, you'll have to pull the differences in length to the front of the loom. In the case of a hairy thread, like some wools, this can be tricky and lead to waste, as you have to cut off and discard extra warp from the too-long threads.

Poorly Beamed-On Warps

A properly beamed-on warp should be an even cylinder from one end to the other, with all of the threads the same length, under the same tension, and following the same path. What you do not want to see are cigar-shaped warps (see page 58) or bow-shaped warps. The latter are less common and represent the opposite problem: warp threads crowding over each other on the outside of the warp. (For a review of how to wind on, see Warping the Loom, pages 56–58.)

The only cure for a badly beamed-on warp is to unbeam it, keep it under tension so it doesn't tangle, pull any too-long threads so the extra length is to the front of the warp, and rebeam. If that seems like a lot of work, rest assured that it's easier than fighting your way through weaving a badly beamed warp.

No (or Teensy) Shed

After you've threaded your loom and tensioned the warp comes the moment of truth: the first time you open a shed. Is it big enough to get your shuttle through without skips or floats? Most rigid-heddle looms don't make a huge shed, which is why I recommend using either a stick shuttle or a thin boat shuttle. But the shed should be distinct, with no threads dangling down in the middle of it, and it should be big enough to pass your shuttle through easily. If your shed is nonexistent or teensy, here are some things to check:

» **NOT ENOUGH TENSION.** Do you have a strong enough tension on the warp? Sometimes clicking the brake a notch or two tighter will cause a mushy shed to spring open.

» **DANGLING THREADS.** Danglers (loose, or dangling, threads) in the middle of a shed like that in the photo above are caused by threads that don't have the same tension as their neighbors. To fix these, untie the bout (group of threads) the dangling thread is in, stroke the threads until any extra slack is brought to the front, and then retie the bout. If your danglers are on the edge of the warp, look at your warp beam: are the threads loose because they slipped off the warp protector and took a shortcut? If that's the case, you'll have to unbeam and rebeam.

- » **THREADING ERRORS** in multiple-heddle weave structures can tie the heddles together in ways that make it hard to open a shed. You should also check that you're raising the right combination of heddles together to create the sheds when you are threading a multiple-heddle project.

- » **OTHER THREADING ERRORS.** Did you thread both the slots and the holes? It sounds like a silly thing to check, but it's easy to forget to thread the holes in your hurry to get weaving.

- » **HEDDLE INCORRECTLY POSITIONED.** Are you putting the heddle in the correct up and down positions? It's not always obvious where the up and down positions are on a rigid-heddle loom. When in doubt, check the owner's manual or ask a weaver who's successfully woven on that brand of loom.

- » **NEGLECTING THE BACK BEAM.** Did you go over the back beam of the loom? Some, but not all, rigid-heddle looms have a back beam that the warp has to go over in order to make a shed. Schacht Flip looms have a back beam; Ashford Knitter's looms do not. (See pages 18-19.)

- » **OVERFILLING THE LOOM.** Is there too much warp on the loom? Looms that don't have a back beam to go over rely on the angle of the loom to create the shed. That's why looms without back beams, such as those by Glimakra and Ashford, are angled, while ones with back beams (Schacht and Beka) lay flat. The upside is that you can put more warp on a loom without a back beam, because it's not there to get in the way. The downside is that if you put on too much warp, the shed may be teensy until you weave off enough warp that the angle changes and improves the shed.

Diagonal Fell Line

Unless you're doing something unusual like weaving a V or pulling warp threads to create shaped fabric, you want the fabric on your loom to be square and level. The fell line (the weft-wise edge of the fabric) should run horizontally, at a right angle to the warp as shown in the photo below, from one side of the loom to the other. If it's not, here are a couple of things to check.

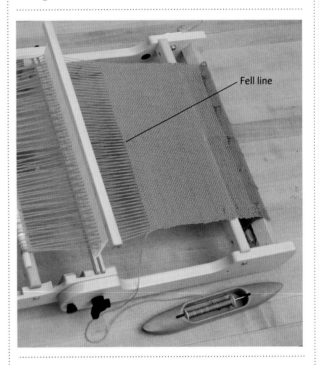

Fell line

- » **ARE YOU BEATING SQUARE?** Check that you're not holding the heddle at an angle when you beat the weft into place. Try to develop the habit of holding the beater in the center to avoid an uneven fell.

- » **IS ONE SIDE OF THE WARP TENSIONED TIGHTER THAN THE OTHER?** If so, that side will become more warp-faced and weave faster than the other side.

Selvedge Problems

Selvedges are the bane of both beginning and experienced weavers. Ask any weaver what part of their craft they'd like to improve, and the answer will likely be selvedges. Achieving better selvedges is one thing you will spend your weaving life perfecting.

Uneven Selvedges

If your selvedges are uneven, it's because you're putting in too much weft in some picks and too little in others. Watch the size of the bubble or the angle you put the weft in at, and make sure that one hand isn't being more generous than the other.

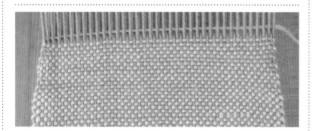

» **TOO MUCH DRAW-IN.** If you're experiencing a lot of draw-in (the cloth is much narrower than the warp in the heddle), you need to put more weft into each pick. Increase the size of the bubble or the angle you're using to insert the weft (see page 75).

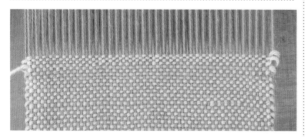

» **LOOPY SELVEDGES.** If there are loops hanging out at the selvedges, you're putting too much weft into each pick. Decrease the size of the bubble or the angle you're using to insert the weft.

Abrading or Breaking Selvedges

New weavers often run into problems with selvedge threads that continually shred and break. Just when you've got one fixed or removed from the project, another one goes. It's a sinking feeling to watch your dreamed-of project becoming narrower and narrower, one broken thread at a time.

The cause of this is almost always too much draw-in. Compare the width of your woven fabric to the width of the warp in the heddle. If it's off by more than ½ inch, you're putting a lot of unnecessary stress on your selvedge threads. What's happening is this: instead of running straight from the back of the loom to the front of the loom, the selvedge threads are bending in toward the fell line of the fabric. Since they are the same length as the rest of the warp but traveling farther (the shortest distance between two points is a straight line), they're tighter than the rest of the warp. Add to that the abrasion from scraping sideways against the inside of their hole or slot in the heddle, and it's no wonder that they fray and snap.

Happily, there's an easy fix: bubble or angle more weft until the draw-in reduces to a reasonable level. You can also try doubling the selvedge threads. The doubled thickness strengthens the selvedge threads and helps them resist the force applied by the weft as it turns around them. A third solution is to use a temple to hold the cloth at a fixed width while you weave (see facing page). All of these things may help, but you need to provide each pick with additional weft to address the underlying problem.

Fabric That's Too Dense or Too Loose

To be successful, a weaving project needs to have the correct sett (see page 33). The sett you should use varies between yarns and the intended use of the final cloth. For example, you set linen cloth differently depending on whether it's going to be used for garment or upholstery fabric.

When you are sampling to determine the correct sett for a project, be sure to check how the fabric feels after you've washed it. Some fabrics, such as rayon chenille, can dramatically change after you've washed them. You might revise your opinion of what the ideal sett for the project would be.

The good news is that you can change the sett of a project that's set too loosely or too tightly, without taking it off the loom. The bad news is that you'll have to rethread the slots and holes of the heddle.

» **IF THE FABRIC IS TOO DENSE,** swap out the heddle for one with fewer threads per inch. If this means that you have too many threads to fit in the heddle, you can leave some of the threads at both edges unthreaded and let them dangle off the back of the loom.

» **IF THE FABRIC IS TOO LOOSE,** swap the heddle for one with more threads per inch. If this makes your project too narrow, add additional warp threads to the project. You can either weight the new threads in a bundle at the back of the loom, as you would a broken warp thread (see page 87), or you can un-beam the warp, tie the new warp threads to the back rod, and re-beam the warp.

USING A TEMPLE

If you are weaving a project (such as curtains) where it's important that the fabric width stays consistent, you can use a temple to counteract the draw-in. Temples are available in different materials: metal and wooden. You can even make one yourself with paper clips, string, and weights. To use a temple, first adjust it until the teeth are as far apart as the width of the warp in the heddle (a). Next, push the teeth on one side of the temple into the cloth just inside the selvedge. Repeat with the other side of the temple and the other selvedge (b). Press the temple flat to spread the warp. Lock the temple in place. The mechanism to do this varies depending on the type of temple. Remove and reposition the temple forward as you weave, every 2" to 3".

Broken Warp Threads

Sometimes, through no fault of your own, a warp thread breaks. Perhaps it was a flaw in the thread or a knot that slipped past you during winding the warp. In any event, it's not the end of the world. Weaving is magic because the warp threads are discontinuous, which is a fancy way of saying they are cut at both ends. This means that you can replace part or all of one warp thread without affecting the others.

The first thing to do when you break a warp thread is stop and evaluate the situation. You have options at this point:

» **DON'T FIX THE BROKEN WARP THREAD.** Instead, toss it over the back of the loom, and weave a project one thread narrower than you'd originally planned. This typically is an option only when a selvedge thread breaks, if you intend to felt the fabric, if the project is a sample where a few missing threads won't be an issue, or when the yarn is so wild (think eyelash yarn in the weft) that you'd never know. Obviously, you wouldn't want to do this more than once or twice in a warp.

» **COMPLETELY REPLACE A BROKEN WARP THREAD.** If you decide to do this, cut a replacement warp thread the same length as you measured for the warp, insert it into the warp to replace the broken warp thread, and, after the cloth is off the loom, replace the broken warp thread entirely, making the mistake as if it never happened. This is an elegant fix that involves hanging weights off the back of your loom to tension the replacement thread. It yields the cleanest end result, but having one or more weights dangling off the back of a rigid-heddle loom can be cumbersome. (see facing page.)

THINGS TO AVOID

Some broken warp threads *are* totally your fault, like when you slam a shuttle into a warp thread or, in an extreme case, drop the loom and break a warp thread while trying to catch it on the way down. Other weaver contributions to broken warp threads include choosing the wrong thread for warp yarn. (For a list of things to consider when choosing a warp, see page 26.)

If the warp yarn snaps because it's weak, you may still be able to weave with it, but you'll have to be more careful and perhaps take other protective steps, such as sizing the yarn (adding a substance that acts as a temporary glue to strengthen the yarn during weaving and then washes out later).

METHOD 1: *How to Replace a Broken Warp Thread*

① Cut a new warp thread the same length as the original warp.

② Push a T-pin into the already woven cloth and wrap one end of the new warp thread around the T-pin in a figure-8 pattern to secure it.

③ Thread the new warp thread in place of the broken one.

④ Secure and weight the rest of the new warp behind the loom. Some weavers use small canisters weighted with pennies inside, wrapping the excess yarn around the outside of the canister. I use kumihimo bobbins. The photo illustrates how to use washers laced on a split key ring. You want the weight to be enough to match the tension of the rest of the warp as closely as possible. Hang the weight off the back of the rigid-heddle loom, providing tension for the new warp thread. The broken warp thread also dangles off the back of the loom. You'll have to take care to unroll it when you advance the warp.

Continued on next page ▷

METHOD 1: How to Replace a Broken Warp Thread, *continued*

⑤ Weave the rest of the cloth.

⑥ After you cut the cloth off the loom, use a square knot to tie the loose end of the new warp thread to the bit of broken warp thread in the fabric.

⑦ Starting at the front of the cloth, pull the broken warp thread (a) until the knot reaches the front of the fabric. The new warp thread now replaces the broken warp thread completely (b).

⑧ Washing and or massaging the cloth a bit will remove any tension irregularities between the new warp thread and the rest of the cloth.

Ta-da! It's like the broken warp never happened!

Another Way to Fix a Broken Warp Thread

An alternate solution is to fix a broken warp thread the way I do it 90 percent of the time. I hate having things dangle off the back of my rigid-heddle loom, where there's an opportunity for dangling things to tangle. So, I've adapted how I repair broken warp threads: it's quicker and more convenient than replacing the entire thread. The trade-off is that after the cloth is finished, there is one warpwise join in the fabric. If you are good at joining, however, this should be barely noticeable. (*Note:* This method is also useful for repairing breaks in painted warps, where it would be nearly impossible to color-match a broken warp thread, unless you planned ahead and dyed a few extra warp threads when creating your painted warp.)

METHOD 2: *How to Replace a Broken Warp Thread*

① Cut a piece of replacement warp 8"–12" long and tie it to the broken warp end at the back of the loom.

② Thread the repair thread through the heddle.

③ Stick a T-pin into the woven fabric and wrap the repair thread around it in a figure-8 pattern to secure it. Do this under tension, so that when you're done, the repair thread is at the same tension as the rest of the warp.

④ Weave off the rest of the fabric and remove from loom.

1–3

Continued on next page ▷

METHOD 2: How to Fix a Broken Warp Thread, *continued*

⑤ When the fabric is off the loom, untie the repair thread and remove it. Thread the broken thread onto a tapestry needle and needle-weave it back up to the front of the cloth, overlapping the warp for 1 inch where the break occurred. You may need to tug on the warp thread as you do this to get enough slack for the overlap.

⑥ Trim loose ends.

→ *You'll have repaired the fabric with the original broken thread (handy if you didn't have extra warp for repairs) and no need to fuss with a dangling and tangling thread weighted off the end. The downsides to this method are that you may have a slightly shorter fringe and a warpwise join.*

Unweaving and Cutting Out

There are times during weaving when you need to go backward and undo some of the cloth you've created. Perhaps there's a huge skip in the fabric or the weft you chose doesn't look good with the warp. At these times, you have two basic choices: unweave or cut the fabric out.

» **UNWEAVING.** If the mistake is only a few threads back, you can try unweaving. Unweaving to fix a float or a skip sometimes leads to more of a tangle than you began with, unless you're careful about pulling the skipped threads out of the way when you go backward through the shed. If your attempts to unweave have ended in a snarl, do the sensible thing and cut the weft below the beginning of the snarl, taking great care not to cut a warp thread in the process, then rejoin the weft and begin weaving again.

» **CUTTING OUT THE WEFT.** If the mistake is several inches back, it's more expedient to cut the weft out instead of unweaving it. To do this safely, loosen the tension on the warp. In the center of the warp, pull the warp threads apart to create an inch-wide gap in the fabric. Then, take care to cut only the weft (a). From the selvedges, pull the cut weft pieces out of the fabric with your fingers or a tapestry needle (b).

On wide warps, or warps made up of thin yarn, you may have to repeat this process in several places across the width of the warp in order to get pieces of weft short enough to easily pull free (c).

GETTING THE PERFECT FINISH

WEAVING IS ONLY A PART OF THE PROCESS OF MAKING A HANDWOVEN ITEM. As you saw at the beginning of this chapter, warping is a large component of making cloth. Another is finishing, taking the cloth from its raw state to completion. Like warping, finishing can take a long time, and like warping, doing it well is crucial to the success of the end result. I think of creating a handwoven item as a three-step process: warping, weaving, and finishing.

There are many ways to finish a cloth, from simple to intricate. The following sections describe the finishing process and several techniques you can use.

Securing the Weft

When you first take your cloth off the loom, you'll notice that there's nothing holding the weft in place except friction. Slippery yarns like rayon will begin to unweave themselves immediately; you'll have a bit of extra time with sticky yarns like wool. The first thing you should do when you finish weaving is control the cut ends of the warp to prevent the weft from falling out. This can be as simple as making overhand knots, or as complicated as a netted fringe. If you will be using your fabric to sew a garment that will be seamed or hemmed, you can secure the raw edges with machine zigzag stitch or serging.

Fringe

Fringe is a finish that doesn't add bulk to the end of the cloth and can be quite decorative, showing off beautiful warp threads. A proper fringe enhances the textile, is durable, and resists tangling. Ideally, you decide whether to have fringe during the planning stages of your project, since fringe requires extra length in your warp. If you are weaving a single item, such as a scarf, you can usually get enough length out of the loom waste and the front knots to create an "afterthought" fringe. If you are weaving multiple items, however, you'll need to leave unwoven warp between the items in order to have length to create a fringe.

Often the final use of the cloth will determine whether you want fringe on your project. A delicate silk shawl might be enhanced by fringe, but fringe might be not be practical on a set of cotton dish towels that will be washed often.

Before you begin your fringe, decide how many threads to have in each fringe bundle. Find a number that will divide evenly into the number of warp threads you have. You can fudge this if necessary by sneaking in extra threads here and there.

Select a number of threads in each bundle that is neither too thick or too thin. A too-thin fringe has fewer than two threads. A too-thick fringe looks awkward and creates gaps in the bottom of the cloth. This happens because it's gathering together warp threads that are spaced too far apart. Typically, fringe is anywhere from two to eight threads in size, with thicker threads having fewer warps in each fringe and thinner threads having more.

The simplest fringe is an overhand knot. The tricky thing about this fringe is that it leaves cut ends of the warp loose, exposing them to abrasion and fraying. If you use this fringe with a tender or loosely spun yarn, you'll soon end up with a row of knots at the end of your cloth and no fringe. I recommend this fringe only for items that won't be washed often (like a table runner or lamp shade) and only for fibers that are tightly twisted and fray resistant, such as linen or tightly spun cotton.

TWISTED/PLIED FRINGE

This style of fringe creates a plied cord out of a group of warp threads. Plying the warp threads together protects them from fraying. You can create this type of fringe using just your hands, a mechanical plying device, or an electronic hair braider (which, despite the name, actually is a hair-plying device.)

There are several mechanical devices that you can use to create a plied fringe. They are a bit faster than using your fingers, and offer the advantage of making it easy to do three- and four-ply fringes, something hard to achieve just using your fingers. The ones made by loom manufacturers tend to be utilitarian, but if you go to conferences or weavers' guild sales, you may find some more whimsical models created by local woodworkers.

Before you begin, decide whether you are creating a two-, three-, or four-ply fringe. The more plies in your fringe, the rounder it will be. Which you use is largely a matter of aesthetics, so you may want to experiment with some cut pieces of extra warp yarn to see what you like before you begin.

BRAIDED FRINGE

A braided fringe can be as simple as the three-strand braid used to plait hair, or as complicated as the patterned square braids woven in the Andes. A three-strand braid forms a fringe that is flatter than a plied fringe and requires no special equipment. As with plied fringe, you braid the fringe and then tie an overhand knot at the bottom in order to secure the braid. I recommend using a ruler to get all the knots at the same length.

How to Make Plain Fringe

(1) Determine how many threads are in each fringe bundle, choosing a number that is a multiple of the total number of warp threads. Tie an overhand knot in each fringe bundle. It's important to snug the knots up against the weft evenly. You can use a tapestry needle inserted into the center of the knot to move it around before you tighten it down all the way.

(2) After you've placed and tightened all the knots, trim the fringe to a consistent length. First, I comb the fringe, so it's even and flat, then I put a clear ruler over the fringe and cut the fringe with a rotary cutter. (You can get the same results with a pair of sharp scissors, but it takes more care.) This gives you a nice, even fringe.

Ply Fringe with Your Hands

(1) To twist a two-ply fringe with your fingers, take a group of warp threads and divide them in half.

(2) With one group in each hand, use your fingers to roll the group of threads to the right.

(3) Pass the group in your right hand over the top of the group in your left hand and the group in your left hand under the group in your right hand and swap each group to a different hand. I call this "passing to the left."

(4) Continue rolling to the right and passing to the left until you've used up the length of fringe. Finish the end with an overhand knot.

AN OLD TWIST

Why roll to the right and pass to the left? Because most commercial yarns are spun Z and plied S, which is spinner's speak for saying spun to the left and plied to the right. By rolling right and plying left, you will be increasing the overall twist on the yarn and strengthening it. If you rolled left and plied right, the rolling left would unply the commercial yarn, thus weakening it, which is not what you want your fringe to do. If you find that rolling right and passing left seems to be creating a loose and floppy fringe, check your yarn: it may be one of the few yarns that was spun S and plied Z (such as a yarn designed for crochet, or a handspun yarn). In that case, roll left and pass right. The other time you should roll left and pass right is if you are working with a singles yarn (see Balanced Twist, page 27) that was spun S.

Yarn plied S

Twisted fringe plied Z

⑤ As you continue to make fringe, use a ruler to check the length of each one. Why use a ruler? Why not just compare the current fringe to the previous one? It seems like the obvious thing to do, but this almost always leads to a diagonal fringe. This is because tiny mistakes you make in measuring the new fringe against the previous one (such as pulling a bit too tightly on the new fringe) add up as you go across the warp.

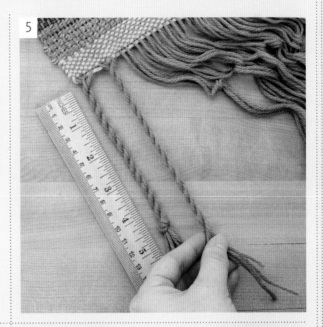

5

⑥ When you've twisted and tied all the fringe, wash the fabric. After the fabric is washed, retighten the knots. Then either cut the excess loose threads off close to the knots (for a clean, polished look) or leave them as tiny lion's tails (for a funky, artistic look.)

6

Securing the Weft

Using Mechanical Twisters

① Load up the alligator clips on the device with your warp threads. For the most consistent fringe, load an equal number of threads into each clip. For a more textured fringe, you can load different numbers into each clip. Whichever you do, make a note of it so you can repeat it across the warp.

② Turn the crank to the right, counting as you go. When the threads seem tight and full of energy, stop cranking and make a note of the number of times you cranked.

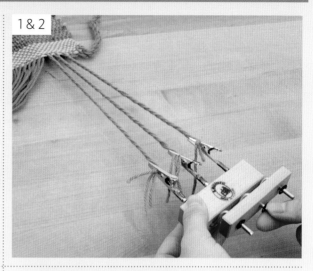

1 & 2

③ Pinching the warp ends so they can't untwist, pull them out of the clips and tie them together in an overhand knot at the length you want your finished fringe to be.

④ Release the fringe. It should ply automatically as the yarn releases the potential energy you added to it by cranking the fringe twister. If the fringe is too tight, undo it and redo it, cranking fewer times with the fringe twister next time. If the fringe is too loose, undo it and redo it, cranking more times with the fringe twister.

⑤ Continue across the warp, cranking each group of fringes the same number of times as you did the first group.

4

Hemstitching

Hemstitching is an elegant edge finish that doesn't add bulk at the end of a fabric. It takes more planning than other fringes because it is performed while the fabric is on the loom. This means that you do one row of hemstitching after you've spread the header but before you begin weaving your item, and another at the end of the item.

As with the plain fringe, hemstitching leaves cut ends of warp threads and thus is best used with tightly spun yarns that won't fray or with projects that won't experience much abrasion. A common use of hemstitching is at the end of linen goods or silk scarves.

How to Hemstitch

① Spread the warp with a few rows of weaving, as described on page 69. Cut the weft.

② Leave a length of warp unwoven; this will become the fringe. You can use a spacer such as a cardboard strip or ruler to make sure the unwoven section is even. I recommend that the unwoven warp be a bit longer than the desired fringe length, so you have some length you can cut off to true-up the fringe length.

③ Leave a loose length of weft at least three times as long as the warp is wide and begin weaving. Weave until you have at least 1" of fabric.

④ Thread the loose end of weft onto a tapestry needle.

⑤ Take the tapestry needle around the first group of warp threads, and come back up out of the woven cloth two or three picks above. Pull gently on the thread to tighten and draw the warp threads together.

5

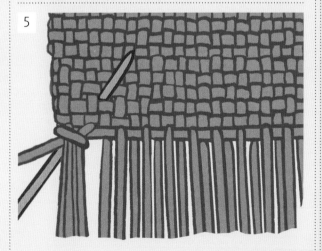

Continued on next page ▷

How to Hemstitch, *continued*

(6) Take the tapestry needle behind the next set of warp threads then all the way around them in a clockwise direction. Come up out of the cloth the same number of wefts as in Step 5, just to the left of the next group of threads you will wrap.

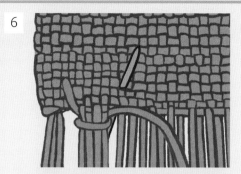

6

(7) Continue across the fabric until you reach the last group of warp threads. Wrap the last group of warp threads. If the weft is a color that blends with the warp threads, take it down into the wrap and tighten into a knot. If the weft is a color that would stand out in the fringe, weave it back into the horizontal line of hemstitching. Pull gently to tighten.

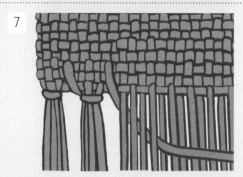

7

(8) Weave the rest of the cloth. Leave a loose end of weft at least three times as long as the width of the warp.

(9) Hemstitch the other end of the cloth. One of the benefits of using a rigid-heddle loom is you can pick up the loom and turn it around so that the hemstitching at the end is done from the same perspective as the beginning. Weavers on shaft looms have to hemstitch at the other end from a backward perspective.

> ### HEMSTITCHING . . . AND MORE
>
> You can use hemstitching in combination with other types of fringe, such as at the top of twisted or braided fringe (see page 91), or in the middle of a fabric to create delicate lacy openings.

Hems

Another common way to protect the warp threads of fabric is to hem it. Because hems encapsulate the cut warp ends, they are one of the most durable ways to finish off handwoven fabric and are commonly used on household goods, such as placemats, dish towels, and garments that are washed often. (For instructions about other types of hems than those covered here, see a basic sewing reference.)

OVERCASTING BY MACHINE

Instead of hand-stitching an overcast hem, you may be able to do this on your sewing machine if it has a setting for overcasting. Or you can use a specialized machine called a serger, which sews an overlock stitch and trims away excess fabric in one pass. The best way to learn about sergers is to go to a sewing shop and ask for a demonstration. You may also find videos on YouTube that show sergers in operation. I use a serger in my studio to protect the cut ends of warp before I wash the fabric.

Note: Be wary of using a serger in a project that you plan to submit to a juried show or competition. Some judges have a bias against machine-stitching in a handwoven project, and especially against the industrial look of a machine-serged finish.

OVERCAST HEM: BLANKET STITCH

To hand-stitch an overcast hem, use a thread and needle to stitch from the top to the bottom of the cloth by going around the cut edge. This causes the thread to wrap the cut ends of the cloth and helps prevent them from unraveling. One advantage of an overcast finish is that it adds very little bulk to the project. A disadvantage of the overcast stitch is that it can be a bit fuzzy, since only some of the cut ends are encapsulated by the overcast stitch. The other cut ends may fray or stick out between the overcasting thread, which is especially true for hand-overcast hems, as they are typically not as dense as machine-serged ones.

One scenario in which a hand-stitched overcast stitch makes sense is in the case of a fulled woolen blanket. The moderate amount of felting that takes place during the fulling process prevents the cut ends from fraying, and the additional support of the overcast stitch adds strength to the edge without adding bulk.

The thread that you use to overcast can either blend into the fabric for an unobtrusive look, or you can pick a decorative thread that adds a design element to the fabric. You often see the latter, for example, along the collars and hems of coats that could use a bit of an accent.

A serger is a great tool for any weaver who plans to use handwoven fabrics for sewing projects. The overlocked edge shown here along the bottom was done on a serger.

How to Hand-stitch an Overcast Hem

① Thread a needle with your overcast thread and secure it to the fabric on the wrong side, either with a few small stitches or a knot.

② To make the first stitch, come out of the fabric on the right side, wrap the thread around the cut edge of the cloth, and go back through the fabric in the same place. Draw the needle through the loop at the edge of the fabric, ready for the next stitch.

③ On subsequent stitches, insert the needle through the fabric from front to back, pass the needle through the open loop of thread, and pull snugly to close the loop.

④ Repeat step 3 until you've finished the edge. Finish off with a couple of small stitches into the fabric or a knot to secure it.

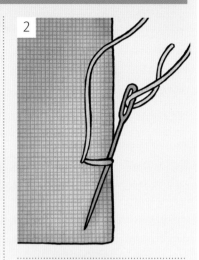

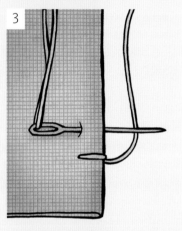

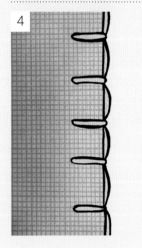

ENCAPSULATED HEMS AND BIAS TAPE

Encapsulated hems use a supplementary cloth such as commercially woven fabric, lace, ribbon, or bias tape to wrap the cut edges of the handwoven cloth. The wrapping cloth is generally lighter in weight and tightly woven so it doesn't fray.

Handwoven and commercial fabrics can complement each other. The handwoven fabric brings high-texture, high-touch uniqueness, along with the ir-regularities that let you know it was handmade. Commercial cloth contributes evenness and smoothness, but it is finer than most of us care to weave. Commercial cloth is great for lining garments, adding strength to the inside of handwoven bags, and for finishing off hems.

While you can save a lot of time by buying ready-made ribbon or lace from a fabric store, for an heirloom-quality project you might choose to make your own trim. Making your own trim can be rewarding and give you trims that exactly match your project. If you weave a band using the same threads as in the warp, for example, you can finish off the inside of a garment in a way that's just as lovely and handcrafted as the outside. Whether you purchase trim or make it yourself depends on the project and your personal preferences.

How to Encase a Hem with Lace or Ribbon

This is often used on the bottom hems of garments such as jackets, skirts, and pants, as well as curtains and table runners, where the wrong side of the fabric won't show.

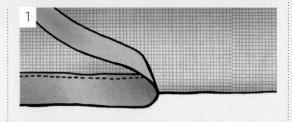

① Overlap the edge of the fabric with the ribbon or lace, and sew close to the edge of the ribbon or lace by hand or machine.

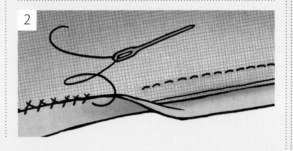

② Fold the ribbon or lace over the fabric edge and hand-stitch the other edge of the ribbon or lace to the fabric, taking tiny stitches into the back of the fabric so it won't show on the front side. Or, for a more refined finish, you can use tiny handsewn slipstitches to tack the edge of the ribbon in place, nearly invisibly.

How To Encase a Hem with Double-Fold Bias Tape

This is often used on the outside edges of projects, such as placemats and pillows. It is also used on the inside seams of garments.

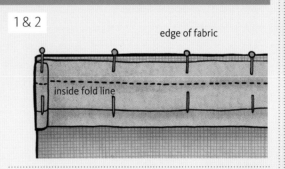

edge of fabric

inside fold line

① Open up the bias tape and pin it to the fabric as shown. You want to pin it so the center fold of the tape abuts the cut edge of the fabric when it is folded around.

② Stitch along in the inside fold line of the bias tape as shown.

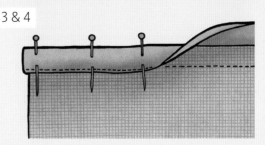

③ Fold the bias tape over the edge of the cloth so that the unstitched fold extends a bit beyond the line of stitching created in step 2. If you put a pin through the previous line of stitching, it should catch the bias binding with about a millimeter of excess.

④ Stitch close to the folded edge of the tape. Or, for a more refined finish, you can use tiny handsewn slipstitches to tack the edge of the bias tape in place, nearly invisibly.

DOUBLE-FOLD HEM

The double-fold hem is the simplest type of hem, but it has some limitations. It may be too thick for bulky fabrics, and it may not thoroughly protect a diaphanous fabric. On the other hand, it has the advantage of being self-contained, meaning that you don't need to purchase or make anything to finish the hem, and it will exactly match the rest of the fabric. If you plan a double-fold hem on the finished project, you can weave the 1½" that will be folded under using a thinner weft than the rest of the project. This reduces bulk in the hem.

To tell where one item ends and another begins, you can also insert one or two picks of a contrasting weft between projects in order to establish cutting lines. Or you may choose to run two lines of zigzag stitching between each item, cutting between the stitching lines after washing to separate them. Be sure to weave enough for both the previous item and the next item you're weaving.

How to Make a Double-Fold Hem

① Secure the weft by serging or zigzag-stitching the cut edges, then wash it so that any shrinkage happens before hemming.

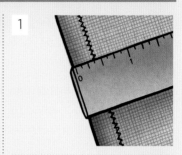
1

② Fold the cut end of the cloth up and iron in place. The amount you fold up depends on the depth of hem you wish to create. For a ½-inch hem, I typically do a first fold that is ⅜" deep.

③ Fold the cloth again to fully encapsulate the cut ends and iron it in place.

2 & 3

④ Hand- or machine-stitch the fold down.

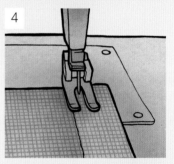
4

⑤ Finish each end of the hem by pushing any raw edges in place with a tapestry needle (a). Ensure the raw ends don't stick out of the tube of the double-fold hem.

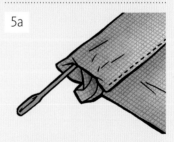

Alternatively, if it will not make the cloth too stiff, or for a high-use item where durability is more important than handle, you can stitch the ends of the tube. I find stitching the ends of the hems closed with a triangle is more durable and more visually pleasing than a straight line (b).

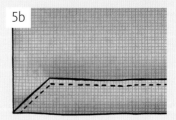
5a

5b

Wet-Finishing Your Fabric

When you take your finished item off the loom, it's a web. It's not until you wet-finish it that it becomes cloth. This transformation can be dramatic or it can be subtle. When you immerse your finished cloth in water, it releases the tension the warp and weft threads experienced while the cloth was on the loom. You'll find that after wet-finishing, the cloth is denser and more flexible as the warp and weft yarns mold in and around each other. This causes dimensional loss in both the weft and warp directions, as the yarn deflects into the thickness of the cloth.

Before you wash your cloth, make sure you have secured the warp ends so the fabric won't unravel in the wash. You can do this using one of the techniques in this chapter (starting on page 90), or simply tie a loose overhand knot at both ends of the warp.

In general, it's best to wash handwoven fabric according to its fiber content. For example, a cotton garment fabric will benefit from being washed in hot water so that it will shrink fully and prevent surprises the first time you wash your handwoven shirt. On the other hand, a cashmere-silk shawl would best be handwashed gently and laid flat to dry.

That said, sometimes washing things in exactly the wrong way reveals wonderful surprises. For example, rayon chenille weaves up stiff as a board. Despite the delicate nature of the rayon yarn, what the fabric really needs is to be beaten up in the washing machine a bit to bloom fully into a soft, velvety cloth.

SAMPLING IS THE KEY

Daryl Lancaster, an inspiring weaving and sewing instructor, taught me this invaluable technique: Weave a sample length, remove it from the loom, then cut it into three parts. Leave one third unwashed, handwash another, and throw the third piece in the washer and dryer with a load of jeans. You may discover fun surprises. For example, singles yarns may develop tracking, which makes organic twill-like patterns in the simplest weave structures, or a multifiber project may distort in an appealing way that you wouldn't have suspected. You may also avoid inadvertently destroying your hard-won fabric if, for example, you discover that a supposedly nonfelting mohair felts into a rock with a bit of agitation.

Unwashed

Hand washed

Machine washed and machine dried

DEALING WITH WARPS THAT GO WRONG

JUST BECAUSE A PROJECT HAS FAILED or you don't want to work on it right now doesn't mean that you've wasted the yarn. You can take a warp off a loom and save it for later. I had one warp, for instance, that I put on three different looms until it found the right fit and I wove it off.

Knowing how to save a warp for later can be a great comfort when you've created a project out of amazing yarn that isn't what you can or want to weave at the moment. Perhaps you chose a yarn that's unsuitable for warp and you want to repurpose it as weft. Perhaps you need to take a project off the loom so you can take the loom to a workshop. Or you have a sudden need to weave a cotton baby blanket for a shower tomorrow and don't want to sacrifice the super-skinny silk warp currently on the loom.

Removing Warp for Future Replacement

Whatever the reason, you can take a project in progress off the loom and put it back on later. The first step is to get the warp off without creating a tangled mess. Remember that a thread under tension is a thread under control. To successfully remove a warp and save it for later, it needs to be kept under tension throughout the process.

If you've already started weaving the project, you'll need to decide whether to unthread the warp or leave it on the heddle. One of the advantages of a rigid-heddle loom is that you can remove the heddle and set it aside, prethreaded to add back to the loom at a later date — something that's hard or impossible to do on a shaft loom. Of course, if you do this, you'll need to own more than one heddle if you want to weave something else while this warp is stored.

This technique is especially useful if you have a rigid-heddle loom that allows you to slide the end loops off the back rod without having to cut them. Schacht looms make this possible from the outset; other brands of looms can be modified to make this possible. Whether or not you choose to leave the heddle in your project (see facing page), you can always take a warp off your loom and restore it later. Hopefully this knowledge will make you a bit more fearless about what you're willing to put on your loom.

TURNING WARP INTO WEFT

If a warp isn't working out, save it for weft. Perhaps the yarn wasn't stable enough for warp, or it didn't work with any of your heddles. In this scenario, I recommend stretching out the warp full length and thread by thread winding it up into a ball. You will have a lot of opportunities to practice joining in new weft in your next project, but you'll also have that thrifty feel of not having wasted a good yarn.

How to Remove a Project without Unthreading the Heddle

(1) Wind the warp (and any partially woven section) onto the front beam. Slide a length of strong waste yarn, such as cotton rug warp, along the back rod, inside the warp. Tie the ends of the waste yarn together. Because the waste yarn is traveling the exact same path as the back rod, you preserve the end loop and make it easy to slide the warp back onto a rod at a later date. Slide the tied loop off the back rod.

(2) Wrap the warp around the heddle tightly, so it can't tangle.

(3) Unroll any woven cloth from the front beam.

Continued on next page ▷

How to Remove a Project without Unthreading the Heddle, *continued*

④ If you tied only the first half of a surgeon's knot when you warped the loom, tie the second half of the knots now to secure them. Slide the tied warp ends off the front rod.

⑤ If your loom attaches the front rod in such a way that this is not possible, untie the knots that attach the warp to the front rod. Tie the loose warp ends together in a loose overhand knot to keep them from tangling. Wrap the cloth and front part of the warp around the heddle. You now have a tidy package that's ready to be put back on the loom at a later date (a). In the meantime, you can weave a different project on your loom with a new heddle. Optionally, you can protect your warp by wrapping it with paper, and note the type and amount of yarn in the warp (b).

How to Put a Threaded Project Back on the Loom

① Unwrap your bundle. Slide the loops back onto the back rod, and distribute them evenly.

② Pulling from the front of the warp, stretch it out to its full length and snap it a few times to even out the tension and get it to lay flat.

③ Wind onto the back beam, using a warp separator (see page 57).

④ Slip the front knots onto the front rod. If your loom is such that you had to untie the front knots, re-tie them now under tension as you would when first warping a loom. Depending on the amount of cloth you'd previously woven, you may need to move the heddle to the back of the loom, or even the back warp beam, to make room.

⑤ Wind any cloth on to the front beam and use the front brake to tension the warp for weaving.

Removing a Project from the Loom and the Heddle

Saving the warp with the heddle in is the most efficient way to reuse a warp because you don't have to rethread it to get it back on the loom. But what if you want to free your loom and your heddle, too? You can save a warp without leaving the heddle in. The thing that saves the threading order and makes this feasible is something called a thread-by-thread cross (see page 41).

If you've wound a warp on a warping board, you're already familiar with a thread-by-thread cross. It's the way you put one thread over a peg and the next one under a peg to make sure that when you take the warp off the warping board the threads can't slide out of their wound order. Creating a cross on a project that's on the loom is easy, simply use the two plain-weave sheds. (If you're weaving a pattern that doesn't have plain-weave sheds, pick the sheds that are most like plain weave or that have the most intersections — that is, the fewest floats.) See below.

How to Remove a Warp from the Heddle

① Raise the first plain-weave shed and tie choke ties around the raised threads behind the heddle. Leave room between these choke ties and the heddle for the next set of choke ties that you'll tie in step 2.

② Create the second plain-weave shed and tie choke ties around the raised threads behind the heddle.

Continued on next page ▷

How to Remove a Warp from the Heddle, *continued*

③ Untie the warp from the front of the loom and pull the warp threads out of the heddle. If you've woven any fabric, you'll have to either unweave, cut the weft threads out of the warp, or cut the cloth off of the warp so you have free warp ends to pass through the heddle.

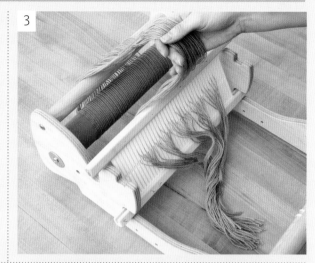

④ Tie the loose ends of warp thread together into a loose overhand knot to secure them and keep them from tangling.

⑤ Chain or use a kite stick to keep the warp threads under tension as you unroll the warp. (For more information about chaining and kite sticks, see pages 46–48.)

(6) Tie a choke tie around the loop that attaches the end of the warp to the back beam. This choke tie should follow the path of the back rod inside the warp loop. Slide the loop off the back beam. Now you have a tidy package that you can store until its ready to go back on a loom. You might want to note the warp length and the heddle that it had been on previously, so you don't have to try to figure out the sett again when you pick the project up later.

How to Put an Unthreaded Project Back on the Loom

(1) Put the end loops of the warp onto the back rod and spread them out between the ties.

(2) Put the cross onto two sticks that are at least 2" longer than the warp is wide, and either tie or tape the sticks together so the cross can't slide off the sticks.

(3) Thread the heddle from the cross, taking the threads in the order that they appear in the cross.

(4) Grab the front of the warp and snap it a couple of times to tension and spread it.

(5) Wind the warp onto the back beam with warp separators.

(6) Tie onto the front rod and tension the warp as normally.

Weaving Ugly Things

There will come a time when you'll look down at the fabric on the loom and think, "Dang, that's ugly." Often it's because of the unpredictable nature of what happens when warp meets weft. Colors merge in ways that are unexpected and sometimes unlovely. Perhaps both colors are beautiful, but the proportions are wrong. You were imagining a weft-faced fabric with occasional pops of warp color, but the warp color is so strong that it's dominating the fabric. Perhaps a fuzzy yarn, instead of providing a playful contrast to the smooth yarns, looks like a tiny stripe of road kill.

The problem may also be the yarn quality. Perhaps the warp yarn was weaker than you thought and is snapping continuously; perhaps it's a hairy linen that has glued itself together with its fellows so you can't raise a shed. Perhaps your weft yarn has started to shed dye all over your hands and the loom. Perhaps halfway through a cone of weft, baby moths started fluttering out.

If you're at the beginning of the warp when you realize things have gone awry, you have several options:

» **CHANGE THE WEFT.** Try a darker color, a lighter color, a different color. Try a thicker or thinner yarn or something you had dismissed as too boring. Try something completely crazy cakes.

» **CHANGE THE SETT.** This alters the proportion of warp and weft and also changes the hand and look of the fabric. A looser sett makes the fabric more weft dominant; a tighter sett makes the

fabric more warp dominant. If you're using different colors in the warp and weft, the color of the fabric will shift as well. If you're weaving fabric that feels like cardboard, try loosening the sett up, keeping in mind that some fabric softens markedly in the wash. If you're weaving something that doesn't hang together, or your weft is completely covering your warp (and you don't want it to), try tightening things up.

» **CHANGE THE WARP.** This is harder than changing the weft, but doable. You can either unroll the warp to revise it, or simply cut threads out and replace them just as you would for a broken warp thread (see page 85). Try different yarns, both ones that you think will work and those you think won't.

» **REMOVE THE WARP AND SAVE IT** for another project, give it to a weaving buddy, or use it to teach a new weaver (who will be so overwhelmed by the "Holy Cats! I'm making cloth!" of it all, that aesthetics will be less of a concern). Or in extreme cases, bury it in the backyard.

If you've finished weaving, and you're still disappointed in the cloth, you can:

» **WASH THE UGLY OUT.** Cloth often improves with wet-finishing. Fabric that's stiff can soften, threads can migrate to new and more pleasing positions. The transformation is sometimes astounding. Try a gentle wash at first, and if that doesn't make it better, you can get more aggressive with it.

» **DYE THE UGLY AWAY.** If the problem is disharmonious colors, you can bring them into alignment by overdyeing the entire cloth with a single color. Take a moment and think about how various colors will interact with the colors in the fabric. For example, a predominantly green project overdyed with red will produce muddy colors, whereas overdyeing with blue would produce soothing blue-greens.

A DOG ON THE LOOM

A "dog on the loom" is a weaverly term for a project that is just too horrible to continue with. If not dealt with promptly, the dog will camp out on your loom for months, perhaps even years, and prevent you from weaving anything fun.

» **PUT IT IN THE MAGIC DRAWER.** You wove it, you washed it: it's still ugly. This is often because what you see in front of you doesn't match what you wanted to create. Put the fabric away for a week or two (or a year or two), and then come back to it with fresh eyes. Sometimes it's only after you forget what you wanted to see, that you can see what's really there.

If after all that it's still ugly, look at it and learn from it. Why is this ugly? What do I wish were different about this cloth? And then get rid of it. No one needs resistant ugly hanging around. Whether it was a poor choice in yarn, weave structure, color, or simply a "dog on the loom," there comes a time when it's best to cut your losses (and your warp) and start over. If the current project is failing, and it's not even worth the effort to save the yarn, do not hesitate to pick up the scissors and cut that disaster off the loom. Don't save a miserable warp that you hate. Don't tell yourself that a couple of more washes will fix that bleeding weft yarn; don't try to freeze or microwave the moth-ridden wool. You won't have a project to show for that day's work, but you'll have learned a valuable lesson about what isn't worth weaving. Your stash will have been improved, and your loom will be free and waiting for your next success.

Before and after: The cotton towel at the top was an unappealing gray, much improved by being overdyed with a rich purple (below).

CHAPTER 4

COLOR THEORY
in a Nutshell

ONE OF THE FIRST THINGS YOU NOTICE ABOUT A TEXTILE IS ITS COLOR. A garment can be beautifully woven and masterfully tailored, but if it's the wrong color, it can be hard to look at. Picking the right color or set of colors is important.

This is the point where some weavers get stuck. Color is so subjective and such a large factor in a textile's success that they freeze up and become afraid to combine colors for fear of weaving something that clashes. Adding to the danger is the way color works in weaving, combining like pixels in a pointillist painting to create new colors, some of them wonderful, others dreadful.

The Courage to Make Colors Sing

To avoid trouble, some weavers stick to monotone, single-color projects or to a few known-to-be-successful color combinations. If that's your joy, great! For some weavers, pattern and yarn texture are more important than color. But if you've found yourself reaching for the same few colors over and over in your work and you're starting to get bored, the following sections provide ideas and tools for how to branch out.

Admiring the work of master colorists Kaffe Fassett and Randy Darwall, I noticed that the work I love best — rich and complex fabric that delights the eye — is comprised of many different colors. As Randy Darwall says, "Why use five colors when fifty will do?" Our eyes love to bounce back and forth between different colors; they give depth to the

These fabrics are all woven plain weave: The colors and textures are what make them come alive.

piece. That's why we're drawn to the hand-painted skeins in the yarn store. (On page 135, I show you how to make the most of these painted skeins in a project.) Next time you're planning a project, throw in more colors than you're comfortable using, and add a few colors that make you squeamish. It's often those few strands of acid green or tangerine orange that make the piece sing.

The Language of Color

Color is such a visual concept that it's hard to describe in words. How often have you tried to describe a color to a friend (or yarn-store employee) without a sample handy and found yourself saying something like "It was red, but an orangey red, kind of pale and translucent, sort of like the inside of a watermelon, but up near the rind." The good news is that there is a language to describe color. It's no replacement for a visual representation, but it should get you closer to the mark than describing produce.

(On page 135, I show you how to make the most of these painted skeins in a project.)

SEEING VALUE

One of the best ways to see value without the distraction of color is to view the yarn through a piece of red acrylic, often sold at quilting shops under the name Ruby Beholder. If you don't have red plastic, you can get a similar effect by squinting. Another way to achieve this is to use a digital camera set to take black-and-white pictures instead of color.

» **HUE.** This is what we think of when we think of color. It defines whether something is red, blue, green, or yellow. Pure hues are the colors you find in a rainbow and the smallest box of crayons.

» **TONE.** If you mix gray with a pure hue, you get a tone. Steel blue is a tone of blue.

Pure hue   *Mixed with gray*

» **TINT.** If you mix white with a pure hue, you get a tint. Sky blue is a tint of blue.

Pure hue   *Mixed with white*

» **SHADE.** If you mix black with a pure hue, you get a shade. Dark blue is a shade of blue.

Pure hue   *Mixed with black*

» **VALUE.** The color's representation on the gray scale is its value. If you take the color out of the piece, how light or dark is it? Red has a dark value and yellow a light value.

» **INTENSITY.** Intensity refers to the saturation of a color. Rich jewel tones have high intensity.

Color Combinations

Color is often represented as a wheel of pure hues, but if you look at the world, you'll notice most colors aren't on the wheel. Really, color is more like a sphere with the color wheel at the equator and light colors at one pole, dark colors at the other. The interior of the color sphere is filled with innumerable color mixes. Since we can't replicate a sphere on the two-dimensional pages of a book, the color wheel is one traditional way to understand the terminology most people use when talking about color.

» **PRIMARY COLORS.** Primary colors that are used to mix paint, dye, or ink are red, yellow, and blue. All the other colors on the color wheel can be generated from these starting points.

» **SECONDARY COLORS.** Secondary colors are created by mixing together two of the primary colors. The secondary colors are purple, green, and orange.

» **TERTIARY COLORS.** Tertiary colors are created by mixing a primary and a secondary color: red-purple, red-orange, blue-green, yellow-green, yellow-orange, and blue-purple.

» **TRIAD.** Three colors that are evenly spread around the color wheel form a triadic color scheme. Purple, orange, and green form a triadic color scheme. This creates a vivid color palette. One way to tone down a triadic color scheme is to adjust the proportion of colors so that one dominates and the other two are used as accent colors.

» **ANALOGOUS.** Colors that are next to each other on the color wheel form an analogous color scheme. Blue-green, green, and yellow-green form one analogous color scheme. This combination is harmonious and rarely clashes. The downside of analogous color combinations is that their lack of visual tension can make them subdued and low energy.

» **COMPLEMENTARY.** Colors on opposite sides of the color wheel, such as red and green, are the complement of each other. This combination creates a lot of visual tension, especially when the colors are used in the pure hue form.

» **SPLIT-COMPLEMENTARY.** Combining a color with the two colors on either side of its complement creates a split-complementary color scheme. This combination has strong visual contrast, but less tension than you have in a straight complementary color scheme. This is one of my favorite color schemes to work with, since it has energy, but not so much as to be overwhelming. Green, red-purple, and red-orange form a split-complementary color scheme.

» **TETRADIC (RECTANGLE OR SQUARE).** Two pairs of complementary colors form a tetradic color scheme. If the color pairs are evenly spaced around the color wheel, it's also a square color scheme. One tetradic color scheme is red, green, blue, and orange.

Getting Color Proportions Right

There are many ways to put colors together. The simplest is to use equal amounts of each color in a scheme. Sometimes, however, this can cause too much visual contrast and/or create a too-predictable pattern. To break things up, you can change the proportions, or let one color lead and the others play subordinate roles as accents.

Many factors affect the visual strength of colors: bright colors come forward, dark colors recede. Shiny threads come forward, matte threads recede. (This is because the reflective nature of the shiny threads makes them visually lighter than matte threads.) Thick threads come forward, thin threads recede. You can use these properties to create a color landscape that pleases you.

You know how some colors only work in small doses? Bright yellow, for example, is hard to take in large amounts. Yellow napkins on a table work, whereas a yellow tablecloth can be overwhelming. This property of colors was studied by Johann Wolfgang von Goethe, who developed a system by which he assigned a numerical value to colors to represent their relative strength. You can use his values as a way to balance the colors in a project. For example, if yellow (9) is three times as visually powerful as violet (3), you can use one-third as much yellow to violet in a fabric to make it more visually balanced. Barbara J. Walker, a master weaver, uses this strategy when designing color-and-weave fabrics with yarns colored in pure hues.

Dark and light

Thick and thin

Complementary colors

COLOR PYRAMID

Combining color effectively is both an art and a science. You can approach design-ing intuitively, by putting a pile of yarns together and arranging them until they look good. Or you can approach designing with color theoretically, by using principals and strategies to set the proportions of color. Ideally, you want to develop both sets of color skills.

Randy Darwall uses color masterfully in his work, layering structure and texture on top of dozens of colors. He talks about using a pyramid of color: First he lays a foundation of a base color that makes up 70 percent of the piece. He then adds addi-tional colors in smaller and smaller amounts as he goes up the pyramid, with the most outrageous color choices at the top of the pyramid, where their small proportions keep them from overwhelming the fabric.

Examples of Randy Darwall's weaving: (top) Eyelash Scarf woven in wool and silk, at the Smithsonian American Art Museum; (bottom) handwoven vests

COLOR GAMPS

▶ *One of the fascinating and unpredictable things about weaving is the interplay of warp and weft and how this affects color.*

In weaving, the threads interact in tiny intervals of over and under, and this close interaction works on the human eye the same way pointillism does, causing the colors to visually merge into a new color. It's quite common for the look of a warp to change completely when you cross it with a weft. Even experienced weavers have a hard time predicting exactly what colors are going to work best together without sampling. These endless color surprises are one of the reasons I love to weave. But not all surprises are pleasant ones, and you want to weave projects that look good. How do you learn what colors harmonize? The only way to know for sure is to sample.

A useful and efficient tool for sampling how colors work together is called a color gamp. In this, you create stripes of color in the warp, and cross it with weft stripes, usually in the same set of colors. Weaving a color gamp gives you information about how colors work together with a minimum of weaving. If you have a set of yarns that you often weave with, a color gamp of all the colorways can be a reference and an inspiration for endless projects to come. If you haven't settled down into one type of yarn (or like me, never will), a color gamp is still a good reference to have as a starting place for color inspirations.

The most frequently woven color gamp is the pure-hue gamp, which uses the colors of the rainbow: red, orange, yellow, green, blue, indigo, violet, often with subcolors like blue-green and red-violet added to increase the color options. What's most useful is to weave a color gamp with the colors you're most likely to weave with. If pastels are your thing, weave a pastel color gamp. If your tastes run to the gothic, a dark palette of colors will be more useful to you than a rainbow. Often the best color gamps are woven with yarns you already own since, ideally, your stash is filled with the kind of yarns you like to work with. For instructions on how to weave a color gamp, see pages 207–209.

By isolating sections of a color gamp as shown above, you can develop a palette that's perfect for what you want to weave.

Designing Warp-Wise Stripes

One of the most straightforward design elements for working with color is stripes. Begin your stripe design by deciding whether you want the stripes in the warp or the weft (or both, as in the case of checkerboards and plaids). Warp-wise stripes are the most common, because they have the advantage of making the textile (and, if used lengthwise for fabric, the wearer) look longer and leaner. Put one color next to another across the warp and you will end up with a striped fabric. Although they take somewhat longer to warp, they're easier to weave than weft-wise stripes, because you can use a single-colored weft and avoid multiple color changes and weaving in ends. Another advantage is that you can design and assess your colors and textures as you wind the warp, but the flip side of that is that the design is set once you thread the warp on the loom.

Theory-Based Designs

You'll find quite a few options for designing stripes. Here are techniques for those who like to plan.

STRIPE DESIGN PROGRAMS

If you like to play with computers, nearly all weaving-specific software lets you design stripes in both the warp and weft. If you're not interested in purchasing fully featured weaving software, there are free online tools that you can use to generate stripes. These were written to help web designers create striped backgrounds for websites, but they work just as well for planning textile stripes. To find them, Google "stripe generator."

The upside to using software to plan your stripes is that it's easy to quickly prototype different striping schemes without using up any yarn. The downside is that it's hard to get the colors on a monitor to exactly match the colors of your yarn, so often what you see on the screen is just an approximation of what you'll get in the fabric.

Thicker warp yarns interspersed with thinner yarns create stripes through texture.

Bold black and white yarns offer a classic stripe combination.

Yellow-green and lavender are both tertiary colors and opposites on the color wheel.

Thick and thin stripes are enhanced by the softly variegated yarns.

The "sparks" of hot reds and oranges in this fabric enliven the subdued dark violets and blacks of the background palette.

MATHEMATICAL THEORIES

A more analytical way to design the number and placement of stripes is to plan your stripes using a mathematical sequence. The Fibonacci sequence generates terms that converge to the "golden ratio," which can be approximated as 1.618. This ratio occurs in nature, such as in the seed patterns of sunflowers and in human DNA, and is considered by most a pleasing proportion. Because of its relationship to the golden ratio, the Fibonacci sequence is often used by weavers to plan stripes, and it's easy to generate. Starting with 0, 1 (or in some systems, 1, 1), add the last two numbers in the series to generate the next. (For example, $0 + 1 = 1$; $1 + 1 = 2$; $1 + 2 = 3$; $2 + 3 = 5$; $3 + 5 = 8$; and so on.) You can use the results to plan the size of each unit (stripe) in your design, basing either the number of threads or actual measurements on the series. For example, if your chosen unit was 1 inch of warp width, you would use the Fibonacci sequence to create stripes that were 1" wide, 2" wide, 3" wide, 5" wide, an so on. The actual number of threads in each stripe depends on your chosen sett. The widths of the stripes in the yarn wrapping at the left are based in the Fibonacci sequence.

Fibonacci isn't the only mathematical series you can use to plan stripes. Some other mathematical concepts to look at include hailstorm sequences and prime-generator functions. Or you can simply roll a dice to generate random-stripe sequences. Gaming stores, such as the ones selling Magic the Gathering cards and role-playing games are a great source of dice with 4, 8, 12, and 20 sides. There are even percentile dice that generate random numbers from 1 to 100.

SPARK COLORS

Another color concept to keep in mind when designing stripes is the idea of a spark color. This is a color that contrasts with a specific stripe and is used in a tiny amount (usually one or two threads) in the center or along the edges of a stripe to highlight it and set it off from other stripes or the background. This unexpected pop of color can often take a textile from good to exciting.

MONOCHROMATIC STRIPES

Though we usually think of stripes being different colors, you can vary the other properties of color as well. You could vary the values of a set of blue stripes, for example, by making some stripes darker and others paler, but all still blue. This would create an elegant and understated fabric. You could weave a somber and businesslike fabric using shades of black and gray, or a lively fabric using shades of orange. The effect of color in monochromatic weavings depends on hue and intensity.

GRADUATED STRIPES

Instead of having sharp boundaries between your stripes, you can slowly shift from one color to another. It takes a lot of intermediate colors to make the shift subtle. Graduated stripes mimic nature — think autumn leaves or sunsets where orange blends into gold — and they are very pleasing to the eye. People who claim not to like stripes often like graduated ones. You can create graduated stripes by purchasing or dying dozens of colors that gently shift from one color to the other. (See Spider-Silk Shawl, page 240, for an example of this technique.)

One of the most effective ways to create a customized look is to combine several threads together as one to shift the color of the group slowly. For example, hold three threads of one color together and treat the group as a single yarn when you warp (AAA). As you move across the width of your warp, trade out one of the yarns for another in sequence (AAB). Use this combination for the next stripe, then substitute another of the As for a B (ABB). Swap the remaining A for another B so that the three warp threads are all the second color (BBB). If you also vary the weft color as you weave, from AAA to AAB to ABB to BBB, you'll create a subtle plaid in the finished project.

SHADES IN FRENCH

Ombré is a French term meaning "shaded" and often refers to a monotone scheme, in which graduated stripes all of the same color slowly shift into its tint or shade. (See page 128 for an example.)

SECRET MESSAGES IN STRIPES

You can also use stripes to encode meaning into your cloth. Some weavers translate music into weaving, using the position of the note on the music staff for the color and the duration of the note for the width of the stripe. Others assign colors to letters of the alphabet and "write" inspirational messages into their fabric. You could use Morse code, having one width for "dit" and another for "dah" in a monotone cloth. DNA is made up of only four nucleotides: you could even weave part of your genetic code into your rigid-heddle cloth. There are all kinds of ways to encode meaning into cloth using the color and size of stripes. It can be a fun exercise and add special meaning to your finished project. And I confess, I always wanted to be a secret agent — this may be the closest I get. The Morse Code Scarf that follows is an example of this approach.

This wrapping creates a blend by first winding four threads of blue, followed by one of dark gray and three of blue, then two of each, then three of dark gray and one of blue, and so on, introducing each color as one of four and changing the proportions in the same manner.

MORSE CODE SCARF

This scarf, with its somber tones of gray, is manly enough for even the most conservative of men. Yet within its pattern of monotone stripes is the message that's woven into all the fabric we make as gifts: "I love you." (Turn the book upside down and see if you can read it!) In this case, it's encoded as Morse code; the Morse code for "I love you" is

.. .-.. --- ..-. • -.-- --- ..-

There are several ways to encode this series of dashes and dots in weaving. You could do it by color (orange for dashes, pink for dots), by length of stripe (six threads for dashes, two for dots), or even by weave structure (weft floats for dashes, warp floats for dots). In this example, I've used narrow silver stripes for dots, and wider silver stripes for dashes. Whichever method you choose, be sure to leave a way of indicating the spaces between letters. In this example, I've used narrow black stripes for the space between dots and dashes, and wider black stripes for the space between letters.

You can weave this project to send a message to someone you love, or weave a meaningful saying into a scarf for yourself. You can either encode your words into Morse code using a book, or use an online Morse-code translator (see the appendix, page 284, for website address).

LOOM AND HEDDLE

Rigid-heddle loom with a weaving width of at least 13"
One 12-dent heddle

WIDTH IN HEDDLE

12½"

WARP YARN

Harrisville Designs Shetland, 100% virgin wool (1.75 oz/217 yd skeins): one skein each of Black and Silver Mist

WEAVE STRUCTURE

Plain weave

WEFT YARN

Harrisville Designs Shetland, 100% virgin wool (1.75 oz/217 yd skeins): one skein of Black

EPI

12 ends per inch

PPI

10 picks per inch

MEASUREMENTS

PROJECT STAGE	WIDTH	LENGTH
Off the loom	11½"	70"
After wet-finishing	10¾"	61½"
Shrinkage	7%	12%

WARPING

Wind a warp 2½ yards long and 148 threads wide, following the color order in the chart below, which spells out "I love you" in Morse code. The 2-thread silver-gray stripe indicates a dot and the 4-thread silver-gray stripe indicates a dash. The 2-thread black stripe indicates a space between dots and dashes and a 4-thread black stripe indicates a space between letters. The threading begins and ends with an 8-thread black border. Thread the heddle as described on pages 59–62.

WEAVING

Weave the entire warp off with the black yarn. Make 3½" long fringe, using 4 threads for each fringe.

FINISHING

Wash the shawl in warm water using a wool-safe soap or shampoo. Agitate slightly, but not so much that the fabric felts. Gently squeeze dry. Remove excess water by rolling the shawl in a towel and stepping on it with clean, bare feet. Hang to dry.

WARP THREADING ORDER FOR MORSE CODE SCARF

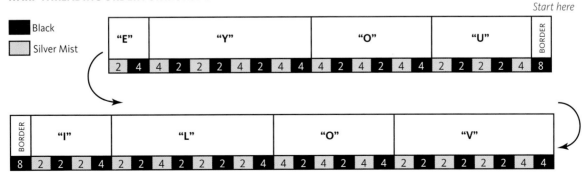

Design-as-You-Go Stash-Based Stripes

One thing nearly all weavers eventually have in common is a stash, often composed of odds and ends of yarn left over from other projects. (If you are a long-time knitter or crocheter, you most likely already have a stash. If you don't have a stash, keep weaving — one is almost certain to follow you home.) Designing with stripes is an ideal way to take advantage of that potential gold mine of miscellaneous yarns. The principle works whether you're weaving towels or blankets. The Random-Striped Blanket on page 124 provides just one way to take all those leftover scraps and weave something wonderful.

The first step in planning your project is to pull out the yarn you want to use and put it in a big pile. Take out any yarns that aren't suitable for warp. (See page 26 for a description of what makes a good warp yarn.) Now squint your eyes and pull out any colors that seem too bright or too dark. When you squint, you're less influenced by hue and are able to focus on the value of the colors. You can leave a few things that are a different value for accents, but you'll find the colors harmonize best if they have similar values.

Designing from stash. *Pile up all your possibilities, then whittle your selection down to those that you feel are most suitable and harmonious.*

» **IDENTIFY THE FIBER.** Is your pile of yarn mostly wool? Mostly cotton? Different fibers shrink at different rates, and if you don't account for this when you're winding your warp, you may inadvertently reinvent seersucker. To prevent differential shrinkage from becoming an issue, you can stick to one type of fiber, such as all wools and animal hairs, or all plant fibers.

If you want to use both animal and plant fibers in the same warp, intersperse them (one plant fiber, one wool, and so on). By avoiding stripes of all one fiber or the other, you can balance out the differential shrinkage. It won't be as smooth and flat a cloth as in the safe option, but I rather like the lively texture that ensues.

» **EVALUATE YARN STRUCTURE.** If wool, are the yarns mostly worsted weight? Mostly sock yarn? Find the average weight of yarn and pick the heddle with the sett that best fits the average. (For an explanation of sett, see page 33.) Make sure all the threads will fit through either the holes or the slots. Skinny threads can be combined to make up a thicker thread, but too-thick threads should be discarded; they'll stick in the heddle and won't be any fun to weave.

» **CHOOSING THE WEFT.** Because I put so much craziness in my warps, I tend to use a dark, solid-colored weft to pull everything together. Some colors that work well with most warps are dark teal, brown, maroon, dark green, and navy blue. Black seems an obvious choice, but it's such a strong color that it will intensify the warp, and can push some warps over the edge. The other caution about black is that it is an unforgiving color as weft because it will highlight all your irregularities in beat — which is good if you're practicing weaving with an even beat, but frustrating if you're trying to weave a good-looking project.

Pale wefts will bleach out a warp, which in some cases might be exactly what you want. Grays will mute the colors. If you put stripes in the weft, or use a hand-painted or variegated weft, you'll get an interesting plaid effect, which may or may not be to your liking.

» **KNOW YOUR WARP LENGTH LIMIT.** The ideal length is the length of your finished piece, with extra warp to account for take-up, shrinkage, and loom waste. Some rigid-heddle looms have bars near the back beam that limit how long a warp you can put on, but most let you put on at least 4 yards.

» **WARPING RANDOM STRIPES.** Pulling at random from your pile of warp, take different yarns and wind a warp. Change colors every thread, cutting the warp yarn and tying it to the next color with an overhand knot (see below) every time you reach the peg or the back rod of the loom. You can build in repetition, such as using one color every five threads, to give the piece a cohesive look. Or you can go wild and place colors as the spirit moves you. If color terrifies you, let fate take a hand. Line up the cones and use dice to pick the next one.

After you've created your warp, stand back and take a look at it. If something isn't working out the way you'd like, change it. When you're satisfied with the colors, finish warping the loom.

RANDOM-STRIPED BLANKET

The fun thing about weaving blankets on a rigid-heddle loom is the joy of creating something large from a small loom; it's so improbable! The secret, of course, lies in piecing narrow strips together, either invisibly on the selvedge using the mattress stitch (page 274), or as a piecework design element, like creating a quilt of handwoven fabric.

The goal of blankets is to be warm and cuddly, so this is a place to use soft cotton yarns and Merino wools. Truly decadent and warm blankets can be woven out of luxury fibers such as cashmere and silk. This can get expensive, unless you use recycled yarns, for example by unraveling thrift store sweaters.

LOOM AND HEDDLE

Rigid-heddle loom with a weaving width of at least 15"

One 10-dent heddle

WIDTH IN HEDDLE

15"

WARP AND WEFT YARNS

Mixed fibers, weights, and colors, including mostly wools and wool blends, approximately 1,600 yards

WEAVE STRUCTURE

Plain weave

EPI

10 ends per inch

PPI

7 picks per inch

OTHER SUPPLIES

Tapestry needle

Bias binding (optional)

FINISHED MEASUREMENTS

42" wide × 48" long, not including 4" twisted fringe at each end (3 panels wide)

STANDARD BLANKET SIZES

Crib	45" × 60"
Lap	36" × 40"
Twin	66" × 90"
Double	80" × 90"
Queen	90" × 90"
King	108" × 90"

Wind three 2-yard warps of 150 threads. For each one, follow the color suggestions on page 122. Thread the heddle as described on pages 59–62.

WEAVING AND FINISHING THE BLANKET

1. Weave your blanket panels in plain weave. (Textured weave structures, such as weft floats, page 144, are also good choices for blankets.) The blanket will be three panels wide, and for each of the three panels, weave 53". To make sure each panel is the same length, measure it as you go, or be willing to unravel a bit at the end if one panel is too long. Some weavers cut a ribbon or twill tape to the panel length and pin it to the fabric as they weave.

2. Remove the woven fabric for the first blanket from the loom. Warp the loom again and weave two more panels the same length as the first one. Make twisted fringe at each end of each of the panels (see page 92).

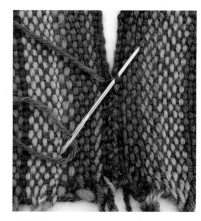

3. With a length of yarn you used for the warp, use mattress stitch to attach the panels together along the selvedges. (See photo at right and also instructions on page 274.)

4. Wash the blanket in lukewarm water, and lay flat to dry. When the blanket is completely dry, brush it with a stiff brush (such as a new, unused scrub brush) to bring up the nap of the wool.

BLANKET VARIATION

Instead of finishing the ends of your blanket with twisted fringe, you can bind the edges with commercial fabric. Cut strips 5" wide, following the grain of the fabric. Fold the strips lengthwise and iron. Sew the strips together to make a binding long enough to go around the perimeter of the blanket, plus enough to join the ends of the binding together. Machine- or hand-stitch the binding in place. Thrift shops are a great source of luxury fabrics for creating binding: A stained silk shirt could find new life as trim for your blanket — simply cut the stained portion away.

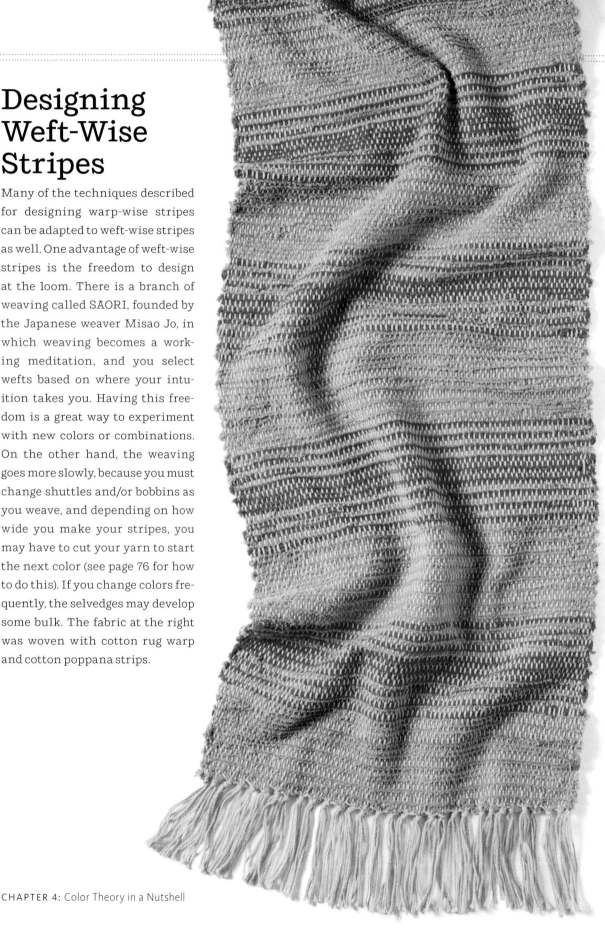

Designing Weft-Wise Stripes

Many of the techniques described for designing warp-wise stripes can be adapted to weft-wise stripes as well. One advantage of weft-wise stripes is the freedom to design at the loom. There is a branch of weaving called SAORI, founded by the Japanese weaver Misao Jo, in which weaving becomes a working meditation, and you select wefts based on where your intuition takes you. Having this freedom is a great way to experiment with new colors or combinations. On the other hand, the weaving goes more slowly, because you must change shuttles and/or bobbins as you weave, and depending on how wide you make your stripes, you may have to cut your yarn to start the next color (see page 76 for how to do this). If you change colors frequently, the selvedges may develop some bulk. The fabric at the right was woven with cotton rug warp and cotton poppana strips.

Weft-Wise Color Blending

An easy way to get a blended effect similar to the one described for warps on page 119 is to pick a yarn with a long, slow shift between colors. Some examples of yarns that would work with this strategy are Noro Kureyon, Noro Silk Garden, Freia, and Kauni. For the most gradual change between stripes using these yarns, weave short, narrow widths.

When your weft yarn has long color repeats, you need to figure out a way to load the shuttles so that you maintain the color shifts. When you wind from the ball onto the shuttle, the beginning of the color shift goes into the inside of the shuttle, but you'll begin weaving from the outside of the shuttle. If you wind only one shuttle, this means that you'll start weaving from a color somewhere in the middle of the ball of yarn, which will be hard to match up when you go to weave the second shuttle. There are several strategies to address this:

» Weave small projects, so that the entire weft fits onto a single shuttle.

» Wind the entire yarn supply into smaller balls, each of which can entirely fit on a shuttle. Pulling from the outside of the ball, wind the yarn onto a shuttle. Weave each small ball in reverse order, starting from the first one wound.

Another challenge of using self-striping yarns is figuring out what to do if you hit a knot and the color shifts abruptly.

» If you have more than one ball of yarn, you can look through the others and see if any of them start at the color where the break occurred.

» If that's not the case, wind yarn from the ball until you return to the color repeat that matches the color where the break occurred.

» If neither of the above is possible, you can soften the jog between colors by picking a color close to the one where the break occurred or by alternating weft picks between two colors for a span before continuing on with just the new color.

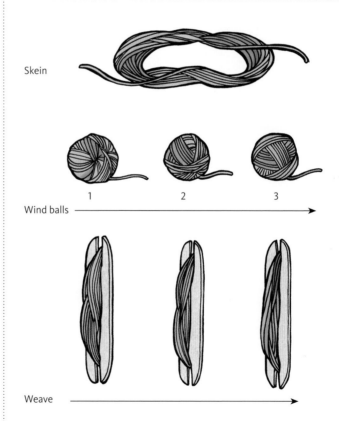

Skein

Wind balls 1   2   3

Weave

Winding a multicolor yarn. *To understand why you have to wind the shuttle from the outside of the ball, study the illustrations above. Winding the balls hides the starting color on the inside of each ball. By then winding the shuttles from the outside of each ball, you bring the starting color back up to the outside of the shuttles. You are using the extra step of winding the ball to reverse the reversal that occurs when you wind a shuttle.*

OMBRÉ SCARF

I wove this as a scarf, but with enough yardage, this could be garment fabric as well: I think it would make a lovely fall or winter skirt. I chose a solid-colored warp to highlight the subtle color shift in the weft. Notice how the dark warp color deepens the appearance of the weft colors. If I'd chosen a light-colored weft, it would have muted the weft color.

LOOM AND HEDDLE

Rigid-heddle loom with a weaving width of at least 10"
One 12-dent heddle

WIDTH IN HEDDLE

9"

WARP YARN

Jamieson and Smith, 100% virgin wool (1 oz/150 yd skeins: 2 skeins of Lilac (123)

WEFT YARN

Kauni Effekt, 100% wool (150 g/660 yd balls): 1 skein of EC (gray/white/black)

EPI

12 ends per inch

PPI

6 picks per inch

MEASUREMENTS

PROJECT STAGE	WIDTH	LENGTH
Off the loom	8½"	62"
After wet-finishing	8"	60"
Shrinkage	6%	3%

WARPING

Wind a warp 2½ yards long and 108 threads wide. Thread the heddle as described on pages 59–62.

WEAVING

The easy part about this project is that the long-repeat, self-striping Kauni yarn does most of the work. The tricky bit is maintaining the color order as you weave. Use the procedures illustrated on the previous page to ensure the color order is correct. Cut the scarf off the loom, and make 3" long twisted fringe, using 4 warp threads for each fringe.

FINISHING

Wash the scarf in warm water using a wool-safe soap or shampoo. Agitate slightly, but not so much that the fabric felts. Gently squeeze dry. Remove excess water by rolling the scarf in a towel and stepping on it with clean bare feet. Hang to dry.

Designing Plaids

When you cross warp-wise stripes with weft-wise stripes, you get plaids and checks. You can look to history or your own heritage for plaid patterns. Patterns of color have identified countries (in flags) and clans (the Scottish Highlands) for centuries. You could weave a blanket based on the Swedish flag, for example, or re-create your grandfather's tartan.

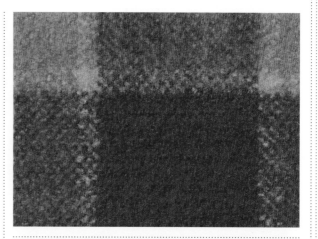

One of the intriguing characteristics of plaids is that you get at least twice as many colors in the fabric as the yarn colors you are working with. Study the color gamp on page 116, and notice that where one color crosses another, the threads interact optically and produce the illusion of a third color. The three warp colors in the fabric used for the pot holder (see photo top right) — orange, magenta, and green — are also used for the weft. The effect, though, is of six colors: orange, orange-magenta, orange-green, magenta, green-magenta, and green. This is assuming that orange-magenta looks the same as magenta-orange, which is true for balanced plain weave, but not the case for all weave structures. Twills, textured weaves, and other patterns can change appearance depending on which color appears in the warp versus the weft. Your three starting yarn colors could look like up to nine colors. It's like getting extra colors of yarn in your stash!

Tartans are a specific kind of plaid, usually woven as plain weave or a 2×2 twill, in which the color, order, and proportion of stripes identifies a Scottish clan. Tartans have also been designed and registered for companies (Harley Davidson), states, and even cartoon characters (Donald Duck). You can peruse all of the currently registered tartans online at the Scottish Tartans Authority, and you can also register new tartan designs through the Scottish Register of Tartans (for website addresses, see the appendix on page 284).

Top and bottom: *Balanced plaids*
Middle: *Checked fabric, woven as a series of 2×2 warp and weft stripes in alternating colors*

TARTAN TABLE RUNNER

This project, woven in wool, makes a substantial fabric that can be used as a table runner, or you can weave it as yardage for a skirt. The pattern I've chosen here is the Mitchell clan tartan (for obvious reasons), but you can weave any tartan pattern you like. Go to the Scottish Register of Tartans online for examples of other tartan patterns (see appendix on page 284 for website address).

LOOM AND HEDDLE

Rigid heddle loom with a weaving width of at least 14"

One 8-dent heddle

WIDTH IN HEDDLE

13¼"

WARP AND WEFT YARNS

Harrisville Designs Highland 100% wool (900 yards per pound):

200 yards each of Cobalt (31), Black (50), and Hemlock (8)

25 yards of Russet (39)

15 yards of White (44)

WEAVE STRUCTURE

Plain weave

EPI	PPI
8 ends per inch	8 picks per inch

MEASUREMENTS

PROJECT STAGE	WIDTH	LENGTH
Off the loom	12"	69½"
After wet-finishing	11"	64½"
Shrinkage	8%	7%

TARTAN TABLE RUNNER THREADING ORDER

2	16	16	2	16	2	16	2	16	16	2

WARPING

Wind a warp 3 yards long of 106 ends, following the color order shown in the chart above. Thread the heddle as described on pages 59–62.

WEAVING

It's important to keep careful count of the number of weft picks you throw as you weave the tartan pattern. The order of colors you'll weave in the weft is the same as the order of colors in the warp as shown in the chart at the right. Repeat the sequence as many times as desired, weaving only 2 picks of Black between each repeat.

Tartans are woven "to square," which means that ideally you should have as many picks per inch as you do ends per inch, and that when you've woven 16 weft picks of a color that has 16 warp threads, the area you create should be square.

FINISHING

If you are planning to use the fabric as a table runner, encase the ends with twill binding as shown here (see instructions on page 99) or make twisted fringes at each end (page 92). If you'll use this as garment fabric, serge or zigzag-stitch the fabric to secure it. Hand wash in warm water, agitating gently to full the fabric, and dry flat.

Detail of tartan fabric, showing twill binding used to finish the ends.

2
16
16
2
16
2
16
2
16
2

Repeat for desired length

WEAVING ORDER

LOOM AND HEDDLE

Rigid-heddle loom with a weaving width of at least 13"
One 5-dent heddle

WIDTH IN HEDDLE

12⅖"

WARP AND WEFT YARNS

Cascade 220, 100% Peruvian Highland wool, worsted weight (3.5 oz/220 yd skeins): 1 skein each of Citron (#8910) and Burnt Orange (#9465B); 2 skeins of Magenta (#7803)

WEAVE STRUCTURE

Basketweave

EPI	PPI
5 ends per inch (threads doubled)	5 picks per inch

MEASUREMENTS

PROJECT STAGE	WIDTH	LENGTH
Off the loom	12"	70.2"
After wet-finishing	7"	39"
Shrinkage	42%	57%

Makes five 7" by 7" pot holders, two 3½" by 3½" coasters, and two 1" by 3½" needle holders (see cutting plan in appendix, page 275)

Double (or Triple) Your Money
PLAID FELTED POT HOLDERS

The main requirement of a pot holder is that it protects your hand from heat. Wool is an excellent choice for the warp and weft as it both insulates the cook from heat as well as resists igniting. Make sure to weave the fabric as densely as possible, because having a hole open up in a pot holder when you're carrying a hot pan is not a fun moment. Felting the fabric after it's woven results in a sturdier, more protective fabric. (If you use a wool other than what is suggested here, be sure it is not machine-washable, as that process prevents felting.)

WARPING

Wind a 3-yard-long warp using doubled strands of the Cascade 200 — in other words, holding two strands together as one: 62 (doubled) threads as shown in the chart on the facing page. Another way to think of this is that you are threading both slots and holes with loops instead of individual threads.

CHAPTER 4: Color Theory in a Nutshell

THREADING

Following the color order in the chart below, thread the slots with two loops (four threads) in each slot. Keep in mind that the numbers in the table below are counting loops, not individual threads. Wind on as usual.

To thread the holes, pull one of the loops through each hole. There should now be two threads in each slot and two threads in each hole.

WEAVING

Weave to square (see Tartan Table Runner, Weaving on page 131) with doubled Cascade 220, 2 threads wound together on a shuttle. Weave using the color order in the chart below for a total length of about 100", or 8 repeats of the pattern. A neat trick is to wind the shuttle using both the inside thread and outside thread of a ball of yarn.

Beat loosely; you should be able to see the surface beneath the loom through the cloth. (In order to felt, the fibers need room to move.)

When switching colors, just dangle the loose ends off the sides of the fabric; do not weave them back into the cloth, as this would create thick areas in the cloth after it is felted. Felting will secure these ends, so you can just trim them after felting.

PLAID FELTED POT HOLDERS THREADING ORDER

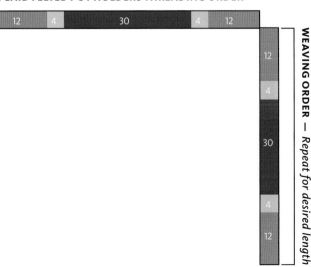

FINISHING

Machine wash and dry on hot with a load of towels, heavy agitation.

Trim the loose threads at the selvedges where you changed colors.

Cut apart in the middle of the orange sections, following the cutting layout in the appendix, page 275.

SIZING POT HOLDERS, COASTERS, AND PLACEMATS

POT HOLDERS vary in size, but they are generally square, in the range of 8 squares inches. Instead of making a square pot holder, however, you can create a pot-holder mitt by tracing your hand, thumb extended, and adding an extra 1¼" to the outline to allow for a ¼" seam allowance and ease.

COASTERS. You can use the same felting technique described for pot holders to weave coasters. For a woolen coaster, cut the felted fabric into a standard coaster size (3½" × 3½" or 4" × 4").

PLACEMATS. Placemats come in two basic sizes, a large placemat (12" × 18" to 14" × 20") meant to hold an entire place setting and a smaller placemat (12" × 12") that holds only the plate, with the napkin, flatware, and stemware laid on the table.

WEAVE AND FELT

Have you ever accidentally thrown a sweater in the wash with your jeans and had it come out smaller and thicker than before? That's felting. Technically, if you start with a knit or woven fabric, the process is called fulling instead of felting. True felting starts with loose locks or roving. But modern crafters have moved the term along and you can find many patterns in the knitting world that talk about felting a project at the end.

To create felt, you must start with a fiber that has microscopic scales. Wool is the classic example, but you can felt many other types of furs and fleeces as well, including angora, cashmere, cat, and dog. You use heat and alkalinity (provided by laundry detergent) to open up the scales, and then agitate the fibers until they entangle. Once the fabric is felted to your liking, remove the heat and alkalinity by rinsing the piece in cold water. The scales close, locking your changes in place.

In order to get the thickest felted cloth, you need to weave a fabric that's loose enough for the yarns to move during the felting process. If you weave a tight, dense fabric, it will full but you won't get the super-thick fabric you might be looking for.

Felting has many variables, not least of which is the fiber. Whether it was a warm or cold winter when the sheep was growing the wool, the breed of sheep, the type of grass it ate, how alkaline the soap you're using is — all these factors contribute to how the finished felted fabric turns out. Because so much is out of your control, I recommend that you sample when planning a felted project. Cut off a piece of the woven fabric to a length equal to one-third the width of the warp and divide it into three equal pieces, serging or zigzag-stitching around the edges to protect them. Leave one sample unwashed and wash the others with the method you plan to use for felting. Process one sample lightly and the other with more vigor. Keep notes about the temperature, soap, and length of time you agitated each sample. When the samples are rinsed and dried, you can look at them to decide how to process your end fabric. For an example of this, see Sampling Is the Key, page 101.

▶ **By hand.** You don't need any tools other than your hands to felt fabric. However, I also have a toilet bowl plunger (bought new and used only for felting) that I use to give my hands a break from the hot, alkaline water. What isn't good for wool isn't good for the skin on your hands either.

▶ **In the washing machine.** With vigilance and good timing, you can felt using a washing machine. To do so, use a setting that provides hot water and a lot of agitation. Top-loading washing machines are preferred for machine felting because you can interrupt them to check on their progress. You can felt with a front-loading washing machine, but since you won't be able to stop the cycle in mid-process, you should sample and figure out which cycle is going to give you the results you want.

Using Painted Skeins Cleverly

I adore hand-painted skeins. The problem comes when I try to use them in a project. Most painted skeins are marketed to knitters, but, knitted up, a gorgeous skein sometimes looks like — let's be frank — the cat's breakfast. Colors pool and muddy and create odd zigzag patterns. The subtle shading that drew me to the skein has vanished. There are ways around this, such as knitting from alternate skeins or stranding a solid-colored yarn along with the multicolored one. But those are improvements to the problem, not solutions.

The weaver in me wanted to be able to use those gorgeous painted skeins in a way that worked with the colors and somehow recaptured the look of the skein in the finished piece.

My first attempt to achieve what I wanted involved using a multiple of the circumference of the skein. The skein was 50" around, so I tried winding a warp 100" long. However, when I hit the end of the warp and turned around to go back to the start, the order of the colors reversed. In most cases, this caused alternating thread-by-thread stripes, with one set of threads showing one color pattern, and the other showing another. It wasn't the smooth flow of color I wanted.

Very occasionally when I tried winding a warp with a painted skein, like magic, the colors did match up and I effortlessly got something that looked like a hand-painted warp. All I had to do was figure out what was going right on those occasions. Looking closely, I discovered palindrome skeins.

Handpainted skeins issue their own siren calls. The challenge comes in how to use them most effectively.

Theory: Palindrome Skeins

To create a handpainted palindrome skein, the dyer lays out the skein and paints across it from top to bottom (a). This is a very efficient and common way of hand-painting skeins. Why are palindrome skeins magic? Because the color pattern has mirrored symmetry, just like a palindrome. In (a), the color changes (starting at the left and going clockwise) are gray, blue, red, blue, gray, blue, red, blue, gray. See the symmetry? The color sequence in the palindrome skein is the same no matter whether you start from the left or right. This means that when you turn around at the end of your warp and go the other direction, the colors match.

> *palindrome \PA-lin-drōhm*
> *A phrase or sequence that is the same backward as forward, for example, "never odd or even."*

This symmetry appears only if you fold the skein at the pivot points (in the bottom photo, gray at both ends). If you fold the skein another way (b), you won't see the symmetry. When you are looking at a skein and trying to decide if it's a palindrome skein, you may have to play with folding it a couple of different ways.

Here are three ways to wind a warp using a palindrome skein. Each results in a different effect.

The top photo shows the palindrome skein arranged as the dyer positioned it while dyeing. Notice how the colors match across the skein.

METHOD 1: *Winding the Warp for Random Colors*

If you don't care about duplicating the effects of a painted warp, you can simply wind a warp without trying to create any special effect. The result is a series of random dashes of color. It doesn't capture the look of the painted skein, but it can be pleasing. To create this effect, start with any kind of painted skein, and simply wind a warp.

METHOD 2: *Winding the Warp for Color Blocks*

With a palindrome skein and a little planning, you can quickly wind a warp that gives the look of a painted warp, where color flows from one hue to another along the length of the fabric.

(1) Fold a palindrome skein to find the two pivot points.

(2) Measure the folded skein to find its folded length (L). (In other words, L is half the circumference.) *Note:* L can be tricky to measure, especially with a stretchy yarn, because you have to decide how much tension to put on it while measuring. Ideally, use the same tension that it will undergo during warping. For example, in the photo below, L is 32" when the yarn is held taut at weaving tension. Don't obsess about this number, however; take your best guess. You'll be able to tweak the warp length to make the colors match in step 6. The important thing is to be close.

(3) Once you have identified the length of the skein and determined the pivot points and color sequence, wind the skein into a ball before you being the warping process.

2

Continued on next page ▷

METHOD 2: Winding the Warp for Color Blocks , *continued*

(4) Starting with a pivot-point color, tie a loop so that the middle of the pivot point is in the center. Slide this loop onto the loom's back rod. The idea here is that you want to start the warp so that the middle of the pivot point is centered on the back rod. You'll know you have the loop tied right when the colors line up as you begin warping.

(5) Clamp the rigid-heddle loom to a table, and clamp the warping peg a distance away that is a multiple of L (such as twice L or three times L).

(6) Starting with the yarn that is tied around the back rod, pull a loop through one of the rigid-heddle slots, and carry it over to the peg.

(7) Center one of the pivot point colors on the peg. If you are weaving an even multiple of L, it will be the same color as you have at the back of the loom. If you are weaving an odd multiple of L, it will be the color of the other pivot point. In order for the colors to line up as the warp is wound, you must have a pivot point at the two "turnaround" points: the back rod and the warping peg. Look at the color shifts: Do the colors on the two yarns match up? If not, adjust the distance between the loom and peg until they do.

(8) Continue pulling loops through the rigid-heddle's slots until you have wound the full width of the warp. Cut the warp from the cone or ball of yarn, and tie the last string onto the back rod.

(9) Pull the loop off the peg and wind the warp onto the back beam under tension, inserting warp separators as you go.

(10) When the end of the warp gets near the front rod, cut the peg loops in half to free the yarn. In each slot you will find 2 threads. Take one of those threads and feed it through the hole next to the slot. Continue all the way across the warp.

(11) Tie onto the front beam, making sure the tension is even across the warp.

METHOD 3: *Winding the Warp to Create Stripes*

I'm a fan of the work of the talented weaver Sara Lamb, especially the fabrics where she blends two painted warps to create stripes of alternating colors. It turned out to be remarkably easy to achieve this effect using a palindrome skein. The basic procedure is the same as for the Color Blocks (page 137), with the addition of one simple trick: tying off lengths of warp to flip the pivot points. (*Note:* This method works best if you have a skein where the pivot points are contrasting colors.)

① Warp the first stripe as described in Color Blocks. (You decide how wide to make each stripe.)

② When you are done with the first stripe, use a simple overhand knot to tie off a loop that takes up exactly one L of yarn length (a). (Remember that about 1" of length goes into the knot itself.) When you tie off one L of yarn in the loop, it causes the pivot point at the back rod to shift to the color on the other side of the skein. This shift occurs all the way down the length of the warp. Notice how in the photo at the right, you can clearly see the pivot point change from red to orange and back again at the peg (b).

③ To switch back to the original stripe, tie off a second loop the same length.

④ Continue winding the warp, tying off loops whenever you want to create a new stripe, until you have wound the entire width of the warp. The rest of the warping process is the same as steps 7–10 in Color Blocks on the facing page.

2a

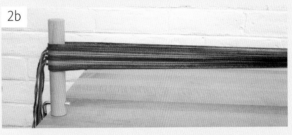

2b

Each of these scarves was warped differently to achieve three very different effects (from left to right): stripes (method 3), color blocks (method 2), and random (method 1).

LOOM AND HEDDLE

Rigid-heddle loom with a weaving width of at least 10"

One 8-dent heddle

WIDTH IN HEDDLE

15"

WARP

Shown here: Schaefer Nancy, 95% Merino/5% nylon, DK/light worsted weight (1,200 yards per pound. Use any similiar-weight yarn. You will need 240 yards for each scarf.

WEFT

Dale of Norway Baby Ull, 100% superwash Merino, fingering weight (1,645 yards per pound; available in 1.75 oz/180 yd skeins): 150 yards of Dark Blue for each scarf (#5545)

WEAVE STRUCTURE

Plain weave

EPI

8 ends per inch

PPI

6 picks per inch

OTHER SUPPLIES

Fabric glue (optional)

MEASUREMENTS

PROJECT STAGE	WIDTH	LENGTH
Off the loom	10"	82"
After wet-finishing	9½"	74"
Shrinkage	6%	10%

THREE SCARVES FROM PALINDROME SKEINS

In each of the scarves shown here, I used a single solid-colored dark yarn for the weft to let the color play of the warp carry the piece. Dark shades make the warp's colors pop.

WARPING

Following the instructions beginning on page 136 for whichever color strategy you choose. Find L and wind a warp of 80 ends between 2½ and 3 yards long, altering the length to ensure the placement of the pivot point colors. This is enough for one scarf. Thread the heddle as described on pages 59–62.

WEAVING

Weave in plain weave for 90".

When beating in the weft, don't beat too hard. The fabric will look a bit like cheesecloth on the loom. That's normal. It's because the warp yarns are stretched out under tension. When the fabric comes off the loom, it will relax, and those holes will fill in, especially after you wash it during finishing.

FINISHING

Remove the fabric from the loom, and add fringe along top and bottom edges (see page 92 for directions).

Wash your scarf gently in warm-to-hot water with baby shampoo or a product designed for washing wool. Agitate by hand if you want to felt it a bit for a firmer fabric. Rinse well.

Gently squeeze out most of the water. Remove even more by rolling your scarf in a towel and stepping on the towel. Hang the scarf to dry.

Trim the knots after washing, if you like. Washing lets the knots felt a bit and reduces the chance that they will come untied.

CHAPTER 5

Slow & Fancy

PLAIN WEAVE IS THE SIMPLEST WEAVE STRUCTURE. It's the one kids learn in kindergarten: the weft goes over one warp and under the next one, alternating on the second row. If you're a knitter, you can think of plain weave as the garter stitch of weaving.

Rigid-heddle looms are plain-weave machines; plain weave is built into the structure of the heddle. But does that mean plain weave is the only structure you can weave on a rigid-heddle loom? Not at all. One of the fun challenges of rigid-heddle weaving is figuring out how to weave complex cloth on a simple loom. Throughout the ages, clever weavers have used rigid heddles and other simple looms to weave amazing textiles.

In this chapter and the next, we'll explore ways to create structures other than plain weave in rigid-heddle cloth. What I'm calling "slow and fancy" includes leno, Brooks bouquet, Spanish lace, Danish medallion, soumak, tapestry, transparencies, and pickup patterning. But before we get into those, let's take a deeper look at weave structure.

TRANSPARENCY

SOUMAK

TAPESTRY

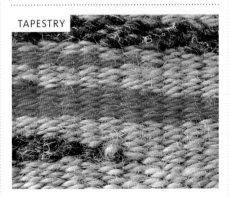

Weave Structure Basics

In woven cloth there is warp — the threads running up and down the loom — and weft — the thread you throw across the loom on a shuttle. Where they interlock is cloth. In the photo at right, the plain-weave sample shows a cloth with no floats: all threads are locked down at the top, bottom, and both sides in every pick. There's no way they can slip past each other. Now look at the photo below it, a 1×2 twill. The weft thread travels under one warp thread and then over the next two warp threads. These jumps are called "floats" in the parlance of weaving because they float over the top of other threads.

Floats serve several purposes in cloth. When the fabric is taken off the loom and washed, the threads that float over others aren't tied down as strongly as they would be in plain weave and can migrate around a bit in the cloth. This is why a twill fabric shrinks more than plain weave when you wash it, and it tends to be thicker than plain weave. It's also why twill fabrics are more flexible. The tiny bits of slack provided by all the floats throughout the fabric let it be more fluid. In fact, the longer the floats, the more flexible and fluid the cloth, but you have to balance stability against motion in the cloth. For example, the extreme case of a long float would be a thread that doesn't interlock at all (a loose thread). It's the most flexible structure you can create with that yarn, but I wouldn't want to make a skirt out of it. (There are cultures where string skirts exist, but they tend to be warmer than Seattle.)

Because the floats allow the threads underneath to slide closer together during wet-finishing (see page 30), twills need to be sett more densely than the same yarn woven in plain weave. If you don't set the warp threads more densely, your weft will pack in too far and ruin the diagonal line of the twill, or, if you beat lightly to maintain the line, the fabric will be sleazy.

No matter what weave structure you're working with, a rule of thumb used by most weavers is to limit floats to a maximum of floating over three other threads. There are specialty fabrics where you might want a longer float length to allow for big migrations in your cloth: honeycomb is one example. In those cases, we're trading stability for a dramatic effect. The important concept to learn about structure is how to make the design-versus-stability trade-off in your cloth consciously, instead of having it crop up in your cloth as an unwelcome surprise.

PLAIN WEAVE

1×2 TWILL

TRANSLATING WEAVING LANGUAGE FOR KNITTERS

Weave structure is a lot like stitch patterns in knitting. Weavers use warp and weft floats in much the same way as knitters use knit and purl stitches. Like any translation from one language to another, it's not a perfect match, but here are some weaving/knitting structure analogies.

Weaving Structure	Knitting Stitch Pattern
Plain weave	Garter
2×2 twill	2×2 ribbing
Huck lace	Lace
Leno	Knit through the back loop

One of the wonderful things about simple looms is that you can still weave complicated structures and patterns on them. You can weave fabric where each thread is controlled independently, like in those most complicated of looms, the Jacquard loom. This is what native weavers in Guatemala, Laos, Ghana, and other places across the world have done for millennia on simple backstrap and rigid-heddle looms. They didn't let the lack of a computer-controlled, multi-harness loom prevent them from creating the fabrics of their dreams, and neither should you. By hand-manipulating the threads to create custom sheds, you can weave a tremendous variety of cloth. I like to think of this as slow-and-fancy weaving.

The trade-off, however, is time. Hand-manipulating threads is slow, which is, of course, why the electronically driven Jacquard loom was invented. In this section, we'll embrace the slow and look at ways to hand-manipulate threads to create intricate fabrics. In the following chapter, Fast and Fancy, we'll use a bit of cleverness and get the loom to store the pattern we're weaving. In that section we'll make cloth faster, but we will have a more limited selection of pattern options.

When you're hand-manipulating the threads, each pick is a new adventure. You can change your mind at any time and weave it differently. The equipment doesn't lock you into any particular pattern. In our fast-paced world, we often don't appreciate the value and freedom of the slow. I think of these weave structures as a reminder that faster doesn't always mean better.

TABBIES & TWILLS

▶ **TABBY.** If you go on to read other weaving books (and I hope you do), you might run across the term tabby. This is not a new structure — it's another term for plain weave. The difference is that tabby is used when plain weave is serving the purpose of tying together a looser weave structure, usually by alternating with it, for example, one pick of a pattern weave, such as overshot or summer-and-winter, and one pick of tabby.

▶ **TWILLS** are named by the location of weft floats in the structure: the first number indicates how many warp threads are up, and the second number indicates how many warp threads are down. So in a 1×3 twill, the weft travels under one warp thread and then floats over three warp threads.

An interesting aside: If you flip a 1×3 twill over, you'll find a 3×1 twill fabric on the other side, as, from this perspective, the weft travels under three warp threads and then floats over one warp thread. Knowing that the complement to your twill is on the other side of your fabric is useful both in design and troubleshooting.

In this 1×2 twill, the fabric at the left shows the red weft traveling under 1 blue warp thread and floating over 2 blue warps. At the right, which shows the reverse side of the same fabric, the weft travels under 2 warp thread and floats over 1.

Leno

Leno uses twist to create openness in the threads, resulting in an airy fabric often used for curtains or areas of lace in clothing. It is an ancient weave structure, with examples of its use all over the world. Leno is created by twisting one set of warp threads over an adjacent set of warp threads. You use your fingers to make this twist, store it on a pickup stick, and then turn the pickup stick on edge to create a shed. It takes a bit of dexterity at first, but the motion is easy to master with a bit of practice. It's easier to manipulate the warp threads if you loosen the tension one click of the brake. You can work these twists on an open or a closed shed, with slightly different results depending on which you choose.

If you want to have an even number of leno twists across the width of your warp, make sure that the bundle size multiplies evenly into the number of warp threads on the loom. If you aren't concerned about each leno twist matching exactly, you can sneak any extra threads into the last few bundles on either side of the warp.

STICKS TO PICK UP

A pickup stick is a wide, flat stick that is at least as long as the warp is wide. They're often pointed on one or both ends to make them easier to slide under and "pick up" threads. You can use them to open a shed in the threads you've picked up by turning them on edge. When purchasing or making a pickup stick, check that it's wide enough to create a good shed when turned on end. I prefer pickup sticks that are between 1" and 2" wide.

How to Weave Leno

Leno is always woven in pairs of rows: in the first pick you manually insert the twist, and in the second pick the warp releases the twist, giving you a "free" pick of leno. If you kept adding twist each pick without allowing the corresponding untwist row, the warp would eventually become too tight to weave (unless you were weaving on a warp-weighted loom, which is outside the scope of this book).

(1) Place your heddle in neutral. Press down into the warp to pop up the threads you plan to twist. In this example I'm popping up four warp threads in preparation to weave a 2×2 leno.

(2) Separate the threads you intend to twist over each other onto your index and middle finger. Because I'm weaving a 2×2 leno, I have two threads on each finger. Then, twist one set of threads over the other. I find it most natural to twist the set of threads on the right under the threads on the left.

(3) Store the twist on a pickup stick.

→ *Continue steps 1–3 all the way across the warp.*

Continued on next page ▷

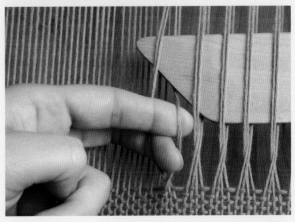

How to Weave Leno, *continued*

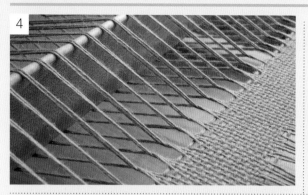

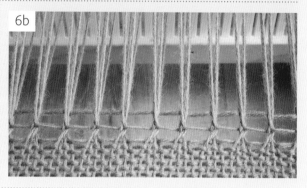

④ Turn the pickup stick on edge to open up the shed.

⑤ Pass the shuttle through and beat. This weaves the first pick of leno. Remove the pickup stick.

⑥ Change the shed by moving the heddle, throw the shuttle (a), and beat (b). This weaves the second pick of leno.

LENO VARIATIONS

One of the fun things about leno is how many different ways you can weave this simple technique. Here are some variations to play with (study the photos on page 146 for more examples):

▶ **DIRECTION OF TWIST.** You can twist some bundles to the left, others to right, to create a subtle undulating effect in your cloth (a).

▶ **BUNDLE SIZE.** Experiment with the number of threads in your bundles. A 1×1 leno creates a delicate, refined lace, whereas as 6×6 leno is a bold architectural element in your cloth. The number of threads in your bundles depends on both the size of your yarns (typically you'll want more threads per bundle for finer yarns) and the scale you want for your lace (more threads mean bigger lace holes). You can even mix different-size bundles in the same row (c). If you do this, however, be aware that larger bundles will be taller than bundles with fewer threads, causing some unevenness in your cloth that will either bug or delight you, depending on your goal. Be aware that you'll get a lot of draw-in when you weave leno. If you combine it with plain weave, expect wavy selvedges.

▶ **UNEVEN GROUPINGS.** There is no rule that says you have to twist the bundles evenly. Experiment with a 1×2 leno, or a 2×3 (b). Having uneven groupings adds texture to leno and highlights the direction of twist.

▶ **PICKUP DESIGNS.** You can combine areas of leno with areas of plain weave to create lacy designs in your cloth. This is especially fun for cloth such as curtains or lamp shades that will be backlit, illuminating the open areas as in the candle cover on the next page. *Note:* One caveat to leno pickup designs inside plain weave cloth is that rows of leno are taller than rows of plain weave, so to keep the areas of plain weave solid, you'll have to weave extra rows in the plain-weave areas. As you can see in the photo at the bottom of this page (d), the weft weaves three rows of plain weave on the right, before entering the leno section of the cloth. It then weaves the leno, and then three rows of plain weave on the left before going back to weave the second pick of leno. The number of plain-weave picks needed may vary, depending on the scale of the leno.

LENO CANDLE COVER

Alternating twists of leno and plain weave create interesting patterns of light and shadow when the candle is lit inside this fabric-covered candle holder.

WARPING

Wind a warp 1 yard long of 80 threads. Thread the heddle as described on pages 59–62.

WEAVING

(1) Weave a 1" header in plain weave. This will become the hem at the back of the candle sleeve.

(2) Weave a row of 2×2 leno, as described on pages 147–48.

(3) Weave 4 picks of plain weave.

(4) Alternate steps 2 and 3 until the cloth is 10" long.

(5) Weave a 1" border of plain weave.

(6) Cut the fabric from loom.

FINISHING

Wrap the fabric warp-wise around the glass cylinder. Fold a hem at both ends, drawing the ends together until the piece fits tautly. Press the hem firmly with a hot iron. Trim the hem and secure the ends and edges with Fray Check. When the Fray Check is dry, use sewing thread and whipstitch or mattress stitch to sew the seam. (For mattress stitch, see page 274.)

Light the candle, and enjoy!

LOOM AND HEDDLE

Rigid-heddle loom with a weaving width of 7" or greater
One 12-dent heddle

WIDTH IN HEDDLE

6⁷⁄₁₀"

WARP AND WEFT YARN

Valley Yarns Undyed Wetspun Warp Linen 8/4 (330 yards per 8.8 ounce tube): 90 yards of Natural (000)

WEAVE STRUCTURE

2×2 leno

EPI

12 ends per inch

PPI

8 picks per inch in plain weave;
4 picks per inch in leno

OTHER SUPPLIES

Glass cylinder 3⅜" in diameter and 6" tall

Pillar candle 3" in diameter and 4" tall

Hand-sewing needle and 18" of sewing thread to match the color of the linen

Fray Check, or similar fabric glue

MEASUREMENTS

5¼" × 12" (including 1" hem at the back of the candle sleeve)

Brooks Bouquet

Brooks bouquet is a structure in which you deliberately wrap the weft thread around bundles of warp threads to tie them together like bouquets of flowers or sheaves of wheat. It is believed to be named after Marguerite Brooks, a popular weaving teacher, who was also an expert in bobbin lace. In traditional Brooks bouquet, the bundles are picked up against an open shed, which creates warp float lines across the back. When weaving this form of Brooks bouquet, you should weave a few picks of plain weave between picks of bouquet to tame those floats.

How to Weave Brooks Bouquet

① Open a shed.

② Push the shuttle into the shed under the threads you wish to wrap.

③ Pull the shuttle up through the top warp and out of the shed.

Continued on next page ▷

How to Weave Brooks Bouquet, *continued*

④ Insert the shuttle into the shed behind the same threads you passed behind in step 2, and draw the weft through. This wraps the threads and creates the bouquet. Continue across the row in the same shed to the edge.

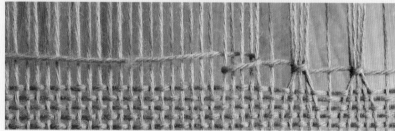

⑤ Weave the next plain-weave shed and beat.

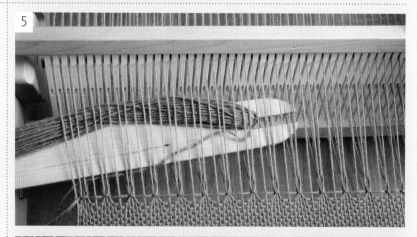

BROOKS BOUQUET VARIATIONS

▶ **CLOSED SHED (a).** Use this wrapping technique on a closed shed for a different look, and to eliminate the warp floats across the back.

▶ **COMBINATION WEAVE.** Combine Brooks bouquet with plain weave in a single pick of weaving. The thing to watch here is that Brook's bouquet, because of the way the warps crowd together in the twist, will not pack weft as tightly as the plain-weave area. You have several options for dealing with this: (1) decide this is the look you want, (2) weave the plain-weave areas back and forth as we did with leno pickup (starting on page 146), (3) double the weft in the plain-weave areas, or (4) use a tapestry fork to pack the weft down in the Brooks bouquet areas.

▶ **ADD RIBBONS.** A fun thing to do with traditional Brooks bouquet is to weave ribbon over the floats on the back of the cloth and under the bouquets.

▶ **STAGGER THE BOUQUETS (b)** between rows to create a fishnet look. This fabric loses a lot of width dimensionally when you take it off the loom, but it has wonderful stretch.

▶ **ADD BEADS (c)** to the weft that wraps the bouquet.

▶ **VARY THE SIZE AND PLACEMENT** of the weft wraps.

How to Thread Beads onto Weft Yarn

Weft yarns are often too thick to go through a needle that is small enough to go through a bead. Here's a way to get around that problem. You may have to experiment a bit to get the right size beads for the weft you are using.

1. Thread a sewing needle with a piece of sewing thread about 6" long. Tie the ends together in an overhand knot.

2. Insert the end of your weft yarn through the loop, leaving a tail long enough that it doesn't easily slip out of the loop.

3. Insert your needle into a bead, and draw it along the loop of sewing thread and then onto the weft yarn.

4. Pull the beads up as needed and push them in place as you wrap the bouquet.

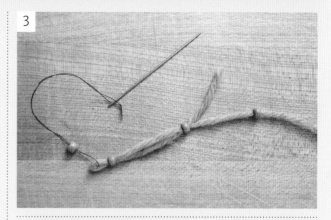

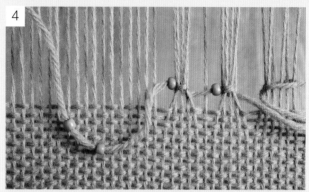

MISTAKE OR DISCOVERY?

I have a theory that many slow and fancy techniques started off as mistakes. Brooks bouquet, for example, looks to me as if a weaver in antiquity dropped a shuttle when she was passing it through a shed, picked it up off the floor, and accidentally twisted the weft around warp threads when she brought it back up. This ingenious weaver, instead of uttering a brief curse, looked at the result and thought, "Huh. That's pretty. Wonder what it'd look like if I did it all the way across." When you make a mistake in weaving, I encourage you to look at it a minute before you fix it. In that moment, you just might discover a new weaving pattern!

Spanish Lace

In Spanish lace, the weft weaves back and forth across a section of warp several times before advancing to the next section. You can use it with a thicker or decorative weft to show off the undulating pattern the weft makes, or you can use a thin weft and pull the woven bundles tight to create eyelets in the cloth. (Spanish lace is sometimes called Spanish eyelet in older weaving books.)

In this structure, the tendency of the weft is to move diagonally upward across the cloth. You can allow this to happen, letting progressively larger warp floats build up in the cloth, or you can smoosh the weft when you beat to prevent this migration. Which option you choose depends on the effect you want. In the 1960s and 1970s, Spanish lace was often woven loosely with large weft threads to create wall hangings where the weft appeared to scribble across the warp threads.

When Spanish lace is packed down, it forms a nice decorative border. Sets of Spanish lace, one woven going left, the other woven going right, create a chevron effect. When I'm weaving Spanish lace to create chevrons, I weave one or two picks of plain weave between each area of Spanish lace to spread the warp threads back out and keep slots from forming in the cloth. (Of course, if you're weaving buttonholes into a cloth, slots might be just what you want.)

Planning Spanish Lace

If you like symmetry and want the sections of Spanish lace to come out evenly across your warp, make sure the number of warp threads in your warp is a multiple of the threads you use in each Spanish lace cell.

For cloth set at the scale of most rigid-heddle projects, weaving under three to five warp threads is a good place to start, though I encourage you to play with other cell sizes and see what pleases you.

An example of Spanish lace

How to Weave Spanish Lace

① Weave under 3 raised warp threads (a), and then pull the shuttle up out of the shed (b).

② Change the shed.

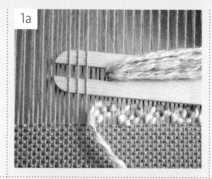

③ Weave back toward the selvedge you began at, under 2 threads (a). Bring the shuttle up out of the shed (b).

④ Change the shed.

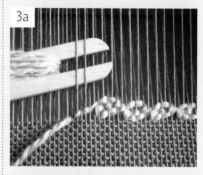

⑤ Weave under 6 threads, and bring the shuttle up out of the shed (a). This step finishes the first cell of Spanish lace and begins the second cell (b).

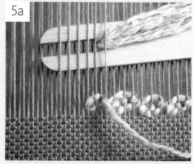

→ *Repeat steps 3–5 until you reach the other selvedge.*

SPANISH LACE VARIATIONS

Spanish lace isn't woven much today, which is a shame. It's a structure with many possibilities. These are some variations you might want to try:

▶ **EXTEND THE HEIGHT** of Spanish lace by adding additional steps. As you do so, keep in mind that the number of steps has to remain odd in order to move forward on the last step. Another thing to keep in mind if you're interested in adding steps is that as your sections get higher, the amount of unwoven warp between the stacks increases, affecting the stability of the cloth. If you're doing a decorative wall hanging, this may be fine; in clothing it could spell disaster.

▶ **THREAD THE WEFT WITH BEADS** (see page 154) and weave Spanish lace. Pull the weft tight and position the beads so they're only on the decorative floats in the eyelets.

▶ **WEAVE SPANISH LACE IN WOOL,** creating long channels of woven cloth with floats between. Full the cloth, and then cut the floats. You've now created tabs of cloth attached at the top (like you'd see in an automated car washer) with no sewing.

▶ **WEAVE SPANISH LACE** with cells of varying sizes.

▶ **WEAVE EYELETS** by weaving sections of Spanish lace using the ground weft yarn and pulling the weft tightly as you go, creating spaces between the Spanish lace cells. This works best as a single row in a field of plain weave, or as rows separated by several rows of plain weave, to make the eyelet rows distinct.

Danish Medallions

This weave structure typically uses a contrasting, or supplemental, weft to draw the fabric up in lozenge or medallion shapes, but you can also use this technique to create flowers, stars, and other flights of fancy. It is a traditional technique in the Scandinavian countries, but it has also been found in weavings in other parts of the world.

You'll need a thicker thread to act as the contrast weft. Usually the rest of the cloth is done with a smooth plain yarn to highlight the design element. The contrast weft should be strong enough to take a bit of abrasion, as you'll be pulling it through the cloth with a crochet hook.

Before you begin to weave, thread one shuttle with the ground weft (this is usually the same yarn as the warp) and another shuttle with the contrast weft. You'll also want to have a crochet hook handy; I typically use a US F/5 (3.75 mm) or G/6 (4 mm) hook, but you should match the size of the hook to the scale of your yarn.

If you want your Danish medallions to come out evenly across the warp, make sure that the number of warp threads in your cloth is a multiple of the number of warp threads you plan to put in each medallion. You can also choose to make medallions of varying sizes, for decorative effect.

How to Weave Danish Medallions

1. Weave a 1" to 2" header using the ground weft.

2. Throw a pick of your supplemental weft.

3. Weave another section of plain weave using the ground weft. How tall a section you weave will determine the height of your medallions. If you don't have a preference, three to five picks is a good starting place.

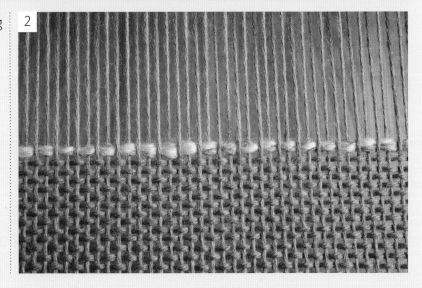

④ Begin to weave a pick of the supplemental weft, stopping at the point where you want the medallion to end. Bring the supplemental weft up and out of the shed.

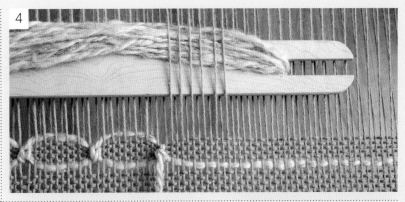

⑤ Using a crochet hook, dive under the first pick of contrast weft, submarine under the cloth, and come up and snag the loose end of the second pick of contrast weft (a). Pull a loop of the contrast weft under the cloth, under the first pick of contrast weft, and up through the woven fabric to the front of the cloth (b).

⑥ Pass the contrast-weft shuttle through this loop (a) and pull to tighten (b).

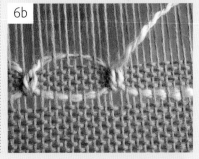

⑦ Put the contrast-weft shuttle back into the shed at the point it came out.

→ *Repeat steps 4–7 to weave the next medallion.*

DANISH MEDALLION VARIATIONS

The lozenge shape is the most traditional way to weave Danish medallions, but you can also get creative with the placement of the loops. Here are some fun things to try:

▶ **WEAVE OTHER SHAPES.** Stars, Christmas trees, and other shapes can be created out of the lines and circles offered by the Danish medallion technique. See specific directions for weaving stars below; these can be a launching-off place for creating your own designs.

▶ **ADD BEADS.** When you pull up a loop with the crochet hook, consider threading a bead onto that loop. It's an easy way to add a bit of glitz to your Danish medallions.

▶ **VARY THE TENSION.** Control how much your medallions distort the fabric by pulling tighter or looser on the supplemental warp in step 6b, page 159.

▶ **USE DIFFERENT-SIZE CELLS.** Change the number of plain-weave picks in step 3 or the number of warp threads you go under in step 4 (pages 158–59) to change the size of the medallions. You can also combine patterns of large and small medallions for a fun effect.

▶ **CHECKERBOARD AND OTHER PATTERNS.** Create one row of medallions and then shift your pattern by a half medallion to create a checkerboard.

How to Weave Danish Stars

① Weave as in steps 1–4, pages 158–159.

② Insert the crochet hook to pull a loop under the cloth, beginning two or three warp threads to the right of where the second pick of contrast weft stopped. This will create the right-bottom leg of the star.

③ Complete step 6, taking care not to pull the tension too tightly. You want the loop to lie flat on the top of the cloth.

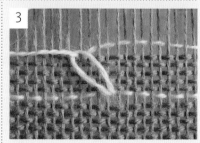

④ Without advancing the contrast weft, insert the crochet hook directly under where the contrast weft in the second pick ends. Pull the contrast weft up and pass the shuttle through the loop as before. This creates the middle-bottom leg of the star.

⑤ Without advancing the contrast weft, insert the crochet hook two or three warp threads to the left of where the contrast weft in the second pick ends. Pull the contrast weft up and pass the shuttle through the loop as before. This creates the left-bottom leg of the star.

⑥ Put the contrast-weft shuttle back into the shed at the point it came out, and repeat the preceding steps all the way across the fabric to finish weaving the bottom row of stars.

⑦ Weave another section of plain weave.

⑧ Start the next pick of contrast weft, pulling the shuttle out just above the left-bottom leg of the star. Starting the crochet hook at the middle of the star (where the three legs converge from the previous row), connect to the contrast weft, and pull a loop through. This creates the left-top leg of the star.

⑨ Put the contrast-weft shuttle through the loop and advance until the shuttle is right over the middle of the star. Pull up a loop from the center. This creates the middle top leg of the star.

⑩ Put the contrast-weft shuttle through the loop and advance until the shuttle is right over the right-bottom leg of the star. Pull up a loop from the center to this rightmost position. This creates the right-top leg of the star.

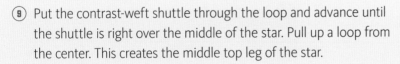
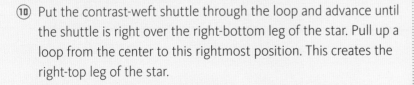

→ *Continue across the fabric to create the top half of the stars.*

Clasped Weft

This is a fun technique you can use to make designs in your cloth. You'll use two different yarns. They're often different colors, but you can play with other aspects such as shiny/matte, smooth/textured, and so on. The point is they must be visibly different, or the technique won't show up well. Clasped weft is a technique that works independently of the weave structure. The basic idea is that one weft goes through the shed, wraps around a second weft, and then pulls the second weft partway into the shed.

In the following instructions, the loom is warped for plain weave and the weaving pattern is plain weave: the heddle alternates between up and down. If you look closely at the resulting fabric, however, you'll see that the weft is doubled in each pick. The actual weave structure of clasped-weft fabric is half basketweave. You'll also notice a bump in the fabric where the two yarns join. That extra bit of thickness is the inevitable result of the yarns bending

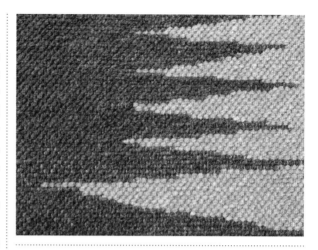

around each other and adds a bit of textural outline to your design.

You can weave many different patterns with the clasped weft technique. My designs tend toward the organic, because I like to play around and design on the fly with clasped weft, but you could also create controlled and precise patterns, such as diamonds and checkerboards.

How to Weave Clasped Weft

① Wind one of the yarns onto a shuttle.

② Have the other yarn in a package that can freely feed yarn, such as a ball or cone. If the yarn is in skein form, wind it into a ball before you begin.

③ Open a shed and pass the shuttle all the way through the shed.

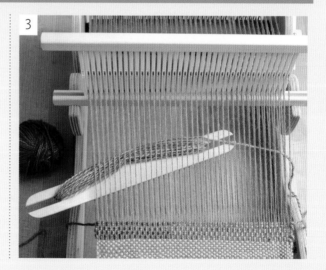

④ Wrap the shuttle around the yarn coming from the other yarn source so the two wefts bend around each other. This is the "clasp": it's as if the two yarns are holding hands.

⑤ Put the shuttle back into the open shed. It is important that you not change the shed between steps 3 and 5. Pull the shuttle out of the shed on the side that it started on in step 3. Keep pulling until the other yarn is drawn into the shed.

⑥ Stop pulling when the other yarn is where you want it in your design.

⑦ Beat, then change sheds. Continue from step 3 to weave the rest of the cloth, alternating between up and down sheds.

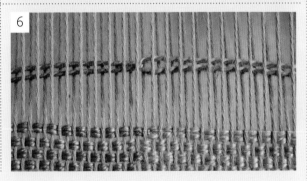

CLASPED WEFT VARIATIONS

After weaving with the extra yarn package on one side of the design, break the weft and start it on the other side. This lets you alternate the sides the colors appear on.

You could do interesting work with clasped weft using yarns of different shrinkage. For example, weave in triangles with yarn that will felt on the edges of a fabric woven with otherwise nonfelting yarn.

Soumak

This technique is one in which the weft yarn wraps completely around the warp while it is flat. In other words, soumak is worked without first creating a shed. Soumak can be used at the ends of a fabric to prevent the weft from unraveling, and it is also sometimes used inside a tapestry design to outline or highlight a motif. The many types of soumak knots can be categorized into two families: Oriental and half hitches.

There are many types of soumak knots, such as single (a half hitch over one thread), Oriental (a half hitch over two threads), Cavandoli (a double half hitch), and Greek (a treble half hitch). In Oriental soumak, the weft circles around the next two warp threads and then moves forward four warp threads. It may be knotted left to right or right to left. The rows will slant in different directions depending on the direction you're knotting. Shots of plain weave, using a thin ground weft, are often woven between each row of knots to lock the rows into place and keep the fabric from stretching.

Soumak is often woven with yarn butterflies (see page 63) or on netting shuttles because of the need to pass the weft source through the loops during the knotting process.

One of the neat features about designing with soumak is that, because it creates half hitches around the threads, it can be tightened down anywhere on the warp. This means that you can weave structurally sound soumak above unwoven sections of warp. Soumak is also free to wander "off the grid," undulating in organic waves across the warp. Both of these features open up interesting design possibilities.

ORIENTAL SOUMAK, WEAVING TO THE RIGHT

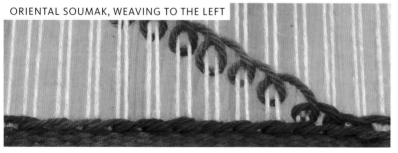

ORIENTAL SOUMAK, WEAVING TO THE LEFT

LOOM AND HEDDLE
Rigid-heddle loom with a weaving width of at least 5"
One 12-dent heddle

WIDTH IN HEDDLE
4¼"

WARP AND GROUND WEFT
Maysville 8/4 cotton carpet warp, 100% cotton (1,600 yards per pound; available on 8 oz/ 800 yd tubes): 120 yards of Linen (#46)

WEFT
Lily Sugar'n Cream, 100% cotton (768 yards per pound; available in 2.5 oz/120 yd balls): 1 ball each of Jute (#00082), Lilac (#01322), and Sage Green (#00084)

WEAVE STRUCTURE
Soumak

EPI	PPI
12 ends per inch	10 picks per inch

MEASUREMENTS
4" × 4"

Note: Netting shuttles like the one shown above, while not required, make it easy to control the pattern weft yarns and knot the soumak stitches. Or, you may use butterflies, as shown here.

SOUMAK-WOVEN COASTER

This project makes a set of four coasters, but the same thick fabric would also be suitable for a small rug or mat.

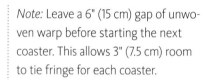

WARPING

Wind a warp 1½ yards long and 51 threads wide. Thread the heddle as described on pages 59–62.

WEAVING

Note: Follow steps 2–5 of the weave pattern below in this color sequence: 5 picks Sage Green, 3 picks Jute, 5 picks Lilac, 3 picks Jute; repeat this sequence once more, then end by weaving 5 picks Sage Green.

1. With the heddle in the up position, use ground weft to weave a pick of plain weave from left to right.

2. Wrap the pattern weft twice around the two left-most warp threads. Wind the wraps so the weft comes out over the warp threads toward the right.

3. With the heddle in neutral position, use the pattern weft to weave a row of soumak going left to right as follows: advance over 4 and back under 2. Each stitch advances the weft by 2 warp threads. Continue across until you reach the last 2 warp threads: leave them unwoven.

4. With the heddle in the down position, use ground weft to weave a pick of plain weave from right to left. The ground-weft picks lock the soumak into place and prevent it from stretching.

5. Wrap the pattern weft twice around the last 2 warp threads. Wind the wraps so the weft comes out over the warp threads toward the left.

6. With the heddle in neutral position, use the pattern weft to weave a row of soumak going right to left as follows: advance over 4 and back under 2. The two rows of soumak should form chevrons, like knitted stockinette stitch turned sideways.

7. Repeat steps 1–6 until the coaster is square. End with one pick of ground weft.

Note: Leave a 6" (15 cm) gap of unwoven warp before starting the next coaster. This allows 3" (7.5 cm) room to tie fringe for each coaster.

FINISHING

Cut the fabric from the loom. Using a tapestry needle, weave the loose pattern weft ends up through the wraps at the edges of the coasters. Using groups of 4 warp threads, tie an overhand knot close to the first and last rows of weaving, 13 knots at each edge. When all the knots are in a line and pulled tight, trim the fringe to ½" (1.25 cm) from the knots.

Tapestry Weaving

Tapestry is a discontinuous-weft, weft-faced fabric. It's woven in plain weave, but with multiple wefts in a single pick. Managing how all of the weft threads interact and creating imagery at the same time makes tapestry weaving surprisingly complex. It is the weave structure most often associated with artistic weaving, and tapestry weavers often call their work "painting with yarn."

Entire books are devoted to the art of tapestry weaving, with vastly more information than I can cover here. (For suggested reading, see the appendix, page 281.) There are many types of tapestry. What I describe here is a variation of slit tapestry, where the ends are woven in as you weave. It's a form of tapestry that's similar to Navajo blanket weaving.

The first step for most tapestry weavers is to create the cartoon, which is an outline of the image you want to weave. For your first tapestry, I recommend a simple geometric design, made up of basic shapes such as squares and triangles. Solid shapes reduce the number of wefts you'll have going at any one time.

Your cartoon should be a life-size representation of the image you want to weave, expressed in simple lines. You can pin the cartoon to the weaving so that it's under the warp, acting as a reference as you weave. Or you can place the cartoon behind the warp and use a waterproof maker to dot the design directly onto the warp. The first method removes any chance that the marker will bleed through onto the weft. The second method prevents you from having to weave around a rattling piece of paper.

BEGINNER'S FOLLY

When I was first learning tapestry, I decided to start by weaving a spiral, not knowing at the time that this supposedly simple shape would require nine different wefts and a lot of fiddly skinny areas of color. It takes experience to be able to look at a cartoon and determine if it's going to be easy or hard to weave. I find that it requires me to bend my mind in the same way that I do when creating a stencil for screen printing.

Warping for Tapestry

The warp doesn't show in tapestry. Tapestry is a weft-faced fabric, which means that the weft completely covers and hides the warp. Because of this, the color of the warp is unimportant, and most tapestry is woven on a white or off-white warp. What is important in a warp yarn is that it be strong, relatively smooth, and a consistent thickness. Suitable yarns include linen and tightly spun wools or cottons. The warp remains under high tension and does not bend: the weft does all the work. Tapestry is often woven under a high tension, and the warp yarn must be strong enough to withstand that force.

The thickness of warp that you use depends on the sett and the thickness of your weft. Typically the warp threads are about half as thin as the weft. You need the weft to have enough room to bend around the warp and yet be able to fill the space between warp threads completely. The best way to determine the proper balance of warp, weft, and sett is to sample. For a place to start, see the project on page 170.

The fiber content of tapestry warp varies among traditions. Some weavers use seine cotton (a strong cotton yarn traditionally used to weave seine fishing nets), others use linen, and yet others prefer a worsted-spun wool. One feature of wool is that it helps lock the weft in place and prevents sliding. This is an advantage, as it ensures that the weft doesn't move out of place and distort your design.

The sett of tapestry is much wider than you'd use for a balanced cloth. This is necessary to allow the weft to sink down between the warp threads and completely encapsulate them. Common setts for tapestry are 8, 10, and 12. This spacing corresponds nicely to the commonly available rigid heddles.

Once you've picked your warp and sett, warp the loom as you would for any other plain-weave project.

Choosing Tapestry Weft Yarns

The design of tapestry typically comes from the graphical placement of color, not from texture. Keeping this in mind, you'll probably want to use weft yarns that are all the same type of yarn, in a range of colors. (If creating tapestries with textured yarns makes you happy, by all means go ahead.)

Because the weft yarn does not need to be as strong as the warp, you can use singles (see page 27) or plied yarns. It should be a yarn, however, that won't fray and that can handle the rigors of being passed through the warp threads and beaten into place.

The size of the weft should be such that it can completely cover the warp threads without distorting them out of position. A quick way to estimate if a weft is the right size is to double it up and slide the doubled weft between the warp threads. The doubled yarn should fill the space without pushing the warp threads out of alignment.

Smooth, strong yarns suitable for tapestry warps

Weaving Tapestry

If you are using a rigid-heddle loom as your tapestry loom, you have two options for weaving tapestry on it. You can use the rigid heddle to beat the weft into place, in which case you would weave the tapestry edge to edge. This means that you would open the shed, advance all of the wefts the entire way across the warp by one pick, and then beat. The other option is to use the rigid heddle simply as a shedding device and to beat areas of weft into place using your fingers or a tool such as a tapestry beater or fork.

The #1 rule of tapestry is "Thou shalt weave plain weave." The reason this is so important is because if you weave any structure other than over one, under one, you will create a visible irregularity in the fabric that will distract viewers from the tapestry image, and the warp threads may show through the weft.

Weaving plain weave sounds easy, until you take into account the fact that you have many different wefts, each of which might be moving left or right in any given pick. Managing all these directions and making sure that you are always weaving a perfect tapestry gives rise to most of the rules and guidelines you'll read in tapestry books. There are many tricks that make tapestry weaving successful, such as moving over a weft by an odd or even number. Here are three simple guidelines that will get you out of most technical difficulties, especially if you keep your design simple.

TAPESTRY TROUBLESHOOTING

▶ **USE THE SUPERPOWER OF THE TURNAROUND.** The warp thread where a weft turns around and goes back the other way counts as both an under and an over. If you run into a situation where threads in two consecutive picks need to go under or over the same warp thread, one way to fix it is to move one of the weft turnarounds over by one thread.

▶ **CHANGE THE DIRECTION OF THE WEFT.** If weft is moving from right to left and causing problems with its neighboring weft, consider breaking the weft and moving it to the other side of the area and weaving in the opposite direction. This often fixes the problem. Overlap the wispy ends of yarn where you broke it, and weave them in as you continue to weave the tapestry.

One of the problems that can come up in tapestry is an uncovered warp thread between two sections weaving in opposite directions.

▶ **ADD ANOTHER WEFT.** What happens if you have an area between two others and on one side you need to be weaving left to right and on the other you need to be weaving right to left? You can add another weft of the same color to the center area so that half of it will weave going left, and the other half going right.

BUBBLING THE WEFT

Remember how you learned to bubble the weft in chapter 2 (page 75) in order to keep the selvedges from drawing in? This is even more crucial in tapestry, where selvedges can exist in the middle of your fabric. In addition to the selvedges at the sides of your tapestry, selvedges exist along the slits created each time one weft turns away from another and goes back on itself. One of the things that makes tapestry such an intriguing challenge is that you might be managing dozens of selvedges in a single pick of weaving, and if you mess up these selvedges, the error might be smack in the middle of your fabric.

To counteract this, bubble the weft more than you think necessary. The weft needs to be long enough to bend around the warp and cover it completely. If you see draw-in where the weft changes direction, you need bigger bubbles. If you see floppy loops where the weft changes direction, bubble less. Bubble just as much on rows with only one weft as on those with multiple wefts. To do this, make several small bubbles across the row.

WEAVE THE BOTTOM FIRST

If you are weaving in the build-up style in which you beat with a fork or your fingers and build up areas across the warp at different rates (as opposed to the edge-to-edge style of weaving), you need to be aware of one potential problem. In the design below, if you weave area A and then area B, you won't be able to weave area C: you have no way to beat it into place because it's overhung by area B. The correct sequence to weave this cartoon is A, C, and then B. Weave from the bottom up.

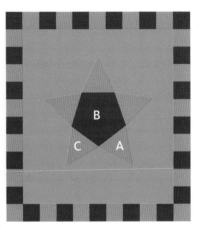

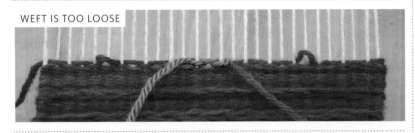

WEFT IS TOO LOOSE

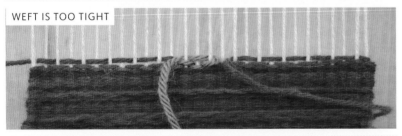

WEFT IS TOO TIGHT

BUBBLES SHOULD BE JUST RIGHT

TAPESTRY COVER
for a Digital E-Reader

This tapestry sleeve is for an e-reader. I have a Kindle Fire (4¾" wide × 7½" long × ½" deep), but you can easily resize this project for a smartphone or iPad, or use it as a cover to protect paperback books. The warp should be as wide as half the circumference of your reader (or book) + 25 percent to cover draw-in, shrinkage, and a bit of extra room to slide the e-reader in and out.

Design a cartoon for your project on a piece of paper that is as wide as your warp, or use the design provided on page 276.

LOOM AND HEDDLE
Rigid-heddle loom with a weaving width of at least 7"
One 8-dent heddle

WIDTH IN HEDDLE
6½"

WARP
Weaving Southwest 3-Ply Worsted Wool Warp, 100% worsted wool (750 yards per pound): 80 yards of Natural

WEFT
Brown Sheep Lamb's Pride Worsted, 85% wool/15% mohair (760 yards per pound; available in 4 oz/190 yd skeins): 160 yards of Kiwi (#M-191), 30 yards of Chianti (#M-28), and 25 yards of Autumn Harvest (#M-22)

WEAVE STRUCTURE
Weft-faced plain weave

EPI
8 ends per inch

PPI
20 picks per inch

OTHER SUPPLIES
Tapestry beater
Decorative button with a long shank
Tapestry needle
Sewing needle and thread to match Kiwi
T-pins

MEASUREMENTS
6¾" × 17½" (unfolded)

WARPING

Wind a warp of 52 threads, 1½ yards long, and thread the heddle as described on pages 59–62.

PREPARING THE WEFT

Wind 6 yarn butterflies of Kiwi, 3 yarn butterflies of Chianti, and 5 yarn butterflies of Autumn Harvest.

Tip: Untwist and pull yarn apart instead of cutting it when you separate it from the skein. If there's a blunt cut edge at the start of the skein, untwist and pull this off. Doing so creates tapering wisps of yarn at the ends of the weft. Weave those in (as you normally would weave the weft) when you start or end weaving with a yarn butterfly. This way you weave the ends in invisibly as you go, and don't have any ends to weave in once your tapestry is complete.

WEAVING

(1) Using warp yarn, weave a couple of rows of soumak (see page 164) to spread the warp and form a firm base for the tapestry. This will not be part of the finished cover.

(2) Working with the pattern upside down, weave the front of the e-reader cover. Use a tapestry beater to beat the weft into place so it completely covers the warp. Bubble the warp generously to achieve minimal draw-in. In areas where you are weaving a single weft thread from one side of the warp to the other, make three to five small bubbles across the warp so the draw-in in those areas matches the draw-in in areas where you weave multiple weft threads across the warp.

(3) When you've woven an inch of the design, secure the cartoon to the back of the fabric, using either straight pins or loose basting stitches.

(4) Continue to weave the design, taking care to always weave plain weave. Weave each row from side to side as you go.

(5) When you've woven the entire tapestry design, continue weaving in Kiwi to create the back of the cover. Be sure to bubble as much as you did when weaving the design. The back is done when it's 1½" longer than the design. This extra length is folded over to make the flap.

(6) Use the warp yarn to weave another 2 picks of soumak to secure the warp. Take the fabric off the loom, taking care not to cut too closely to the fell line. You'll want at least 5" of unwoven warp to use when weaving the warp ends back into the fabric.

(7) Thread the first warp end onto a tapestry needle. Take it over the final weft pick and back down into its own column, taking care not to catch the soumak thread. Bring the warp end out on the surface of the fabric that will be inside the e-reader cover. Pull the warp thread taut, so it tightly encapsulates the last weft row and won't work loose. If this is hard on your fingers, use pliers to pull the needle through. Clip the warp end close to the fabric, being careful not to cut the fabric itself. Repeat for the other warp threads. After all the warp threads are woven in, the soumak threads will not be attached to the fabric and can be removed. Repeat for the other end of the fabric.

(8) Using sewing thread that matches the Kiwi weft, sew closed any slits in the tapestry design longer than ½". Use mattress stitch (see page 274) and pull tight, so the sewing thread is hidden inside the slits and does not show.

(9) Thread an 18" piece of Kiwi weft yarn onto a tapestry needle and whipstitch over the edge of the fabric to conceal the ends of the warp threads and create a firm edge. If the yarn starts to untwist or become overly twisted as you stitch, stop and add or remove twist

as necessary. Repeat for the other end of the fabric.

(10) Hand-wash the fabric using warm water and a wool-friendly wash. Rinse well. Roll it in a towel and gently step on it to remove most of the water. Allow it to dry fully. If you have draw-in irregularities at the selvedges, you can block the fabric by pinning it taut to a firm surface while it dries to reduce or remove them.

(11) Fold the tapestry fabric lengthwise, with 1½" of overlap at the top of the back to form a flap. Seam the selvedges at the sides using Kiwi yarn threaded in a tapestry needle and whipstitch.

(12) Create a braid 12" long using each weft color. This will be used to create the closure. Using sewing thread that

matches the Kiwi weft, wrap and stitch one end to keep the braid from unraveling and trim it close. Tie an overhand knot in the other end and let the raw tapered wisps hang free. Sew the wrapped end down to the inside center of the flap so the rest of the braid hangs straight down the front of the e-reader cover when the flap is closed.

(13) Attach a decorative button to the front center of the cover. You can now close the cover by folding over the back flap and wrapping the braid end around the button.

You've now created a beautiful protective cover for your favorite reading device, phone, table, or book.

Transparencies

Like tapestries, transparencies often depict woven imagery. The difference is in the sett of the cloth and the weave structure. In tapestry, the cloth is a dense plain weave, and the weft is integral to the cloth. In transparencies, the ground cloth is open and airy, often having a window-screen appearance, and the design is woven as a supplemental inlaid weft. You could cut all the pattern weft out of a transparency and end up with an intact ground cloth. Because of this openness, transparencies take less time and yarn to weave than tapestry does. This openness also makes transparencies magical. The inlaid portions block light, while the open areas allow it to shine through. Backlit transparencies create bold silhouettes. With softer lighting, the background cloth visually disappears, creating the illusion that the inlaid designs are floating in space.

I hang this flag up when I'm writing, to remind loved ones not to disturb me. It glows, backlit by the monitor.

Choosing the Yarns

» **THE BACKGROUND WARP YARN** for a transparency needs to be able to weave an open and yet stable cloth. Traditionally, transparencies are woven in linen, because that material is inherently stiff and has tiny little fibers poking out of the yarn that make it sticky and that hold open the holes in the fabric. Other fibers you might consider are the wool stainless-steel yarns by Habu Textiles sett at 12 to 16 ends per inch (see appendix, page 284, for address), worsted-spun wool, wire, and monofilament fishing line (though this last option can be tricky to work with).

» **INLAY WEFT YARNS** need to be thick and flexible enough to fill in the holes of the background cloth without deflecting it. Wool, silk, and rayon are good choices here.

Designing Transparencies

Keep in mind that each time a horizontal line in the pattern is interrupted by empty space or a color change, you'll need a separate yarn supply. Start with simple, solid designs, rather than a trio of spirals. (My passion for spirals has gotten me into trouble on several occasions.)

Weaving Transparencies

You will find that when you are weaving the inlay yarn, sometimes it's ambiguous about exactly where you should end the weft pick. Neither warp thread you could turn around on exactly matches the cartoon. My advice? Color inside the lines. Err on the side of keeping the weft inside the lines on the pattern.

You will need a separate butterfly (or bobbin) of pattern yarn for each noncontiguous part of the pattern. Because transparency inlay is woven edge to edge, you will start every element on the same pick at the same time.

AT HOME

This charming transparency glows and looks especially lovely when hung in front of a window, backlit by the sun. You'll need a rigid-heddle loom with a 12-dent heddle to weave this project. The tapestry bobbins for the cotton weft are optional: you can instead simply wind the cotton into yarn butterflies. The cartoon for this design is on page 277.

WARPING

Wind a warp 2 yards long of 96 warp ends (48 loops). This will give you plenty of room for loom waste and will let you make two or three designs.

Thread the heddle as described on pages 59–62.

In order to deal with linen's inelasticity, I recommend tying onto the front with the heddle in the up or down position (that is, not neutral). This adds a bit of extra length to the hole threads and ensures even tension while weaving. When you put the heddle in the neutral position, you'll notice this extra length. Don't let it bother you. It's the tension while weaving that's preserved in the cloth.

WEAVING THE HEADER

1. Weave an inch or so of plain weave using the linen yarn (which you will use throughout as the background weft). Practice gently pressing this weft into place. You want the background cloth open and lacy so the pattern yarn can float between the linen picks. Ideally, you should be weaving to square, with 12 weft picks to the inch. This section of your cloth will look very cheeseclothy; it's supposed to. The linen yarn is sticky and stiff enough that it will hold its shape. It is the openness of the background cloth that makes the transparency work.

LOOM AND HEDDLE
Rigid-heddle loom with a weaving width of at least 8"
One 12-dent heddle

WIDTH IN HEDDLE
8"

WARP AND BACKGROUND WEFT YARN
Bockens 16/2 linen yarn (available on 8.75 oz/1,250 yd tubes): 350 yards of natural

PATTERN WEFT YARN
Cotton Clouds Softball .75, 100% unmercerized cotton, 850 yards per pound: 10 yards

WEAVE STRUCTURE
Plain weave

EPI
12 ends per inch

PPI
12 picks per inch

OTHER SUPPLIES
Shuttle for linen weft
Tapestry bobbins for the cotton weft (optional; you can also wind the cotton into yarn butterflies: see page 63)
Tapestry needle
Fray Check

MEASUREMENTS
7" × 10", hemmed

② Now that you have a bit of cloth woven, pin the transparency cartoon under the fabric. Now comes the fun part: you will alternate weaving the background (linen) weft with the pattern weft (wool). The fluffy wool yarn should fill in the gaps between the linen background cloth and create solid areas.

③ Open a new shed. Place the pattern weft in the areas outlined by the pattern, and gently squeeze it into place.

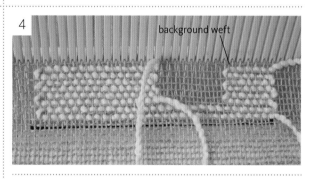

④ Open the same shed as in step 3. Throw the background weft, and beat it gently into place.

⑤ Open the next shed and repeat steps 3 and 4 until the entire pattern is woven.

background weft

You might find yourself wanting to simply beat both the pattern and background wefts into place at the same time. Don't. This will cause the pattern yarn to slip under the background weft in an unbecoming way. Take the extra time to place and beat in the pattern weft separately.

When you turn the pattern weft yarn to fill the image sections, pay attention to the way you wrap the warp threads. For the verticals, take care always to wrap the same warp thread; for diagonals (such as the roof), choose threads that will move smoothly along the angle of the line.

MAINTAINING THE PATTERN LINE

WEAVING THE CASING

When you are done weaving the pattern, weave another inch or so of background cloth, and then weave 3" of fabric with the linen weft, beating firmly. This will be hemmed to make the casing for the knitting-needle hanger. It needs to be more firmly woven to support the hemstitches and the weight of the transparency.

FINISHING

Cut the fabric off the loom, leaving about 5" of unwoven warp. Thread each warp end through a tapestry needle and weave the ends up into the fabric for about 1" to form a neat hem (a). Trim the ends. Apply a line of Fray Check to secure ends. *Note:* This is a delicate and fragile edge finish. For a more durable finish, hem or fringe to finish off the warp ends.

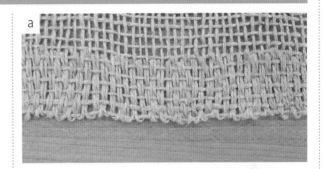

Weave in the ends of the pattern-weft yarn by taking a tapestry needle and carefully retracing its path in the fabric (b). After two or three rows, trim it close to the surface of the cloth; the stickiness of the yarn will hold it in place.

To create a casing at the top, fold over ½" of the firmly woven cloth twice and hem it by hand using the linen yarn and a tapestry needle. Slip the knitting needle through this casing (c).

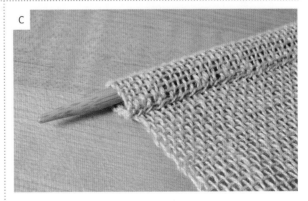

Make the hanger by plying the linen yarn into a rough cord. The hanger pictured on page 174 has 8 ends total. Start with a single length of yarn about 9 feet long. Fold it in half twice, then fold it once more; you will have two bundles of 4 threads each. Twist the bundles of 4 until they begin to ply back on themselves, then tie them together with an overhand knot at the cut ends to maintain the twist, and slip the loop at the other end over the knitting needle. Insert the tip of the needle through the cord near the knot.

Weft-Pile Weaves

Pile weaves refer to those with loops or cut ends coming vertically out of the face of the cloth. These may be weft threads, as we'll see in this section, or warp threads, as when weaving velvet. Both kinds of pile weave can either be cut to create a velvety plush surface, or left uncut to create loops reminiscent of the loops in a terry-cloth bath towel or candlewick bed coverings.

As I mentioned earlier, I'm a sucker for interesting yarn, so I wasn't able to resist when I ran across two handspun yarns from Nepal. One was hemp and the other aloo (nettle.) Both were singles yarn, naturally colored, and with a rough, rustic texture. My plan was to weave organic, exfoliating spa-style washcloths and give them as gifts with a bar of artisan soap. Hemp, being naturally antibacterial and moisture resistant, is perfect for bath items, and aloo smells great and is good for buffing skin. You may be able to find hemp yarn online at websites like Etsy.

Plain weave, however, seemed a bit *too* plain, especially given the rustic nature of the yarns. I wanted a weave structure that would show the two yarns off to best effect, keeping them distinct and special. I also wanted something that could be made on a simple, rigid-heddle loom so I could weave them during my summer travels.

Inspiration hit: handwoven looped pile, which you can weave on a rigid-heddle loom since it's just a hand-manipulated variant of plain weave. When I was done weaving my rustic yarns, I was thrilled with the results. They looked like something you'd see in an upscale spa: rare, funky, and authentically textured.

You can substitute 20/2 wet-spun linen for the hemp warp. Linen is also great for bath linens and can be easier to work with than the high-energy singles yarn. The aloo is more flexible than the hemp, so I used it as the weft, because it made pulling up the pile loops easier. You can also use the hemp singles as the weft, though it is less flexible and more abrasive. It all depends on how exfoliating you want your scrubby washcloth to be.

Because not everyone shares my hippy-granola aesthetic (or can get their hands on handspun hemp and aloo), I've also included directions for weaving the washcloths in Lily Sugar'n Cream, an inexpensive worsted-weight cotton available from most yarn and craft stores.

A rya sample woven using yarn from leftover bobbins as the pile weft. Designed and woven by Elisabeth Hill.

MISTY MAGIC

Bast fibers, like hemp and linen, behave better when there's humidity in the air. If you live in a dry climate, spritzing the yarn with water occasionally will help even out the warp tension and help the weft turn. I keep a spray bottle full of water on hand when weaving with bast fibers.

LOOPED-PILE WASHCLOTHS

A quick and satisfying weave, these looped-pile washcloths make a great gift, especially when paired with a bar of handmade soap.

MEASUREMENTS

FIBER	PROJECT STAGE	WIDTH	LENGTH
Hemp/aloe	*Off the loom*	9"	8½"
	After wet-finishing	9"	8"
	Shrinkage	0%	6%
Cotton	*Off the loom*	8½"	8"
	After wet-finishing	8"	7½"
	Shrinkage	6%	6%

LOOM AND HEDDLE

Rigid-heddle loom with a weaving width of at least 9"

One 8-dent heddle

WIDTH IN HEDDLE

9"

WARP YARN

Hemp/aloo version: Windhorse Imports, 100% Himalayan hemp, single ply (640 yards per pound): for four washcloths, 144 yards

Cotton version: Lily Sugar'n Cream, 100% cotton, worsted weight (768 yards per pound; available in 2.5 oz/120 yard balls): 144 yards of White (#00001)

WEFT YARN

Hemp/aloo version: Himalaya Yarn Aloo (nettle) 100% aloo handspun singles (available in 100 g/approximately 150 yd skeins): 1 skein of Natural (#AL-00). *Note:* The amount of weft needed depends on the density and length of your pile, but I've found one skein is more than enough for four washcloths.

Cotton version: Lily Sugar'n Cream, 100% cotton, worsted weight (768 yards per pound; available in 2.5 oz/120 yard balls): 160 yards of Lime Stripes (#21712).

WEAVE STRUCTURE

Plain weave with weft pile

EPI	PPI
8 ends per inch	7 picks per inch

OTHER SUPPLIES

A knitting needle or dowel to form the pile loops (I used a US 8/5 mm needle, but anything close to that will do.)

A small crochet hook to help pick up the loops (optional)

For four washcloths, wind a warp 2 yards long of 72 ends, and thread the heddle as described on pages 59–62.

WEAVING THE WASHCLOTHS

1. Weave 1½" of plain weave. This will be folded into a hem later.

2. Change the shed and throw the shuttle. Leave the shed open. Do not beat the weft into place.

3. With the shed open, use a knitting needle (or other pointed stick) to pick up loops of the weft between the raised warp threads. I find a small crochet hook helpful for lifting the loops and sliding them on the knitting needle. Make sure the weft has slack when you are picking up the pile loops. You'll need a lot of weft to form the loops. I like to leave a plain-weave border on the edge of my pile block. To do so, I simply do not pull up pile loops between the first four and last four raised warp threads in the shed.

4. Leaving the knitting needle in place, beat in the weft. You can angle the heddle back to beat under the knitting needle.

5. Weave one to three picks of plain weave to secure the pile. The number of plain-weave picks between each row of pile loop is up to you. Fewer picks of plain weave makes a denser pile. Experiment until you get the cloth you want. I used three plain-weave picks for the hemp/aloo version and two plain-weave picks for the cotton version.

6. Remove the knitting needle and begin again at step 2. Continue in this manner until you have woven 8".

7. Weave a second 1½" of plain weave for the second hem.

Repeat the steps above for each washcloth. *(Note: Remember that this means you'll have 3" total between washcloths.)*

→ *If you have extra warp at the end, you can weave the rest as plain weave and sew a soap bag (a simple drawstring bag that you tuck scraps of soap into and then use as a washcloth).*

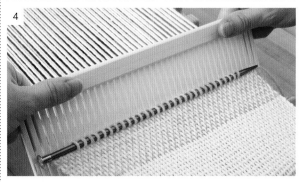

Cut the washcloths off the loom and hem them with a ½" double-fold hem as shown on page 100. Wash in a load of machine laundry on hot.

BEFORE WASHING

AFTER WASHING

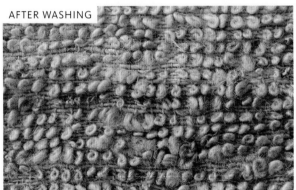

LOOPED-PILE VARIATIONS

You know how you created a plain-weave border by not picking up pile loops between the four threads on the edge? You can actually do that anywhere along the pile row. Each potential loop can either be picked up or left down to create patterns or designs in the pile. The photo below shows what I did in a free-form heart design.

Think about it: you could weave in a message, an initial, a teddy bear, a skull and crossbones — whatever you desire. Needlepoint books and counted cross-stitch patterns are a great resource for creating your own designs. Or you can design your own on graph paper.

Think of these little washcloths as a small, fun, creative palette, and in no time you'll have a pile of these little treasures to hand out as hostess gifts or during holidays.

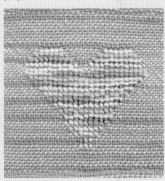

CHAPTER 6

Fast & Fancy

IN THE LAST CHAPTER WE LOOKED AT HAND-MANIPULATED WEAVE STRUCTURES. These offer much in the way of design potential, but they have the downside of taking a long time to weave. In this chapter we look at ways to make the loom do more of the work.

Floats as Design Elements

In plain weave, any floats that occur are regrettable mistakes that we learned how to fix. Now we're going to make floats on purpose, to create patterns in the cloth.

One of the first things to understand about floats is that every warpwise float on the front of the fabric corresponds to a weftwise float on the back of the fabric, and vice versa. (Compare the right and wrong sides of the bottom photo at right.) This occurs because if a warp thread is floating over the top of the fabric, it is not catching the weft on the underside of the fabric.

The other thing to know about floats is that they allow the fabric to deflect. Where floats occur, the warp and weft are more loosely tied together than in areas of plain weave, and threads can shift around, especially when the cloth is wet-finished and the threads relax the tension they had on the loom.

By combining warp and weft floats, you can create lacy and waffle-weave patterns in cloth. One caution though: don't let your floats get too long, or the structural integrity of your cloth will suffer. Depending on the size yarn you are working with, a float that crosses over three threads is generally safe; floating over more threads than that may create open or loose areas in your cloth. Sometimes, however, that's exactly what you want.

Warp and weft floats

Warp and weft floats

Weft floats (left); *warp floats on reverse side* (right)

Using a Pickup Stick to Create Pattern

In the previous chapter, when a pickup stick was used to make a shed, it was placed in front of the heddle and, as a consequence, had to be reinserted for each pick of weaving. Betty Davenport, a rigid-heddle pioneer, popularized placing the pickup stick behind the heddle. This allows you to save the pattern in memory, and makes weaving much faster. We'll use this technique in the following sections to create floats in the warp and weft directions to add texture and create new patterns in rigid-heddle cloth. There are several principles necessary for making this work:

» **PUT THE HEDDLE IN THE DOWN POSITION WHEN YOU PICK UP THREADS.** You do this to ensure that you pick up only slot threads on the pickup stick. This is important because hole threads are locked in place by the hole and can't create a shed when you turn the pickup stick on end. Only slot threads have enough space to slide and open up a clean shed. If you start working with this technique and aren't getting a good shed, check that you haven't inadvertently picked up hole threads.

» **PICK UP THREADS BEHIND THE HEDDLE.** This makes it possible for you to store the pattern between weft picks. If you pick up in front of the heddle, you'll have to repick them with each pick.

» **"TURN STICK" MEANS TURN THE PICKUP STICK ON EDGE.** In the pattern notation below, where I've written the instruction "turn stick," it means, with the heddle in the neutral position, turn the pickup stick on edge to make the shed.

» **"UP AND SLIDE STICK" MEANS SLIDE THE STICK.** Here's how: Put the heddle into the up position. This raises the hole threads. Then slide the pickup stick forward without turning it on edge. This raises a subset of the slot threads. If you do this properly, the stick should be easy to move, and you'll have only one shed. If you find yourself with two sheds, check to make sure you haven't turned the pickup stick on edge.

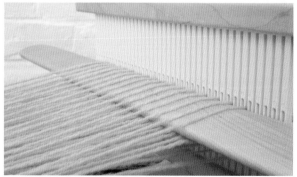

Introducing Weft Floats

This first structure creates a series of weft floats across the fabric. It's a simple and easy-to-weave structure that's a good introduction to this technique.

PICKUP STICK SETUP

Put the heddle in the down position, so only the slot threads are up. Insert a pickup stick into the slot threads so that the first slot thread is on top of the stick, and the next slot thread is beneath the stick. The easiest way to do this is to wiggle the tip of pickup stick up and down so that it weaves into the slot threads. Continue to do this across the warp. You've now stored the pattern shed "in memory."

WEAVING WEFT FLOATS

This cloth is essentially plain weave, with the exception of some weft floats every fourth pick. It's simple to weave and creates a richly textured fabric. Here is what's happening in the fabric: Steps 1–3 are pure plain weave; step 4 creates floats in some areas (where the threads were picked up above the stick) and plain weave in others (where the threads were below the stick). After a few repeats of the pattern, you'll find it easy to remember.

① Put the heddle in the up position. Throw a pick of weft, and beat. (This is a plain-weave shed.)

② Put the heddle in the down position. Throw a pick of weft, then beat. (This is a plain-weave shed.)

Continued on next page ▷

Introducing Weft Floats , *continued*

③ Put the heddle in the up position. Throw a pick of weft, and beat. (This is a plain-weave shed.)

④ Put the heddle in the neutral position, turn the stick on edge, throw a pick of weft, and beat (a). (This shed creates floats. You can use the same yarn that you use for the plain-weave sections, or, as shown here, use a different color for the floats(b).)

→ *Repeat steps 1–4 until the entire cloth is woven.*

Now that you understand how the technique works, I've written it and the following patterns in tabular form, so they're easy to parse. The patterns that follow are a subset of what's possible. Experiment and you may discover your own patterns.

WEFT FLOATS WEAVE PATTERN

Pickup stick setup: 1 warp up, 1 warp down, repeat across all slot threads.

ROW	HEDDLE POSITION
1	Up
2	Down
3	Up
4	Turn stick (neutral heddle)

Repeat rows 1–4 to continue lace pattern.

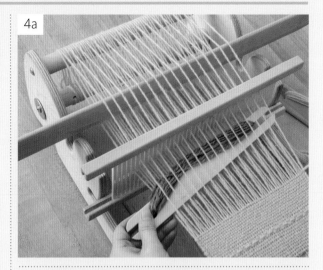

4a

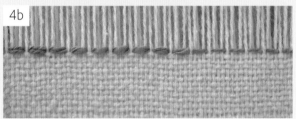

4b

WEFT FLOAT VARIATIONS

▶ Change the number and pattern of threads picked up on the stick.

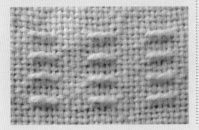

▶ Insert the pickup stick so it weaves floats only in certain areas across the warp.

▶ Create a checkerboard of floats by changing where the pickup stick is creating floats.

Introducing Warp and Weft Floats

This pattern is similar to the preceding one, but it adds warp floats in addition to the weft floats, creating a windowpane effect around areas of plain weave. You can weave it on the same warp as the preceding example without changing the pickup stick. The pattern weaves the weft floats in the same manner as the preceding pattern, but extends the last step to also weave a series of warp floats. It's a good approximation of waffle weave on the rigid-heddle loom.

If you turn the cloth over (one nice thing about rigid-heddle looms is that it's easy to flip them over and view the underside of the fabric you're weaving), you'll see that warp floats on one side of the fabric correspond to weft floats on the other side.

You can use a contrasting colored thread in the fabric where the warp and weft floats are. The color change will emphasize the windowpane effect. This is particularly attractive if you use black to outline brightly colored plain weave, or vice versa.

WARP AND WEFT FLOATS WEAVE PATTERN

Pickup stick setup: 1 warp up, 1 warp down, repeat across all slot threads

Row	Heddle Position
1	Up
2	Down
3	Up and slide stick
4	Down
5	Up
6	Turn stick (neutral heddle)

Note: Advance the fabric frequently. As the fell gets close to the heddle, it can be hard to get a good shed on the "up and slide" sheds.

CONTRASTING COLOR WEFT FLOATS

WARP AND WEFT FLOATS

Honeycomb

Honeycomb is an interesting weave structure in that it creates undulating waves in the fabric. These can be outlined with a thicker or contrasting yarn. The way you get curves is to weave floats next to areas of plain weave, so that when the fabric is washed, the threads in the densely woven areas of plain weave push out into the float areas, creating waves and curves. This weave structure is ideal for highlighting an expensive or precious yarn, as very little yardage is needed for the yarn that outlines the cells. The caution with honeycomb is that there are long floats on the reverse side of the fabric, making honeycomb best used in textiles where only the front of the fabric shows, such as pillows and lined jackets.

If your pattern goes all the way from selvedge to selvedge, there will be some picks that do not catch the edge warps. To avoid that problem, plan your design so that five or six warp threads on each side weave a plainweave border.

MANAGING TWO PICKUP STICKS

You use two different patterns, A and B, to weave honeycomb, so it is useful to have two pickup sticks. You'll store the first pattern (A) on the pickup stick closest to you and the second pattern (B) on a pickup stick behind that (1). As you switch between weaving pattern A and pattern B, you'll remove pickup stick A to weave pattern B. When you weave pattern A again, you'll pick it up in front of stick B. Pickup stick B stays in place the whole time. This halves the amount of time you spend inserting pickup sticks. If you use only one pickup stick, you'll have to insert it into the new pattern each time you switch between pattern A and pattern B.

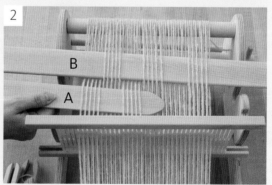

How to Weave Honeycomb

HONEYCOMB WEAVE PATTERN

Pickup stick A setup: 5 up, 5 down

Pickup stick B setup: 5 down, 5 up

ROW	HEDDLE POSITION	YARN
1	Down	Pattern weft
2	Up and slide stick A	Ground weft
3	Down	Ground weft
4–7	*Repeat steps 2 and 3 twice or more*	
8	Up and slide stick A	Ground weft

Repeat rows 1–8 with pickup stick B

ROW 1

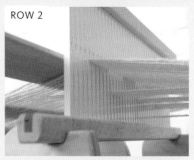

ROW 2

Note: To get a complete honeycomb, when you begin a section of honeycomb on a plain-weave fabric, start your design with row 8, which weaves the bottom of the cell consisting of the pattern weft.

HONEYCOMB VARIATIONS

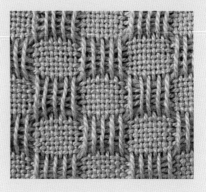

- Change the number of threads in each cell, such as 3 up, 3 down.

- Vary the size of the cells, such as 5 up, 3 down.

- Use a larger amount of plain weave repeats between pattern picks for taller cells.

- Use a heavier or thinner pattern yarn.

HONEYCOMB PILLOW

Here's an exotic and soothing pillow for your couch or bedroom. This project uses the honeycomb weave structure to make the most of an expensive yarn. By weaving most of the fabric in 3/2 mercerized cotton and using the recycled silk yarn just to outline the cells, you can weave a substantial amount of fabric and use only a bit of your special yarn. Sewing the fabric into a pillow hides the long floats on the reverse side of the honeycomb fabric.

LOOM AND HEDDLE

Rigid-heddle with weaving width of at least 17"
One 12-dent heddle

WIDTH IN HEDDLE

17"

WARP & GROUND WEFT YARN

UKI 3/2 100% mercerized cotton (1,200 yards per pound): 600 yards of Persian Green (#106)

PATTERN WEFT YARN

Frabjous Fibers Hand Picked Hues, 100% recycled silk, worsted weight (455 yards per pound; available in 100 g/100 yd skeins): 20 yards of Fuchsia (#17)

WEAVE STRUCTURE

Honeycomb

EPI	PPI
12 ends per inch	9 ground weft; 1 pattern weft

OTHER SUPPLIES

A 16" × 16" pillow form (available at fabric stores)
16" zipper (optional)

MEASUREMENTS

PROJECT STAGE	WIDTH	LENGTH
Off the loom	16"	33"
After wet-finishing	14½"	30"
Shrinkage	9%	9%

Wind a warp 2 yards long and 204 threads wide. Thread the heddle as described on pages 59–62.

HONEYCOMB WEAVE PATTERN

Pickup stick A setup: 4 up and 4 down

Pickup stick B setup: 4 down and 4 up

ROW	HEDDLE POSITION	YARN
1	Down	Pattern weft
2	Up and slide stick A	Ground weft
3	Down	Ground weft
4–7	Repeat steps 2 and 3 twice more.	
8	Up and slide stick A	Ground weft

Repeat rows 1–8 with pickup stick B.

Weave a 3" header in plain weave using the ground weft.

Work the Honeycomb Weave Pattern for 33".

Weave another 3" section in plain weave using the ground weft.

Cut the finished fabric off the loom and serge or zigzag-stitch the ends. Do not be concerned if the honeycomb cells look rectangular at this point; the honeycomb structure doesn't fully bloom until the fabric is washed and the yarns have shifted into the less-densely woven areas. This is one example where wet-finishing substantially changes the cloth.

Handwash the fabric in warm water, agitating gently. Rinse, and allow to dry.

With right sides together, fold the fabric in half, and sew a ½" seam along each selvedge. Press the seams open, and then turn the fabric right side out. Insert a pillow form into the pillow cover and hand-stitch the final seam closed. Alternatively, if you would like a removable pillow cover, insert a zipper in the opening before sewing the side seams.

PILLOW COVERS

The main feature most people want in a pillow is something soft to snuggle. Pillow covers are a great way to use up odds and ends of fabric — pieces too big to throw away but too small to make something else. You can also patch together scraps of handwoven fabric to make a pillow cover. They can be made of almost any material: cotton, linen, silk, rayon, wool, as long as the cloth is durable enough to hold the stuffing in and take a bit of squeezing. You may want to check what size pillow forms are available at your local fabric store and plan your handwoven fabric accordingly. Another option is to stuff your pillows with woolen thrums (waste yarn from your weaving projects), a thrifty way to recycle weaving waste into a new project.

Weaving Spots

If you design your fabric with floats interspersed with plain weave so there are isolated areas of floats, you create spots. An attractive way to weave spots is in a checkerboard pattern. Depending on the sett and the yarn, this can result in deflection around the spot areas, creating diamonds or circles in your cloth.

SPOT-BRONSON WEAVE PATTERN

Pickup stick A setup: 4 up, 2 down (across)

Pickup stick B setup: 1 up (do this once to shift the pattern), 2 down, 4 up

ROW	HEDDLE POSITION
1	Up
2	Turn stick A (neutral heddle)
3	Up
4	Turn stick A (neutral heddle)
5	Up
6	Down

Repeat steps 1–6 with pickup stick B.

WASHED FABRIC

UNWASHED FABRIC

SPOT-BRONSON SCARF

This Spot-Bronson Scarf pattern features a checkerboard of spots. Although I used a slightly heavier pima cotton set at 10 ends per inch, the scarf also looks lovely woven in 3/2 mercerized cotton with a sett of 12 ends per inch. It makes a lovely addition to a spring or summer wardrobe. Or weave this project 20" wide and create delicate placemats for your table.

WARPING

Wind a warp 2½ yards long of 86 ends. Thread the heddle as described on pages 59–62. Insert two pickup sticks as follows:

Pickup stick A: 8 up, *2 down, 3 up; repeat from * four more times; end 2 down, 8 up.

Pickup stick B: 6 up, *2 down, 3 up; repeat from * five more times; end 2 down, 5 up.

WEAVING

Weave a 1½" header in plain weave.

Work the Spot-Bronson Weave Pattern for 65" starting with stick B. When you are done weaving with stick B, remove it and weave with stick A. To weave stick B again, reinsert it into the warp in front of stick A.

Work another 1½" section in plain weave.

FINISHING

Cut the fabric from the loom and finish the ends with a braided or twisted fringe (see pages 91–93).

Wash the scarf in a washing machine on a normal setting and tumble-dry in the dryer. Remove while the scarf is still slightly damp to avoid wrinkles.

LOOM AND HEDDLE
Rigid-heddle loom with a weaving width of at least 9"
One 10-dent heddle

WIDTH IN HEDDLE
8⅗"

WARP AND WEFT YARN
Nashua Handknits Natural Focus Ecologie Cotton, 100% pima cotton, worsted weight (50 g/110 yd skeins): 400 yards of Chestnut (#80)

WEAVE STRUCTURE
Spot-Bronson

EPI
10 ends per inch

PPI
10 picks per inch

MEASUREMENTS

PROJECT STAGE	WIDTH	LENGTH
Off the loom	7½"	68"
After wet-finishing (not including fringe)	6¾"	60"
Shrinkage	10%	12%

Supplemental Weft Inlay

This weave uses two wefts, one to weave a plain-weave background cloth and a second supplemental weft that floats on the surface of the background cloth to create pattern. What makes the second weft supplemental is that it's not an integral part of the fabric. You could cut it out of the cloth and the background fabric would remain, holding everything together.

SUPPLEMENTAL WEFT INLAY WEAVE PATTERN

Pickup stick setup: 1 up, 1 down on a down shed

ROW	HEDDLE POSITION	YARN
1	Up	Ground weft
2	Turn stick (neutral heddle)	Pattern weft
3	Down	Ground weft
4	Turn stick (neutral heddle)	Pattern weft

With supplemental weft inlay, the pattern yarn needs to be thick enough to cover the background yarn, but not so thick that it distorts the ground cloth. If you have a really thick pattern weft and the background cloth is being stretched thin beneath the inlay, you can weave a couple of extra picks of plain weave (picks 1 and 3) so the ground cloth can catch up and fill in under the pattern weft. The goal is for the background cloth on the reverse side of the inlay areas to look like the plain-weave areas of the rest of the background cloth.

SUPPLEMENTAL WEFT INLAY VARIATIONS

Alter the pattern you use when you insert the pickup stick into the slot threads (a), for example:

1 up, 1 down

1 up, 3 down

Weave with a heavier supplemental weft and omit step 4 (b).

Do free-form inlay (c).

Weave with two pattern wefts of different colors, one on step 2 and the other on step 4 (d).

Doup Leno

Remember how time-consuming weaving leno was (page 146)? How you had to insert the twist by hand on each row? Wouldn't it be great if you could establish the twist pattern once and then reuse it row after row?

You can, by using doups, a type of string heddle. On a shaft loom, the string heddles are threaded on one shaft, and when that shaft is raised, the doups twist the warp threads. The same technique can be woven on a rigid heddle by using a rod instead of a shaft to control the doups.

In addition to the normal weaving tools, you'll need the following to weave doup leno:

» Pickup stick or weaving sword: A weaving sword is like a pickup stick, but one or more of the edges are beveled to make it better for use when packing in the weft.

» Tapestry fork

» Doups: loops of a thin, strong thread that are all the same size. You can make doups by tying nylong string into loops. Or, you can use pre-made Texsolv heddles that are designed for shaft looms for this, as they meet all these requirements and are already formed into loops that are all precisely the same size.

» A rod to thread the doups on and raise them to create a shed

Because leno has a tendency to draw in, if you are weaving a project (such as curtains) where it's important that the leno stays a consistent width, you may want to use a temple to counteract the draw-in. For information about temples and how to use them, see page 83.

How to Set Up the Loom for Doup Leno

① Using a pickup stick or weaving sword, pick up the leno pattern in front of the rigid heddle, just as you would if you were weaving traditional leno.

② Take a doup and fold it around one of the threads on top of the pickup stick.

③ Thread it onto the rod that you'll use to raise the doup shed.

④ Repeat steps 3 and 4 all the way across the warp until all the threads on the top of the pickup stick are threaded.

⑤ Tie a safety string from one end of the rod to the other to ensure the doups do not fall off the stick

⑥ Remove the pickup stick from the warp and raise the stick holding the doups. You should see the same shed open up. If it's not a huge shed, don't worry; you'll use a pickup stick during weaving to open it wider.

How to Weave Doup Leno

(1) With the heddle in neutral, raise the doup stick to open a shed. It'll be small, so slide a pickup stick into the shed and turn it on edge to widen the shed.

(2) Throw the shuttle.

(3) Beat the thread into place with the pickup stick or a tapestry beater (as shown below).

(4) Put the rigid heddle into the up position to open a shed. If the doups prevent the shed from opening wide, insert the pickup stick into the shed and turn it on edge to create a wider shed.

(5) Throw the shuttle and beat the weft into place with a tapestry beater.

(6) Put the rigid heddle into the down position. If you have trouble opening up a shed, use a tapestry beater to push the doups back toward the rigid heddle.

(7) Throw the shuttle and beat the weft into place.

DOUP LENO CURTAINS

Leno makes a light and airy curtain fabric for windows where you want to filter the incoming light and don't need to provide total coverage. The size of the curtain you weave depends on the window you're trying to cover and whether you'll mount the curtain inside or outside of the window frame.

WARPING

Wind a warp 55" long of 216 threads. (*Note:* Measure your window and adjust length accordingly.) Thread the heddle as described on pages 59–62.

WEAVING

1. Weave a 6" header in plain weave for the sleeve that holds the curtain rod.

2. Weave a row of 2×2 doup leno, as described on page 197. (It's desirable to use a temple to prevent the sides of the curtain from drawing in; see page 83.)

3. Weave 2 picks of plain weave.

4. Alternate steps 2 and 3 until the cloth is 32" long, or as long as desired.

5. Weave a 2" border of plain weave.

6. Hemstitch over groups of four warp threads, as described on page 95.

7. Cut the fabric from loom.

FINISHING

1. Trim the fringe to 1" past the hemstitching.

2. Secure the top edge by machine zigzag or serging. To create a casing for a curtain rod, make a double-fold hem (see page 100) by turning under ½" and then 2½" and machine stitch close to the second fold.

LOOM AND HEDDLE
Rigid-heddle loom with a weaving width of at least 18"
One 12-dent heddle

WIDTH IN HEDDLE
18"

WARP AND WEFT YARN
UKI 3/2 100% mercerized cotton (1,260 yards per pound): 550 yards of Willow Green (#57)

WEAVE STRUCTURE
Leno

EPI
12 ends per inch

PPI
10 picks per inch in plain weave; 4 picks per inch in leno

OTHER SUPPLIES
Texsolv 12⅜" (blue-tie) heddles to use as doups. (You can also tie your own doups, in loops 8 inches long, if you prefer.)
Rod to hold the string heddles
18" wide temple
Rotary cutter or scissors
Ruler
⅝" dowel or curtain rod for hanging the curtain
Hooks to hold up the dowel

MEASUREMENTS
18" × 37", hemmed and including fringe

HANDWOVEN CURTAINS

Cotton and linen are traditional curtain materials, as these fibers stand up to sunlight. When designing curtain fabric, keep in mind that most curtains are translucent, unlike drapes, which are opaque. Here are some ways to weave a fabric that lets light through:

- Weave a thin fabric with light-colored yarns.

- Create holes in the fabric using a weave structure like Brooks bouquet (page 151) or leno (page 146).

- Use a stiff fiber, such as linen, and sett it loosely. The stiffness of the fiber holds open the holes of the loose sett and lets light shine through.

- Weave a transparency (see page 173) as a window panel. Because transparencies have areas of dense sett (where the image inlay is) and open sett (the rest of the fabric), they don't drape evenly. Instead of making a gathered curtain, therefore, weave a panel, which accommodates the sett differential and displays the design to best effect.

▶ **CURTAIN SIZE.** The size of the curtain depends on the size of the window you're covering. When you measure the window, be sure to allow for shrinkage in the width and length of the fabric (sampling is your friend) as well as extra material for the hem and a casing or other top edge treatment to attach the curtain to the window.

▶ **ATTACHMENT TO ROD.** There are several treatments you can use to attach a curtain to a curtain rod: a sewn sleeve (casing) at the top of the curtain, tabs, grommets, and curtain hooks. A trip to the home decor section of a fabric store will give you ideas.

▶ **HEM.** If you don't want the bulk of a hem at the bottom of your curtain, you can finish the bottom with hemstitching (page 95) or a series of overhand knots. Because they are not washed often or subject to much handling, you can use delicate finishing techniques on curtains.

▶ **LIGHTFASTNESS.** Curtains are exposed to sunlight and subject to fading. This is one reason why light-colored fabrics are traditional. If you want to use a dark fabric, test the yarn for lightfastness first, or line the curtain.

DOUBLE YOUR HEDDLE, DOUBLE YOUR FUN!

AN ADVENTUROUS THING TO DO WITH YOUR RIGID-HEDDLE LOOM is to add an additional heddle. For a modest investment, you can open up new vistas in weaving, making it possible to weave cloth set more finely than 12 ends per inch and new weave structures, like the Theo Moorman technique. And, as we'll see on page 216, adding a third heddle gives you even greater possibilities.

A rigid-heddle loom is the equivalent of a two-shaft loom, with an important difference: one of the "shafts" is passive. The holes do all the work: raising "shaft 1" by going up when you raise the heddle and raising "shaft 2" when you lower the heddle, getting out of the way so the slot threads are on top.

A common misunderstanding about rigid-heddle looms is that each heddle adds the effect of two more shafts, meaning that two heddles are the equivalent of a four-shaft loom. This is wrong. When you add another heddle to the rigid-heddle loom, you get another set of active threads that can move independently, but the slot threads in the second heddle act exactly as the slot threads on the first heddle. They don't move. So adding additional heddles after the first is like adding one more shaft to your loom, not two. In other words, a rigid-heddle loom with two heddles is the equivalent of a three-shaft loom, a rigid-heddle loom with three heddles is the equivalent of a four-shaft loom, and a rigid-heddle loom with seven heddles (if you could manage it) would be the equivalent of an eight-shaft loom.

If you only have two heddles, you can create four-shaft patterns by using pickup sticks to create additional sheds. In most cases, however, I find it easier to use a third heddle instead of juggling both pickup sticks and heddles. This also has the advantage that a third heddle won't fall out of your warp if you pick up your loom to move it to another room. We'll see how to use three heddles on page 216, but first let's find out what we can do with two heddles.

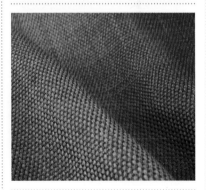

All of these fabrics feature fine threads, such as (top to bottom) Tencel, bamboo, and silk, which need to be woven at setts finer than 12 ends per inch. Using two heddles together (two 12-dent heddles create 24 epi) makes it possible to weave fine fabrics like these on a rigid-heddle loom.

Fine Cloth with Two Heddles

One of my favorite uses of a second heddle on a rigid-heddle loom is to weave fine cloth. Most people associate rigid-heddle loom cloth with thick cloth because the finest heddle you can buy is 16 ends per inch. If the plastic were milled any finer than this, the uprights would be too thin and likely to crack.

With two heddles, you can double the sett and weave 24 ends per inch (two 12-dent heddles), 20 ends per inch (two 10-dent heddles), and 16 ends per inch (two 8-dent heddles.) This adds a whole new range to the weight of cloth you can weave.

A 24 ends-per-inch fabric woven with 10/2 Tencel, for example, makes lovely garment fabric. Remember to adjust the thickness of your threads when you add a second heddle: trying to weave 3/2 cotton at 24 epi would create a super-dense fabric with sticky sheds that would be unpleasant to weave. (If you need a reminder about how to pick the proper sett, go to page 34.)

Weaving fine cloth with two heddles is easy. You simply raise and lower the two heddles together to make the shed. It's exactly the same as weaving plain weave with one heddle. To beat, you can either use just the front heddle, or bring both heddles forward together. On my looms, I rubber-band the two heddles together and treat them as one, which makes the weaving motion smooth and fast.

Threading Double Heddles

Threading two heddles to weave plain weave is a technique well worth learning. There are many ways to get the threads into position. Some folks thread one heddle at a time; others thread both together and shift threads around later. As long as the end result matches the diagram on page 204, it will weave correctly.

The main thing to keep in mind as you thread two heddles for plain weave is that any time you have three threads together in a slot, they need to get split up on the next heddle into left slot, hole, right slot in order to maintain the plain-weave structure. If you look at the diagram for step 6, on page 204, you'll see this occurring going forward for the threads together in a slot on the back heddle, and going backward for the threads together in a slot on the front heddle.

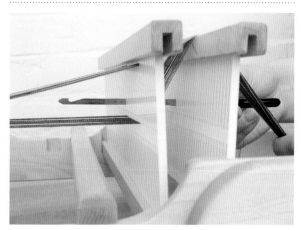

Threading the back heddle of a two-heddle project.

Using Two Heddles to Weave Fine Cloth

These directions assume that you're at the front of the loom, facing the back. Left-handed persons may choose to substitute left for right in these instructions to make them more lefty-friendly.

THREADING

① Set up the loom for direct-peg warping, with one heddle in place (see page 52).

② Pull two loops through each slot instead of one. You will have four threads in each slot. Wind the warp onto the back rod, and cut the loops.

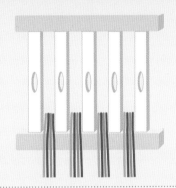

③ Move one of the threads (red) in each slot to the adjoining hole on the right.

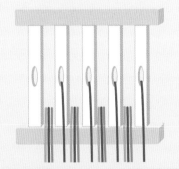
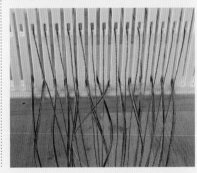

④ Put the second heddle on the loom. Line the heddles up so the slots of the front heddle are directly in front of the slots on the back heddle. I find sticking a threading hook through a slot in both heddles useful for this.

Continued on next page ▷

Using Two Heddles to Weave Fine Cloth , *continued*

⑤ Pull the hole thread (red) into the slot on the right.

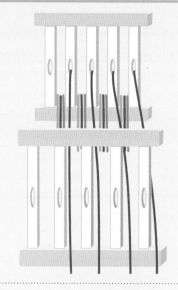

⑥ Break up the three threads together in a slot in the back heddle as follows:

(a) Pull one of the slot threads (blue) to the slot on the right. *Note:* This is the same slot the hole thread went into.

(b) Pull one of the slot threads (green) into the hole on the right.

(c) Pull the final slot thread (yellow) into the slot on the left.

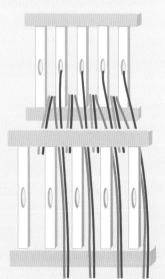

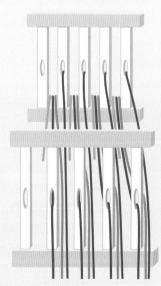

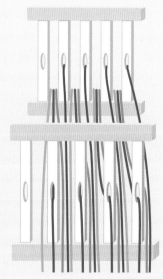

→ *Repeat steps 5 and 6 all the way across the warp. Note that now when you move the hole thread from the back heddle into a slot in the front (step 5) there will already be a thread in that slot from the last substep of step 6. You will end up with 3 threads in each slot of both heddles and 1 thread in every hole in both heddles.*

Check your work:

- Look down between the heddles and make sure you haven't inadvertently wrapped one thread around another. (See Crossed Threads, page 206.)

- Holding onto the front of the warp so it doesn't unthread, check that you have a clean up shed by raising both heddles (a), and check that you have a clean down shed by lowering both heddles (b).

- When you are satisfied that the heddle has been threaded correctly, tie onto the front rod as described on page 62.

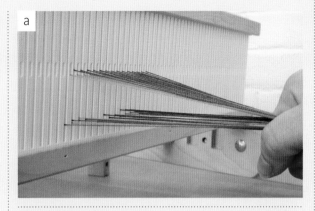

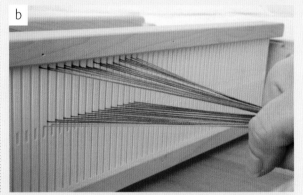

WEAVING

1. Raise both heddles to create the up shed. Throw the shuttle across. Beat.

2. Lower both heddles to create the down shed. Throw the shuttle across. Beat.

→ *Repeat steps 1 and 2 until the fabric is done.*

Crossed Threads

Crossed threads are something to watch out for. They can occur when you're threading the second heddle and inadvertently reach under or over one warp to grab another. Or, you can cross a thread by threading into the wrong slot or hole in the front heddle. This creates a twist between the two heddles that will impede weaving. Before you begin weaving any multiple-heddle project, test your threading by putting the heddles through all the various shed combinations that your project requires. While you do so, look between the heddles to spot any crossed threads.

Fixing a crossed thread is sometimes as easy as sliding the crossed thread out of the heddle, and threading it through the correct path. Sometimes, however, one crossed thread gives rise to another, and you end up rethreading half your warp threads, or perhaps the entire warp. In this scenario, it's a good idea to take a break, stretch a bit, and enjoy a cup of tea before going back and rethreading. In my experience, when you feel like kicking your loom, stepping away is good for both the loom and the weaver.

Crossed thread (blue) caused by twisting one thread around another during threading

HANDLING MULTIPLE HEDDLES

One of the tricky things about working with multiple heddles is keeping them stable on your loom while you're threading them. Some looms, like the Schacht Flip, come with multiple threading slots built in. The Flip can accommodate up to three heddles without any modifications. Other looms, such as the Ashford Knitter's Loom, have add-on kits that modify it for double-heddle use. If your loom does not have a double-heddle kit, or you prefer not to buy one, use a clamp, such as the Irwin Quick Grip clamp, to attach the second heddle to the loom or the table to hold it steady while threading.

COLOR GAMP

This color gamp is a traditional one, made with pure hues. Finding the right mix of pure hues can be a challenging but instructive time at a yarn store. Or, if you are a skilled dyer, you can generate your own palette of yarns. In this gamp, I used the yarns in the Tubular Spectrum series sold by Lunatic Fringe. (These yarns are sold in sets of assorted colors of different-weight yarns.) Whatever yarns you use, take careful notes of the colors and the order they were woven in so you can repeat the combinations you like best in later projects.

LOOM AND HEDDLE

Rigid-heddle loom with a weaving width of at least 15", *Note:* If you have a narrower loom, you can weave this in two panels: half of the colors on one warp, and the other half on another.
Two 12-dent heddles

WIDTH IN HEDDLE

15"

WARP AND WEFT YARNS

Lunatic Fringe 10/2 mercerized cotton (4,200 yards per pound; available on 1½ oz/ 400 yd cones): 50 yards each of 20 colors

WEAVE STRUCTURE

Plain weave

EPI

24 ends per inch

PPI

15 picks per inch

MEASUREMENTS

PROJECT STAGE	WIDTH	LENGTH
Off the loom	15"	15.4"
After wet-finishing (excluding fringe)	15"	14.7"
Shrinkage	0%	5%

green #10, green #5, green-yellow #10, green-yellow #5, Yellow #10, yellow #5, yellow-red #10, yellow-red #5, red #10, red #5, red-purple #10, red-purple #5, purple #10, purple #5, purple-blue #10, purple-blue #5, blue #10, blue #5, blue-green #10, blue-green #5

green #10, green #5, green-yellow #10, green-yellow #5, yellow #10, yellow #5, yellow-red #10, yellow-red #5, red #10, red #5, red-purple #10, red-purple #5, purple #10, purple #5, purple-blue #10, purple-blue #5, blue #10, blue #5, blue-green #10, blue-green #5

WARPING AND WEAVING

Wind a warp 1 yard long of 360 ends, 18 threads of each color. Follow the color order in the chart on this page, placing two loops in each slot on the rear heddle. Then, follow the warping instructions for weaving fine cloth on two heddles, beginning on page 203.

1. Spread the warp by weaving a header with 10/2 yarn.

2. Skip a section of warp to leave unwoven for fringe. Cut the weft and leave a tail at least three times as long as the width of the warp on the loom. (This will be used for hemstitching in step 4.)

3. Weave 14 picks of the first color.

4. Hemstitch across the bottom 3 picks of the fabric. (For information on hemstitching, see page 95.)

5. Continue weaving, switching colors every 11 picks, and keeping the same color order that you used to wind the warp.

6. Weave an additional 3 picks of the final color, and then hemstitch the top edge of the fabric as you did at the beginning.

FINISHING

Wash as you would any cotton fabric. Press. Use a rotary cutter or scissors to trim the fringe to ¾". (See photo, page 92.)

EXAMINING YOUR COLOR GAMP

There is no right or wrong in a color gamp, and as you'll find, it's a tool you can use over and over to help design the color interactions when planning projects. Here are some suggestions for how to make the most of it:

▶ **MOVE THE CLOTH**; do you see iridescence anywhere? This is that marvelous quality of some fabrics to shift colors when you look at them from different angles.

▶ **ISOLATE THE COLOR REGIONS** when you look at them, because you perceive color differently depending on what it's next to. A piece of mat board in black or photo gray with a hole cut in it (or two L shapes that you can combine to make a variable-size opening) is a useful tool.

▶ **WHICH SQUARES APPEAL TO YOU?** Which squares repulse you? Take a look at the relative positions of the warp and weft on the color wheel. Do you like low-contrast combinations of colors close together on the color wheel, or do you prefer the vibrancy of colors on opposite sides of the color wheel? There is no right or wrong here, just what you like and what you don't like.

▶ **LOOK FOR STRIPES OR PLAID PALETTES.** You might want to take a few moments here to find a set of colors on your gamp that works together for designing stripes (see page 117) and plaids (see page 129).

Note that nowhere in the previous section did I call a gamp a "sample." It's a tool for planning projects and improving the resulting textiles. Oh, wait — that's what a sample is! The way to think about samples is not as an onerous task imposed on you from the outside, but as an investigation you undertake to improve your understanding of the weaving craft in general, and this project or aspect in particular.

I write this as a woman who currently has a sweater on knitting needles with a gauge of 3¾ stitches to the inch instead of 4 because she didn't feel like swatching. I'm trying to decide whether to rip back or eat more chocolate. My willingness to sample in weaving (it's fast, and you can do it on the same warp) and my reluctance to knit a gauge swatch is why I'm a better weaver than knitter.

LOOM AND HEDDLE

Rigid heddle loom with a weaving width of at least 18"

Two 12-dent heddles

WIDTH IN HEDDLE

18"

WARP AND WEFT

Bockens Cottolin 22/2, 60% cotton/40% linen (3,200 yards per pound; available on 8 oz/ 1,680 yd cones): 1,000 yards each of wintergreen, wine, and peacock

WEAVE STRUCTURE

Plain weave

EPI

24 ends per inch, using two 12-dent heddles

PPI

12 ends per inch

MEASUREMENTS

PROJECT STAGE	WIDTH	LENGTH
Off the loom	17"	25½"
After wet-finishing	16½"	24¼"
Shrinkage	3%	5%

COTTOLIN KITCHEN TOWELS

Kitchen towels are useful and inexpensive items to weave, and they make great hostess gifts. Best of all, they wear out and get stained on a regular basis, giving you an excuse to weave more. This project creates four towels approximately 16" by 24" each. Cottolin is my favorite yarn for dish towels, as it has the absorbency of linen but is as easy to weave as cotton. Traditional Scandinavian weavers often use cottolin for warp and linen for weft.

WARPING

Wind a warp 4 yards long of 432 threads, following the color order in the chart below, placing two loops in each slot on the rear heddle. Then follow the threading instructions for weaving fine cloth on two heddles beginning on page 203.

WEAVING THE TOWELS

1. Weave a 2¾" wide border with wine.

2. Weave 2" bands of each of the colors in this order: wintergreen, peacock, wine. Repeat the color sequence two more times.

3. Weave 2" more with wintergreen, then 2¾" with peacock.

4. Lay in a single thread of the wintergreen. This indicates where one towel ends and another begins.

Repeat steps 1–4 for the second, third, and fourth towels.

COTTOLIN KITCHEN TOWELS COLOR ORDER CHART

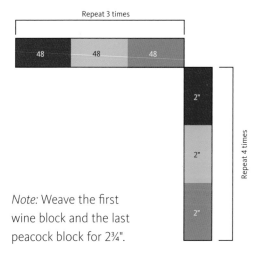

Note: Weave the first wine block and the last peacock block for 2¾".

FINISHING

Cut the cloth from the loom and zigzag-stitch or serge the raw ends of the fabric to secure it.

Wash and dry the fabric in a washing machine as you would any dish towels.

Cut the towels apart at the wintergreen separator threads and turn the ends in a double-fold hem that is ½" wide (page 100).

STANDARD HOUSEHOLD LINENS SIZES

There are myriad forms and uses for towels: fancy linen tea towels, hard-scrubbing dishcloths, and super-absorbent bath towels. Terry-cloth pile bath towels are a modern invention. The towels of yesteryear were thirsty linen yarns woven into plain weave. With a bit of piecing together at the selvedges, you could weave up a satisfying set of vintage towels for your bath. Although weaving a large towel or bath sheet would be quite the undertaking on a rigid-heddle loom, there are many smaller, yet satisfying projects you can weave, such as the Looped-Pile Washcloth on page 179 and Cottolin Kitchen Towels given here.

Dishcloth	**12" × 12"**
Kitchen towel	**16" × 25"**
Washcloth	**13" × 13"**
Fingertip towel	**11" × 18"**
Hand towel	**16" × 30"**
Bath towel	**27" × 52"**
Bath sheet	**35" × 60"**

Theo Moorman Technique

The Moorman inlay technique was developed by Theo Moorman, a twentieth-century British artist and weaver. It's a technique in which you weave a ground cloth, and at the same time have a thinner set of supplemental warps that tie down pattern yarns that float on top of the ground cloth. It's similar to the inlay technique on page 194. Because the pattern weft does not contribute to the stability of the cloth, you're free to move the pattern yarns across the face of the cloth in creative ways. It's like painting with yarn. Theo Moorman technique is most efficient for weaving designs with a plain background and a few focal elements that dance across the cloth. Here are the basic elements of the technique:

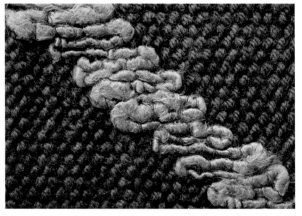

Pattern weft moving diagonally across the ground cloth in a fabric woven in Theo Moorman technique

» The tie-down thread should be one-quarter the size of the ground thread or thinner, and preferably in a darker color that will blend into the background cloth and disappear visually.

» The front heddle controls the ground cloth, alternating the ground cloth threads between holes and slots.

» In the back heddle, the ground-cloth threads pass through slots and don't go through any of the holes.

» The tie-down thread is threaded at half the sett of the ground cloth and is controlled by the back heddle. This means the tie-down thread is threaded through every other hole and slot in the back heddle and in each slot in the front heddles.

How to Thread for Theo Moorman Technique

For steps 1–3 below, line up the heddles and pull the threads through the corresponding slots on both the front and back heddles. The black threads are the tie-down threads; the blue threads are the ground cloth.

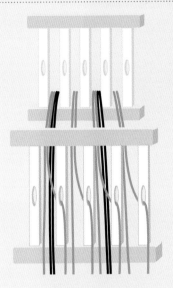

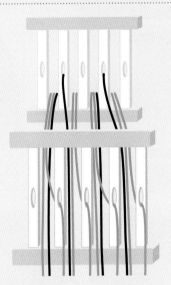

1 Starting from the left side of the heddle, thread as follows:

- A loop of both warps, tie-down and ground.

- A loop of only the ground warp.

Continue in this pattern until the whole width is threaded.

2 Move one ground-cloth thread from each slot into the hole to the right.

3 In the back heddle, where there are two tie-down threads in a slot, pull one out and thread it into the hole to the right. Bring the thread forward to the front heddle and thread it into the slot to the right of the corresponding hole in the front heddle.

CHECKUP

When you are done threading, check to ensure that you have the following:

- One ground thread in every hole in the front heddle.

- One ground thread and one tie-down thread in each slot in the front heddle.

- One tie-down thread in every other hole in the back heddle; the holes between tie-down threads on the back heddle are empty.

- No crossed threads between the heddles; you can make clean sheds.

- Two ground threads, alternating with two ground threads and a tie-down thread, in the slots in the back heddle.

THEO MOORMAN SCARF
Woven with Two Heddles

For this scarf, the ground cloth is woven by raising and lowering the two heddles together. You have two options for inserting the pattern weft: one after the down ground-cloth shed, and another after the up ground-cloth shed. You can add pattern weft on one of these sheds for a sparse inlay, or add pattern weft in both sheds for a dense inlay, or add pattern weft in neither shed to weave the background cloth without any inlay.

What's fun about this technique is that the tie-down threads provide the structure for the pattern weft, giving you the freedom to draw or scribble with the pattern yarn. It has tremendous design possibilities.

LOOM AND HEDDLE

Rigid-heddle loom with a weaving width of at least 9"

Two 10-dent heddles

WIDTH IN HEDDLE

8⅓"

GROUND WARP & WEFT YARN

Cascade 220, 100% Peruvian Highland wool, worsted weight (1,000 yards per pound; available in 3.5 oz/220 yd skeins): 360 yards of Navy (#8393)

TIE-DOWN WARP YARN

UKI 20/2 mercerized cotton, 100% cotton (8,400 yards per pound; available on mini-cones from some suppliers): 110 yards of Soldier Blue (#021)

PATTERN WEFT YARN

Farm Fresh Textiles 100% recycled banana and other fibers (454 yards per pound): 30 yards of Kelp. *Note: If you are unable to locate this yarn, you can substitute Himalaya Yarn Recycled Silk, 100% recycled silk: one 100g/80 yard hank.*

WEAVE STRUCTURE

Theo Moorman

EPI

10 ends per inch for the ground warp, 5 ends per inch for the tie-down warp

PPI

8 picks per inch

MEASUREMENTS

PROJECT STAGE	WIDTH	LENGTH
Off the loom	7¾"	72"
After wet-finishing	7¼"	66"
Shrinkage	6%	8%

WARPING

Wind a warp 2½ yards long with 82 ground threads and 42 tie-down threads. Thread the loom as described on page 213. Insert a pickup stick to weave the bottom half of the tie-down warp as follows: Put both heddles in the down position and use the stick to pick up only the tie-down slot threads. The pickup stick should be behind the heddles when you do this.

WEAVING

1. Spread the warp as usual (see page 69), then leave about 5" for fringe.
2. Moving both heddles together, weave 1" in plain weave with the ground-cloth weft.
3. Following the Theo Moorman weave pattern below, weave the pattern weft back and forth in short rows to create an undulating path across the fabric. Weave until the piece measures 72" from the beginning, and remove from loom.

THEO MOORMAN WEAVE PATTERN

ROW	HEDDLES	YARN
1	Lower both heddles	Ground weft
2	Raise the rear heddle	Pattern weft
3	Raise both heddles	Ground weft
4	Turn stick (heddles in neutral)	Pattern weft

Note: If you are using a pattern weft that is much thicker than the ground fabric, you may find that you need to weave a couple of extra picks of plain weave in the ground fabric. To do so, weave the pattern above, omitting the inlay rows (2 and 4) every other time through the pattern.

FINISHING

Twist a fringe to secure the ends (see page 92).

Handwash the scarf in warm water using a wool-safe soap or shampoo. Agitate slightly, but not so much that the fabric felts. Gently squeeze dry. Remove excess water by rolling the scarf in a towel and stepping on it with clean, bare feet. Hang to dry.

THREE-HEDDLE ADVENTURES

VERTICAL SKIP TWILL

CORD-WEAVE TWILL

IF YOU'VE EVER LOOKED AT A BOOK OF FOUR-SHAFT PATTERNS and sighed because you'd never be able to weave them on your rigid-heddle loom, I have good news. Using three heddles on your rigid-heddle loom gives it the same patterning capabilities as a four-shaft loom. Yes, you can weave overshot, twills, block laces, and more.

The most versatile of four-shaft threadings is straight draw. In straight draw, the threads are connected to shafts 1, 2, 3, and 4 in a repeating sequence: 1-2-3-4-1-2-3-4-1-2-3-4, and so on. With this structure you can weave many types of cloth, including diagonal twill patterns, block weaves, and doubleweave.

The only rigid-heddle loom currently on the market that has three threading slots built in is the Schacht Flip, but you can modify other looms to support three heddles by using clamps or screwing additional heddle supports to the inside of your loom.

As you experiment with using three heddles, here are a few thoughts to keep in mind:

» **ROOM FOR THE HEDDLES.** Depending on the mechanics of your loom, you may find that you need to work closer to the front beam to have room for all three heddles.

» **"TOP" AND "BOTTOM" SHEDS.** In the following descriptions, "weave through the top shed" means to weave through the shed formed above the neutral (all-slot) threads. The instruction "weave through the bottom shed" means to weave in the shed created below the neutral threads, which has the effect of implicitly raising those threads.

» **WEAVING DIFFERENT WEAVE STRUCTURES.** Once you have the loom threaded, you can weave a variety of weave structures on the 1-2-3-4, straight-draw, threading. For ideas, consult a book on four-shaft drafts, such as Marguerite Davison's *A Handweaver's Pattern Book*.

A NOTE ON SETT FOR THREE HEDDLES

In the following sections, we'll be using the additional heddles to affect the pattern of the cloth, not its density. We'll be skipping some slots and holes in order to keep the overall density of the cloth to that for a single heddle. Please choose yarns and sett based on the epi of a single heddle.

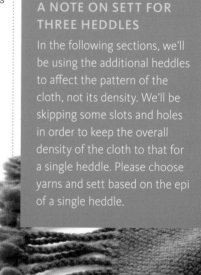

THREE-HEDDLE STRAIGHT-DRAW (1-2-3-4) SAMPLER

This project is purely research, like the color gamp on page 207. Weaving 4-shaft twill patterns on a rigid-heddle loom is exciting, and at the end, you'll have a reference you can refer to when planning projects.

For this sampler, I used three 12-dent heddles. The extra heddles provide pattern control, instead of increasing the sett as in fine-cloth weaving. Normally, I would set a worsted-weight yarn at 8 ends per inch, instead of 12. Because twills have floats, you need to set them at least 20 percent closer than you would for plain weave to create a stable cloth.

In addition to those shown here, you can weave other types of twills, such as point twills and advancing twills, on a rigid-heddle loom. To do so, change your threading to match the 4-shaft threading. For example, for point twills, the threading would be 1-2-3-4-3-2. For more information about how to do this, see the explanation of how to translate 4-shaft drafts to the rigid-heddle loom on page 220.

LOOM AND HEDDLE
Rigid-heddle loom with a weaving width of at least 11" and with room for three heddles
Three 12-dent heddles

WIDTH IN HEDDLE
11"

WARP YARN
Harrisville Designs Highland, 100% wool (900 yards per pound; available on 8 oz/450 yard cones): 270 yards Cobalt

WEFT YARN
Harrisville Designs Highland, 100% wool (900 yards per pound; available on 8 oz/450 yard cones): 200 yards Raspberry

(Optional) A yarn of about the same weight as the warp and weft yarns, in a contrasting color, to insert when you change weave structures. In this sample, I used about 2½ yards of a yellow wool yarn.

WEAVE STRUCTURE
Straight draw (1-2-3-4) threading with various twill weaving patterns

EPI	PPI
12 ends per inch	10 picks per inch

① Place the rearmost heddle on the loom. This will be heddle 3 when you weave. Using the direct-peg method (starting on page 51), wind a 2-yard warp of 132 ends, with 1 loop in each slot. Wind onto the back rod, using a warp separator. Cut the loops.

② Starting from the left side of the loom (as you stand in front of it), thread the heddle as follows:

- Pick up one of the threads in the leftmost slot, and put it into the hole to the left of the slot.

- Skip the next slot and hole.

Continue across heddle 3 following this same sequence. When you are done, you will have threaded every other hole on the heddle; half the slots will have one thread and the other half will have two threads.

Note: Each set of four threads comprises one threading repeat (left to right): hole, slot with one thread, slot with two threads. Repeat this sequence with every group of four threads across the heddle.

③ Place the middle heddle on the loom. This will be heddle 2 when you weave. Line up heddle 2 with heddle 3 so that the holes and slots match. Pull forward the first four threads on the left and thread them from the back heddle to the middle heddle as follows (from left to right):

- The hole thread goes into the slot on the right.

- The slot thread goes into the hole on the right.

- The two slot threads in the same slot continue forward into the same slot in front of them.

Repeat this sequence with every group of four threads across the heddle. *Note:* Each set of four threads comprises one threading repeat (left to right): slot with one thread, hole, slot with two threads.

④ Place the frontmost heddle on the loom. This will be heddle 1 when you weave. Line up heddle 1 with heddle 2 so the holes and slots match. Pull forward the first four threads on the left and thread them from the middle heddle to the front heddle as follows (from left to right):

- The slot thread goes forward into the slot in front of it.

- The hole thread goes into the same slot.

- One of the slot threads goes into the hole to the left. (This is the hole in front of the hole threaded on the middle heddle.)

- The remaining slot thread goes forward into the slot in front of it.

Note: The completely neutral threads (those that go through only slots) represent shaft 4 when you compare the rigid-heddle weaving draft to the 4-shaft weaving draft. Because you can't raise the neutral threads, you'll lower other heddles when you need "shaft-4" threads to be on top of the others.

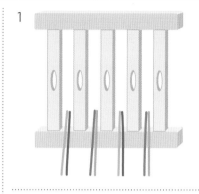

1

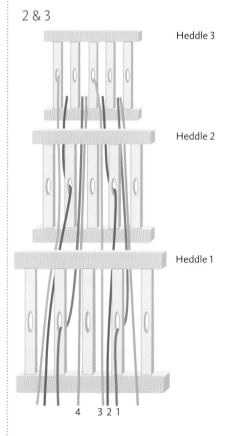

2 & 3

Heddle 3

Heddle 2

Heddle 1

4   3 2 1

Check your threading:

- Go across the warp and pull each group of four threads taut. For each group, a different thread should be going through a hole on each heddle, and one thread should go through only slots.

- On each heddle, only every other hole is threaded.

- When you look between the heddles, no threads should be crossed or twisted around each other.

- The threads should flow through the heddles in a relatively straight manner.

- Each heddle raises and lowers into clean sheds. Hold onto the warp as you check this to keep it from coming unthreaded.

WEAVING

Because the threads are set tightly in this sampler, you may find some sheds hard to put a shuttle through without catching threads in the top or bottom of the shed. If this happens, simply put a weaving sword pickup stick into the shed you've created with the heddles and turn the stick on its side to widen the shed.

WEAVING PLAIN WEAVE

The mother of all weave structures, plain weave has the most interlacements.

PLAIN WEAVE PATTERN

ROW	HEDDLES
1	Raise 1 and 3
2	Lower 1 and 3

WEAVING WEFT-FACED TWILL

In this twill, the front of the fabric shows more weft than warp. (*Note*: The back of this fabric is warp-faced and will be identical to the front of the fabric in the warp-faced twill.)

WEFT-FACED TWILL PATTERN

ROW	HEDDLES
1	Lower 1, 2, and 3
2	Raise 3
3	Raise 2
4	Raise 1

WEAVING VERTICAL SKIP

This twill creates a pleasing pebbled effect. (For photo, see page 216.)

VERTICLE SKIP PATTERN

ROW	HEDDLES
1	Lower 1 and 2
2	Raise 1 and 2
3	Raise 2 and 3
4	Lower 2 and 3

WEAVING 2×2 TWILL

In this twill, you create a diagonal line. When the epi and ppi are the same, the line is at a 45-degree angle.

2 × 2 TWILL WEAVING PATTERN

ROW	HEDDLES
1	Raise 1 and 2
2	Raise 2 and 3
3	Lower 1 and 2
4	Lower 2 and 3

WEAVING ZIGZAG TWILL

For zigzag twill, you change the direction of the diagonal, creating a zig-zag effect.

ZIGZAG TWILL WEAVING PATTERN

ROW	HEDDLES
1	Raise 1 and 2
2	Lower 2 and 3
3	Lower 1 and 2
4	Raise 2 and 3
5	Lower 1 and 2
6	Lower 2 and 3

WEAVING CORD WEAVE

This twill creates strong vertical lines in the fabric. (For photo, see page 216.)

CORD-WEAVE TWILL PATTERN

ROW	HEDDLES
1	Raise 2 and 3
2	Lower 1 and 3
3	Raise 2 and 3
4	Raise 1 and 3

CONVERTING FOUR-SHAFT WEAVE DRAFTS FOR USE WITH A RIGID-HEDDLE LOOM

OVER CENTURIES, WEAVERS HAVE DEVELOPED GRAPHIC SYSTEMS called "weave drafts" to indicate how to thread and weave different fabric structures. Once you understand what they mean and how they work, you'll be able to convert a weave draft written for a 4-shaft loom into a threading and lift plan for a rigid-heddle loom

There are three basic components to a weave draft: (1) the threading, which tells you which shaft a given warp thread is attached to; (2) the tie-up, which tells you which shafts will raise when you step on a given treadle; and (3) the treadling, which tells you the order in which to step on the treadles.

The following explanation assumes that you are dealing with the modern form of a weave draft used in the United States, with a shed created by rising shafts, and with the threading, tie up, and treadling in the positions shown on the facing page. Be aware that other countries and other eras formatted weave drafts differently. If you come across a weave draft that looks odd, take a moment to figure out where the various parts are and how they're encoded before converting it.

Converting Floor Loom Threading to Rigid-Heddle Threading

On a floor loom, each shaft contains a set of heddles, which are wires or strings with loops in the middle that the warp yarns are threaded through. It's as if each shaft is a rigid heddle with only holes and no slots. Following a four-shaft weave draft to thread a rigid-heddle loom with three heddles is fairly simple if you follow a few rules:

» Shafts 1–3 correspond to the holes on heddles 1–3, respectively. Shaft 4 corresponds to threads that go through slots on all heddles.

» Threads that do not go through a hole on a given heddle go through a slot.

» Plan your threading so that threads flow through the heddles as straight as possible.

» Try not to have more than two threads in any given slot. This guideline is the least important, so if you have to cheat, cheat here first.

Converting Floor Loom Tie Up to a Peg Plan

Some weavers find it easier to understand the conversion from a 4-shaft weave draft to a rigid-heddle plan by taking an intermediary step and examining what is known as a "peg plan." (Weave drafts created for table looms and computer-driven looms use peg plans.) Study the three charts on the facing page to see how each system works. To the right of the threading in illustration A, a chart indicates the tie-up, or how the threading maps to the treadles of a floor loom. On a floor loom, you physically tie one or more shafts to a treadle; when you press that treadle with your foot, one or more shafts move to form the shed. Since your rigid-heddle loom doesn't have treadles, you must convert a weave draft with a tie up into a weave draft in peg-plan format (B). A peg plan format has no tie-up, and thus tells you explicitly which shafts need to be raised to create each shed.

Here's how to convert a tie-up and treadling into a peg plan: For each row of the treadling, go straight up to the corresponding line in the tie-up above. This will tell you which shafts need to be raised on that row. On the peg plan, fill in the blocks for those shafts. (Most weaving software has the ability to convert a tie-up draft into a peg plan with a click of a button.)

Converting a Peg Plan into a Rigid-Heddle Weaving Plan

After you've converted the weave draft into a peg plan, you can then convert the peg plan into a rigid-heddle weaving plan (C). This is useful because of the way shaft 4 works on a rigid-heddle loom. Since the "4th" shaft is made up of the passive slot threads, in order to raise it, you instead lower any shafts that aren't raised in that weft pick. For example, let's compare the 4-shaft peg plan to the rigid-heddle weaving plan for a 2×2 twill.

PEG AND RIGID-HEDDLE PLANS COMPARED

PEG PLAN	RIGID-HEDDLE LLAN
Raise 1 and 2	Raise 1 and 2
Raise 2 and 3	Raise 2 and 3
Raise 3 and 4	Lower 1 and 2
Raise 4 and 1	Lower 2 and 3

As you can see, in the rigid-heddle plan, shaft 4 never moves, so you have to figure out how to move the other threads below shaft 4 in order to have shaft 4 on the top of the cloth. It's not harder to weave, just different, and worth figuring out and writing down before you get to the loom. The calculation is easy: Any time shaft 4 threads are raised, make the shed by lowering the heddles with hole threads that should be down for that shed.

A. Standard 4-shaft 2×2 twill draft

threading   tie-up

weaving

B. Threading translated to rigid heddle and tie-up converted to peg plan

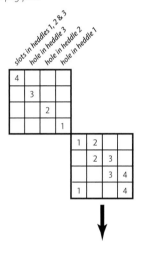

C. Threading translated to rigid heddle and peg plan translated to rigid heddle

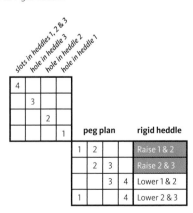

peg plan			rigid heddle
1	2		Raise 1 & 2
	2	3	Raise 2 & 3
		3	4	Lower 1 & 2
1			4	Lower 2 & 3

FOUR-SHAFT WEAVE DRAFT FOR POINT TWILL

The chart shown here is a common 4-shaft weaving pattern: Point Twill. Using the technique from the previous page, you can convert it into a rigid-heddle project. This first chart shows the tie-up version of the weave draft (A).

The next step is to convert the tie-up to a lift plan by mapping the shafts lifted in each treadle step (B). From the lift plan, you can create the rigid-heddle weaving plan (C). Remember to lift heddles on rows where shaft 4 does not rise and to lower heddles on rows where shaft 4 does rise.

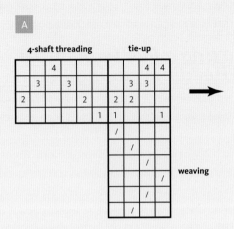

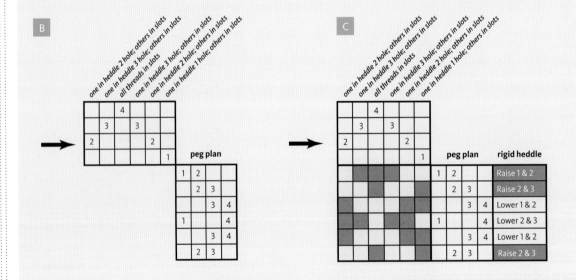

Overshot

Overshot is a two-shuttle weave that uses two wefts. A thick weft creates the pattern, while a thin weft weaves plain weave between the pattern picks. These plain-weave picks are called tabby. Having tabby between the pattern threads gives the pattern threads the freedom to have long floats without jeopardizing the cloth's stability. Overshot makes it possible to create circles and curves that are otherwise difficult to create in woven cloth. Often the warp and tabby weft are the same thin yarn, giving the thicker pattern weft room to spread out over the ground cloth.

Since weaving tabby with three heddles on a rigid-heddle loom means alternating raising heddles 1 and 3 and then lowering heddles 1 and 3, we'll call these tabby up and tabby down.

Detail of overshot fabric in the Nappy's Butterflies pattern, woven on a rigid-heddle loom

WEAVING OVERSHOT ON A RIGID-HEDDLE LOOM

HEDDLE POSITION	YARN
Tabby up	Thin weft
Pattern pick 1	Thick weft
Tabby down	Thin weft
Pattern pick 2	Thick weft

And so on, alternating the pattern picks of the design with tabby up and tabby down.

The pattern picks needed to create the pattern for an overshot design can be long. The pattern used for the Overshot Scarf on page 224 is very simple, and yet it has 32 different picks before it repeats.

One of the tricks of weaving overshot is to keep track of which tabby you're on at any given time. If you always start with the tabby up coming from the left side of the loom and the tabby down coming from the right side of the loom, the position of the shuttle will tell you which tabby pick you're on. It's important to properly alternate the tabby in order to form a solid ground cloth to hold your pattern shots in place.

THREADING HOOK

A threading hook, long enough to reach back through all three heddles, is helpful when you're working with this many heddles. The threading hooks made by AVL for their Production Dobby floor looms are very long and thin and ideal for this work.

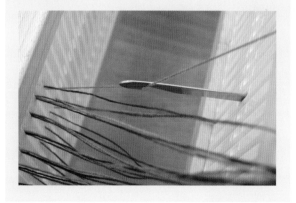

LOOM AND HEDDLE

Rigid-heddle loom with a weaving width of at least 7"
Three 12-dent heddles

WIDTH IN HEDDLE

7"

WARP AND TABBY WEFT

Valley Yarns Valley Cottons, 3/2 100% mercerized cotton (1,260 yards per pound): 400 yards of Willow Green #5604

PATTERN WEFT

Henry's Attic Gaia Worsted, 100% organic Merino wool (305 yards per 8 oz skein), hand-dyed in shades of orange, yellow, and brown: 220 yards (two strands wound together on the shuttle)

WEAVE STRUCTURE

Overshot

EPI

12 ends per inch

PPI

16 picks per inch: 8 of pattern weft, 8 tabby weft

MEASUREMENTS

PROJECT STAGE	WIDTH	LENGTH
Off the loom	6.5"	58"
After wet-finishing	6"	57"
Shrinkage	8%	2%

OVERSHOT SCARF

This scarf is based on the overshot pattern Nappy's Butterflies, from Marguerite Porter Davison's A Handweaver's Pattern Book. *In a wider fabric, this project could make a nice evening wrap or jacket fabric.*

Using a softly variegated pattern weft that contrasts with the ground warp gives color variation to this design. Although I hand-dyed my pattern weft, there are many hand-dyed yarns on the market you can substitute. For instance, you could try Madelinetosh Tosh Chunky (a 100% superwash Merino wool at 165 yards per 100g skein) or Brown Sheep Lamb's Pride Worsted (an 85% wool/ 15% mohair at 190 yards per 4 oz skein). Since these yarns do not need to be doubled, only 110 yards is required for either.

WARPING

Using a single heddle set in the back and the direct-peg method of warping (page 51), wind a warp 3 yards long and 81 threads wide. *Note:* This length gives you extra warp to practive weaving the pattern.

1. Pull a loop through each of 41 slots on the rearmost heddle. There will be two threads in each slot, except only one in the last slot.

2. Wind onto the back beam.

3. Put the other two heddles on the loom, lining them up so that all the corresponding slots are aligned on each heddle.

4. There are two pattern repeats across the warp; each pattern repeat is 42 threads wide. The chart on page 227 shows how to thread the pattern. Starting from the right-hand side of the chart (and the right-hand side of your loom), thread the first 8 threads: 1-2-3-4-3-4-3-2. The threading of these first eight threads is illustrated in the drawing at the right. For the rest of the threads, continue threading the rest of the pattern on page 227. *Note:* For pattern symmetry, do *not* thread the final 3 positions of the second repeat.

- For all shaft 1 threads, the thread stays in its slot in the back heddle, goes through the corresponding slot in the middle heddle, and moves to the hole just to the right on the front heddle.

- For all shaft 2 threads, the thread stays in its slot in the back heddle, goes through the hole just to the left on the middle heddle, and goes back into the corresponding slot in the front heddle.

- For all shaft 3 threads, the thread comes out of the slot in the back heddle, and into the hole just to the right, then goes through the corresponding slots in the middle and front heddles.

- For all shaft 4 threads, the thread stays in the slot in the back heddle and is threaded into the corresponding slots in the middle and front heddles.

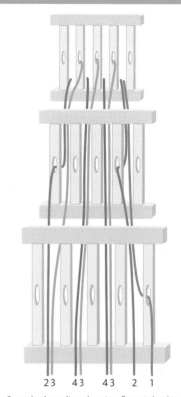

2 3   4 3   4 3   2   1

Sample threading showing first eight threads

As you thread the pattern, check that you are threading things correctly every four threads. Use the following guidelines as you thread the heddle. Look between the heddles: Are there any twisted threads? Does the order of the holes on the heddles match what's in the pattern? Holding onto the ends so they don't unthread, can you get clean sheds by raising the heddle? It may seem tedious to check the threading every four threads, but threading errors you catch right after you make them are easier to fix than those you catch 84 threads later.

⑤ The next four threads in the pattern are 3-4-3-2. Thread them according to the instructions above for each type of thread.

⑥ When you've threaded one complete repeat of the pattern (42 threads), you are halfway done. Go to the right on the weaving draft and thread the pattern right to left again (84 threads in all).

⑦ When you are threading, check your work again. Compare the order of the hole threads in the heddles to that of the threading diagram. I suggest checking this once right to left, and a second time left to right. Yes, you checked them as you were threading them, but it doesn't hurt to check a second time. With added power (a complex weave structure) comes added responsibility.

⑧ When you're satisfied that the pattern is correct, tie onto the front, and tension the warp as described on page 62.

PATTERN CARDS

I write out each shot pick on blank business cards, and then keep them in sequence by my loom so that I can flip them over in order as I weave. To keep the sequence in order, you can punch holes in the cards and run a notebook ring through the holes.

Weave a 1½" header of plain weave using only the tabby weft (the 3/2 cotton). To do this, alternate raising heddles 1 and 3 with lowering heddles 1 and 3. Weaving the header is an opportunity to get familiar with weaving using multiple heddles and with weaving the tabby picks of the cloth.

Begin the overshot section of the scarf using two shuttles: the thin, tabby weft alternates with the thicker pattern weft. In other words, insert alternating picks of tabby up (raise heddles 1 and 3) and tabby down (lower heddles 1 and 3) between the pattern picks shown in the chart on the facing page.

Once you reach the end of the pattern picks, start over from the beginning for a second repeat of the pattern. Remember to weave your tabby picks.

When you have woven nine repeats of the pattern, weave another 1½" of plain weave as header.

Cut the scarf from the loom, and twist 4" fringe (page 92) at both ends. Wash in warm water, agitating firmly, or wash in a washing machine on the delicate cycle. Hang to dry.

Rigid-Heddle Threading:

All threads in slots
One in heddle 3 hole; others in slots
One in heddle 2 hole; others in slots
One in heddle 1 hole; others in slots

Raise 2 and 3
TABBY: Raise 1 and 3
Raise 2 and 3
TABBY: Lower 1 and 3
Raise 2 and 3
Raise 1 and 2
Raise 1 and 2
Raise 2 and 3
Lower 1 and 2
Lower 2 and 3
Lower 1 and 2
Lower 2 and 3
Lower 1 and 2
Raise 2 and 3
Raise 1 and 2
Raise 1 and 2
Raise 1 and 2
Raise 2 and 3
Raise 2 and 3
Raise 2 and 3
Lower 1 and 2
Lower 1 and 2
Lower 1 and 2
Raise 2 and 3
Raise 1 and 2
Lower 1 and 2
Raise 2 and 3
Lower 1 and 2
Lower 2 and 3
Raise 2 and 3
Lower 1 and 2
Lower 2 and 3
Raise 2 and 3
Lower 1 and 2
Lower 1 and 2
Lower 1 and 2

CHAPTER 7

TEXTURAL EFFECTS & "WILD" YARNS

ONE OF THE WONDERFUL THINGS ABOUT YARNS is the different variations you can find: there are smooth yarns and fuzzy yarns, yarns that are a consistent width, yarn with slubs, and wild things like bouclés and eyelash yarns. In addition, you can weave things that aren't yarn at all: twigs, metal, even glass. Every once in a while it's fun to look around and wonder, "How the heck would I weave with that?"

By combining weave structure and the properties of your yarns, you can create textured and interesting fabrics, including shibori. What's fun about the projects in this chapter is that even though you may weave plain weave, the fabric is often transformed into something different and amazing when you wash it.

Elastic Yarns

Lycra and Spandex are brand names for elastane, the stretchy material that holds up commercial socks (look carefully for the thin elastic threads running along the main yarn in your cuffs), adds stretch to elastic, and serves a whole host of other uses in ready-to-wear garments. It's rare to find 100 percent Lycra or Spandex yarns, as they are usually blended with another fiber or produced as a yarn where an elastane core is surrounded by another fiber.

Weaving with elastic yarns can be tricky. You need to warp it under tension, stretching it out to its full extent so it can collapse dramatically when taken off the loom. As a rigid-heddle weaver, however, you have an advantage: the peg-method of warping is ideal for keeping stretchy yarns under control during warping.

LOOM AND HEDDLE
A rigid-heddle loom with a weaving width of at least 2"
One 12-dent heddle

WIDTH IN HEDDLE
1"

WARP YARN
Gütermann Unterfaden elastic bobbin thread (64% polyester/36% polyurethane): 2 spools of white

WEFT YARN
Karabella Yarns Silk Velvet, 100% silk, 25 g/112 m (122 yds); color 50040

WEAVE STRUCTURE
Plain weave

EPI
12 ends per inch

PPI
10 picks per inch, while the band is on the loom

MEASUREMENTS
1¼" × 22"

ELASTIC HAIRBAND

This project uses elastic yarn in the warp. Because the warp is only 1 inch wide on the loom, it's a great first project for working with elastic yarns. The secret to keeping them from tangling is to keep them always under tension. Elastic yarn with a cotton exterior is preferable to 100 percent pure elastic, which tends to snag in your hair.

Once you've woven one hairband, consider other possibilities. You could use this technique to weave a few elastic threads at the edge of a garment fabric, for example, to create gathered cap sleeves on a shirt.

WARPING

Measure a 1-yard warp of 12 ends using the direct-peg method of warping (page 51). It's crucial to keep the warp threads constantly under even tension. You don't need to pull them tight, just taut enough so they won't tangle. Thread the heddle as described on pages 59–62.

WEAVING AND FINISHING THE HAIRBAND

1. Tie your warp onto the front and tension the elastic threads. This step is a bit of an adventure. Work to get the tension on each thread as even as you can.

2. With the warp under tension (you want the elastic to be actually stretching and engaged), use plain weave to weave a weft-faced band 2" longer than the circumference of the head of the person you're making the headband for.

3. Take the band off the loom. Experiment to find the right balance of size and tightness for the intended recipient. You may need to unweave a few picks if the band is too long.

4. Tie the elastic threads from each end together in loose square knots. Try on the band. Once you're completely happy with the fit, tighten down the square knots. Because this is a weft-faced project, the knots should become hidden by the weft.

Do-It-Yourself Yarns

Making your own yarn is satisfying. To see a project progress from raw material, to yarn, to fabric, to garment is magical. In addition, creating your own yarns gives you more control and room for creativity in your weaving. The reasons for making your own yarns are many.

» **CREATE YARNS THAT AREN'T ON THE MARKET.** Perhaps you can't find exactly the yarn you're looking for. When you spin your own yarn, you can engineer yarns to create specific effects in your cloth. For example, I spin highly twisted singles of tussah silk and Merino for weaving. It's something I couldn't find when I went looking for energetic and crepe yarns.

» **REDUCE THE COST OF LUXURY YARNS.** Want to weave with cashmere, but don't want to spend $300 on yarn for a scarf? Thrift shops have a surprising number of cashmere sweaters at reasonable prices. Purchase a sweater, unravel it, and you have cashmere yarn at a fraction of the cost of purchasing new. Silk sweaters to unravel are less common, but you can find silk shirts and cut them into narrow strips to use as weft.

» **ADD MORE OF YOURSELF TO A PROJECT.** A scarf you weave is more yours than a scarf you buy. It has more of your artistry, your aesthetics, more of *you* in it. In the same way, when you create the yarn, it becomes as much your work as the finished fabric. I feel as if weaving projects in which I create the yarn have more "soul" than projects woven with commercial yarn. There's something appealing about the slight irregularities of handcrafted yarn.

*Handspun (blend of silk and Polwarth)
and hand-dyed silk fabric strips*

Fabric Strips

A great way to get started creating your own yarns is with fabric strips. You can recycle old clothing or start with fabric from a store. In either case, it's a quick path to creating weft yarn without the need for special skills or equipment.

PREPARING FABRIC STRIPS FOR WEAVING

If you purchased the fabric new from a store, wash it to remove any sizing and allow the fabric to shrink. If you weave with unwashed fabric strips and then wash the woven item, it may shrink and distort in unexpected ways. If the fabric is used, such as from recycled shirts or jeans, washing is optional.

If you are upcycling used clothes into weft, first remove any findings such as buttons, zippers, and so on. If you'll be making a garment out of your handwoven cloth, it can be fun to reuse the findings from the original clothes. Cut off collars and cuffs and button bands, as they are generally reinforced with interfacing thicker than the rest of the fabric. Remove any patch pockets. You want the fabric for the next step to be as consistent and flat as possible.

If you want a thin weft, cut narrow strips; for a thick weft, cut wider ones. To figure out the width you need, cut a few samples in different widths and then roll them between your fingers. The thickness you see when you roll the fabric is similar to the thickness of the fabric you'll get when you beat the weft into place, depending on whether you gently press it in or beat it more firmly. As with all things in weaving, however, the only way to tell for sure is to sample.

The best shuttles for cloth strips are ski shuttles, poppana shuttles, and stick shuttles. Fabric strips are generally too bulky to work well on bobbins.

WEAVING WITH FABRIC STRIPS

Weaving with fabrics strips is very similar to weaving with yarn; the one difference is how you join cut ends together. Using the techniques on the facing page, you can create long continuous strands of weft, but eventually (unless your project is very small), you will run out of weft and have to join in a new piece.

The easiest way to add new weft is to overlap the cut ends by about 1½ inch. After you wash the piece, the tail ends may work up to the surface of the fabric, where you can snip them off. A neat trick to try if you're weaving with bias tape is to fold the new piece into the ending bias strip. This catches the tail in place and keeps it from escaping.

WHAT IS POPPANA?

Poppana is long bias fabric strips that come prewound on cardboard spools. You can either rewind the fabric onto the shuttle of your choice or use a poppana shuttle, which is designed to accept the cardboard spools without rewinding. Poppana comes in many colors, and once it's woven and washed, it fluffs out into an almost sueded fabric, as the cut edges of the bias strips gently fray.

CUTTING CONTINUOUS FABRIC STRIPS FOR WEFT

Cutting fabric on the bias (at a 45-degree angle to the grain of the fabric) creates a yarn that stretches; cutting fabric on the grain creates a yarn that doesn't stretch.

▶ **CUTTING FABRIC ON THE GRAIN.** With right sides of the fabric facing, sew the fabric into a tube. Fold the tube so that the seam is in the center, and press the seam open. Turn the tube right-side out and place it on a cutting surface with the seam-side at the bottom (1). Cut "fingers" in the cloth running up from the bottom to the fold at the top, stopping at the same distance as the width you plan to cut your strips. (For example, if your strips are 1 inch wide, stop the cuts 1 inch from the top fold.) A rotary cutter and self-healing mat make this step fast and easy. When all the fingers are cut, cut on the diagonal from the end of one strip to the top of the adjacent strip (2 and 3).

▶ **CONTINUOUS BIAS STRIP.** Fold a rectangular piece of fabric so that the bottom edge aligns with the top edge. Cut on a 45-degree diagonal along the fold from the bottom to the top corner to remove a triangular piece (1). With right sides of the fabric facing, stitch this triangle to the other end of the fabric, with "b" sides aligning to create a trapezoid (2). Fold this piece so the diagonal edges (a) align. Offset the fabric seam by whatever width you would like your bias strip to be. With right sides of the fabric facing, sew the offset edges together. You can now cut a continuous strip, as shown by cutting lines in step 3. (Measure the width as you go so that your strip is even.)

You can use a bias strip as a single layer of fabric, in which case the edges will fray decoratively in the fabric. Or, for a smoother fabric, you can fold the bias back on itself to create a bias tape that encapsulates the raw edges (see page 99). Sewing stores sell tools that help fold and iron bias strips into bias tape.

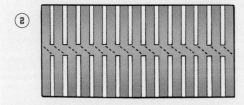

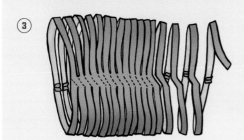

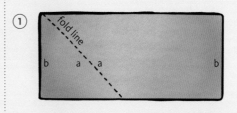

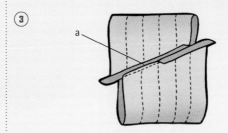

REWOVEN
FABRIC BAG

If you have a fabric that is printed with a bold design, you may want to retain that pattern when you prepare it for weaving, rather than cut it into continuous strips. For this bag, the fabric was cut into strips and woven back together so the design reappears in the finished fabric. Keep in mind that the weaving process foreshortens the image, usually in the vertical direction. The distortion of a compressed flower can still be beautiful, whereas a compressed face might be disturbing. Bold graphical elements without too many fine lines will look the best. Why go to all the trouble of cutting up a design only to reweave it? The practical reason is that the rewoven version is heavier and more suitable for jackets and bags than the original fabric. The aesthetic reason is that the rawness of how the woven fabric strips come together and reshape the refined pattern is intriguing.

LOOM AND HEDDLE

Rigid-heddle loom with a weaving width of 18" or greater

One 8-dent heddle

WIDTH IN HEDDLE

18"

WARP & TIE-DOWN WEFT YARNS

Maysville 8/4 cotton carpet warp, 100% cotton (1,600 yards per pound): 400 yards of Velvet (84), or a color that coordinates with your fabric

PATTERN WEFT

2 yards of 45" wide cotton quilting fabric patterned with bold graphics, cut into fabric strips

WEAVE STRUCTURE

Plain weave

EPI	PPI
8 ends per inch	6 picks per inch (3 of fabric, 3 of tie-down weft)

OTHER SUPPLIES

Rotary cutter or scissors, and ruler

Purse handles that coordinate with your fabric (available at fabric stores)

MEASUREMENTS

PROJECT STAGE	WIDTH	LENGTH
Fabric before washing	15¾"	26"
Fabric after washing	14½"	22"
Shrinkage	8%	8%

WARPING

Using the 8/4 cotton, wind a warp of 144 ends at least 2 yards long. Thread the heddle as described on pages 59–62.

PREPARING THE PATTERN WEFT

Wash and iron the fabric for the pattern weft. Cut the 1½ yards of fabric in half lengthwise, along the grain of the fabric, to create two strips that are 18" wide. Set one 18" strip aside to use later to sew a lining for the bag. Then, cut horizontally across the remaining 18" strip of fabric to create 1" wide fingers of cloth. Do not cut all the way to the edge; stop ½" from the selvedge. Leaving the strips attached in this way keeps them in order until you are ready to use each one. You will be laying each strip separately, so you do not need to wind them onto a shuttle.

WEAVING THE DESIGN

(1) Weave a 2½" header with the 8/4 cotton yarn.

(2) Cut the bottom strip off your fabric and lay it in place in the next open shed. Center the fabric strip across the warp. Fold the strip in half lengthwise by pinching together the fabric sticking out at each edge of the warp. The fold of the fabric should be toward you inside the shed. Folding the fabric makes your woven fabric reversible. *Note:* If you find folding the strip on the loom difficult, you can fold and press the strips before you start weaving.

(3) Do not beat the fabric strip into place. Change the shed and weave the next pick with the 8/4 cotton yarn. Make sure to interlock the 8/4 cotton weft with the fabric strip. In other words, if the last warp nearest the shuttle goes over the fabric strip, your weft should go under the fabric strip before re-entering the shed, and vice versa.

(4) Beat firmly. This packs both the 8/4 cotton weft and the fabric strip weft into place. You should see the fabric fold again, creating a double-folded weft that is one-quarter the width of the original strip.

Repeat steps 2–4 until the cut-strip portion of the fabric is 19" long. Weave another 2½" border with the 8/4 cotton yarn.

Note: Folding the fabric strip in steps 3 and 4 creates a reversible design, but it also has the effect of shortening the height of the image on the fabric. If you have more than one pattern repeat in your fabric, you can counteract this shortening by cutting four versions of the pattern into strips (sets A, B, C, and D) and weaving fabric strips alternately from each set. In other words, weave a bottom strip from set A, cotton warp, bottom strip from set B, cotton warp, next strip from set C, cotton warp, next strip from set D, and so on.

SEWING THE BAG

1. Cut the handwoven fabric from the loom and serge or zigzag-stitch along the raw edges of the header fabric to secure it, and then wash it.

2. Fold the plain-weave header to the inside of the bag and press it in place. With right sides together, stitch up the sides of the handwoven fabric. This is a great opportunity to hide any irregularities in your selvedges. Clip the corners and fold the seam open. To create a flat bottom, sew each corner across the opened seam. Turn the bag right side out.

3. In the project shown, I created fabric tabs to attach the handle to the bag. Using the template on page 275, cut eight pieces of the quilting fabric. With two right sides together, sew a ¼" seam as shown in the template. Repeat for the other three tabs. Clip the curves and turn each tab inside out. Insert the fabric tab through a loop in the bag handle and pin the tab to the bag close to the top edge and about 2" from the side edge. Align the top half carefully over the bottom half covering the raw edges. Stitch close to the folded tab edge all the way around, finishing with a horizontal line at the top to lock the raw edges and purse handle in place.

4. Measure the bag and cut a piece from the remaining quilting fabric to use as lining. Before cutting, make sure to add a ⅝" seam allowance to both sides. With right sides of the lining fabric together, stitch up the sides (a). Clip the corners and press the seam open. Sew each corner across the open seam (b). Fold down 1" of the lining fabric to the wrong side to make a hem.

5. Pin the lining inside the bag so the lining hem is just below the turn of the cloth at the top of the bag. Hand-stitch the lining in place.

4a

4b

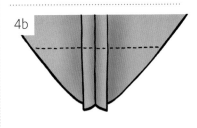

5

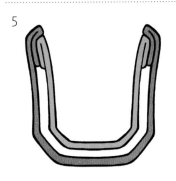

Handspun Yarn

Weaving with handspun yarn creates such a lovely fabric that each weaver should try it at least once in his or her life. The rich texture that handspun yarn brings to a fabric makes it worth learning to spin, or befriending someone who does.

Rigid-heddle looms are one of the best choices for weaving with handspun yarns, for several reasons:

» **PLASTIC HEDDLES ARE GENTLE.** A plastic heddle is gentler on handspun yarn than the metal or string heddles of a shaft loom.

» **TENSION IS LOWER.** Rigid-heddle looms weave at a lower tension than shaft looms, causing less stress on the handspun yarn.

» **THERE'S LESS LOOM WASTE.** Rigid-heddle looms produce less loom waste than a floor loom. On a typical small floor loom, for instance, my loom waste is about a yard. On my rigid-heddle loom, it can be as little as 6 inches. After you've taken the time to spin yarn (or to beg a spinner for their handspun), you don't want that precious yarn to end up as loom waste.

SUITABLE HANDSPUN WARP YARNS

Some weavers will tell you that you can't use handspun yarn as warp. Centuries of textile history prove that wrong; there would have been whole eras of unclothed people if handspun yarn wasn't up to the rigors of being used as warp yarns. What's true, however, is that not *all* handspun yarn makes a good warp. It needs to have a certain amount of structural strength to survive being put under tension and abraded against other warp threads and the heddle. Here are some characteristics that make a handspun yarn useful as warp.

» **SPUN WORSTED.** This is a spinning technique that keeps the fibers in alignment when you create the yarn. Worsted yarns are spun from combed top, in which all the fibers are processed to lie in the same direction. The spinner then pinches and pulls the fibers out of the top as she spins, maintaining the parallel nature of the fibers. This creates a smooth and strong yarn.

» **BALANCED.** A balanced yarn is one in which the spin energy of the singles has been neutralized. Usually this is done by plying (spinning two or more singles together in the direction opposite of the way they were spun), but it can also be done mechanically, by washing singles and drying them with a weight on the skein to add tension. The latter is a temporary measure: energy will return to the singles yarn as soon as you wash the woven fabric, which can result in interesting textures in the final fabric.

Each of the above fabrics was woven with handspun yarn in both warp and weft.

IN FAVOR OF SINGLES

If you're a spinner who hates to ply, weaving has the answer for you. Singles yarns make great weft, and can even be used as warp if spun firmly enough.

» **SMOOTH.** A fuzzy or lumpy yarn can be challenging to use as a warp yarn because it may have difficulty passing through the heddle, may stick to other warp threads, and may be shredded by beating the weft into place. Highly variable and textured art yarns would be challenging to use as warp.

» **STRONG.** Yarns with high twist are stronger than loosely twisted yarns because the fibers are more closely intertwined. It's the spinning equivalent of a fabric woven with a close sett versus one woven loosely. This strength helps these yarns stand up to the rigors of weaving.

Handspun yarn that meets all of these requirements makes an easy-to-use warp that will be a delight to weave. That said, because the rigid-heddle loom is gentle on warp yarns in terms of tension and opening the shed, you can often get away with using handspun warp yarns that meet only some of these requirements. If you use the direct-peg method of warping, you can even tame unbalanced yarns by keeping them under constant tension during the warping process. I've used warps of softly spun yarns, highly energized singles, fuzzy yarns, even beaded yarns. Experimenting is the best way to find out how far you can push the limits.

CHOOSING A HANDSPUN WEFT YARN

Any handspun yarn can be used as weft. The weft undergoes no tension on the loom, and little is asked of it during weaving. Softly spun yarns will get packed down and held together by the warp yarns. Highly twisted yarns can be tamed by shuttles. Fuzzy yarns won't rub against other weft threads during weaving. You can even weave with unspun roving and locks.

SPINDLE-SPUN YARN

Before we close the discussion on weaving with handspun, I have to mention spindle-spun yarn. You can create lovely yarn for weaving on either a spinning wheel or spindle (or just with your hands, if you're very, very patient), but spindle-spun yarn has an advantage in that each inch of it has already been tested for strength. When you spin with a drop spindle, you are forced to spin a yarn that is strong enough to withstand the weight of the spindle

Drop-spindle-spun singles are one of my favorite warp yarns. With the direct-peg method of warping to control the twist (see page 51), even highly energized singles can be dressed onto the loom. I weave the singles I spin into a light and airy fabric at 12 ends per inch. When it's washed it develops a lovely gauzy texture.

Drop-spindle-spun yarns, single or plied, work beautifully as both warp and weft in handwovens.

238

Crazy-Skinny Yarns

If you go to weaving stores or conferences, you'll often encounter yarn that looks as fine as spider silk. It'll be labeled something like 140/2 or 220/2 and be thinner than sewing thread. Most of the time, it'll be silk, since silk is one of the few fibers strong enough to work with that fine. If you're like me, a cone or two of the gorgeous stuff might follow you home. Since there's no such thing as a 120-dent rigid heddle, how can you weave with this on a rigid-heddle loom? Here are some ideas:

» Use the yarn as weft. By using a thin warp yarn (such as 10/2 Tencel) and a super skinny yarn as weft, you can create a marvelously thin fabric on your rigid-heddle loom.

» Run several strands of the thin yarn together as one. Where one thread might be too thin to use as warp, six might be thick enough to weave at 24 ends per inch.

» Use the skinny yarn as nearly invisible tie-down threads for the Theo Moorman technique.

A SKINNY YARN VARIATION

If you're a spinner, you can ply the skinny silk with a handspun single, creating an interesting bouclé. The resulting yarn makes a lovely weft yarn, or if the bouclé is tight enough that it won't be shredded by the holes in your heddle, you can use it for warp as well. You can test a bouclé for warp by threading it through one of the holes in the heddle and pulling it back and forth. If the yarn is damaged, use it as weft only; if it can stand up to this treatment, you can try using it as warp.

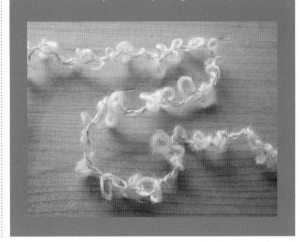

SPIDER-SILK SHAWL

The 120/2 silk yarn in this project is usually set at 72 ends per inch in plain weave, something impossible to do with a rigid-heddle loom. By combining multiple threads together as one working end, you can weave this fine silk on a rigid-heddle loom. Using multiple threads together also makes it easy to do graduated color blending, by swapping out individual fine threads one by one to slowly shift the color of each working end. (See photo on page 242 for my method of managing groups of these very fine threads.)

WARPING AND THREADING

Each color blend in the chart on the facing page is composed of 6 threads. Each bundle of 6 threads is used as one compound warp end. The chart shows the color progression of the compound warp ends. For each color blend, pull 12 loops, following the color-blend ratio, through three consecutive slots. You will have 294 compound warp ends.

Note: Use the direct-peg method of warping beginning on page 51 for this project; it protects the very fine threads from tangling.

① Place one heddle on your loom (this will be the back heddle). Using the peg method of warping, wind a warp 2½ yards long. The color blending is warped as follows:

Pull twelve loops (24 threads) of the first color (purple) through each of the first three slots.

LOOM AND HEDDLE

A rigid-heddle loom with a weaving width of at least 13"
Two 12-dent heddles

WIDTH IN HEDDLE

12¼"

WARP AND WEFT YARNS

RedFish DyeWorks 120/2, 100% silk (30,000 yards per pound): 600 yards each of Purple, Red, Red-Orange, Orange, and Yellow-Orange

WEAVE STRUCTURE

Plain weave

EPI

24 ends per inch

PPI

20 picks per inch

OTHER SUPPLIES

Boat shuttle
30 sewing machine bobbins
Size 6/0 seed beads in colors that complement the silk

MEASUREMENTS

PROJECT STAGE	WIDTH	LENGTH
Off the loom	10.2"	47.25"
After wet-finishing	9.25"	45"
Shrinkage	10%	5%

SPIDER-SILK SHAWL COLOR BLENDING ORDER

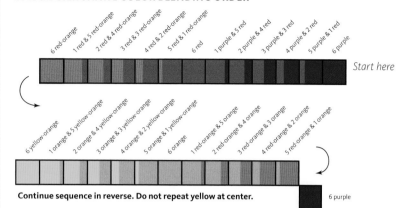

Start here

Continue sequence in reverse. Do not repeat yellow at center.

Next, pull twelve loops of the next color blend (10 purple, 2 red) through the next three slots.

Continue working across the color chart to the last color (12 loops of yellow-orange). At that point, turn around and go back across the color chart. Fill the next three slots with 12 loops of (10 yellow-orange, 2 orange), and so on.

You will have a warp 12.25" wide, with the lightest section in the center, blending to deep purple at each edge. *Do not cut the loop at the peg!*

(2) Wind the warp onto the back beam, using the peg loop to keep the warp under moderate tension as you wind. This is one warp you don't want to tangle. When you're done winding on, cut the peg loop.

(3) Thread the back heddle as follows: Pull 6 of the fine threads out of each slot and put them into the hole to the right. You don't need to obsess about the exact colors of these six threads (unless you want to). Slight variation in the color blending is part of the charm of this project.

(4) Place the second heddle on the loom. Thread the second heddle as described on pages 203–205 for plain weave using two heddles, treating 6 fine threads together as one warp end.

(5) After the heddles are threaded, tie the warp onto the front rod with even tension.

WEAVING ORDER

6 purple
5 purple & 1 red
4 purple & 2 red
3 purple & 3 red
2 purple & 4 red
1 purple & 5 red
6 red
5 red & 1 red-orange
4 red & 2 red-orange
3 red & 3 red-orange
2 red & 4 red-orange
1 red & 5 red-orange
6 red-orange
5 red-orange & 1 orange
4 red-orange & 2 orange
3 red-orange & 3 orange
2 red-orange & 4 orange
1 red-orange & 5 orange
6 orange
5 orange & 1 yellow-orange
4 orange & 2 yellow-orange
3 orange & 3 yellow-orange
2 orange & 4 yellow-orange
1 orange & 5 yellow-orange
6 yellow-orange

Spider-Silk Shawl

WEAVING

Note: I recommend using a boat shuttle with this project, due to the fineness of the yarn.

Preparing the weft: Using a sewing machine or a stand-alone bobbin winder, wind 6 sewing machine bobbins of each of the 5 colors of silk (30 bobbins total). Each weft pick contains 6 threads. To make it easy to do the same graduated color blend used in the warp, you will place six sewing bobbins on the shaft of a boat shuttle and change out the bobbins as you weave.

(6) Weave 1½" of each color blend, following the same color chart that you used for warping, and reversing after the Yellow-Orange section as you did before. As you weave, take care that all 6 threads turn the selvedge together. Make sure there are no loose loops of fine threads. Weave in the fine threads as you change out the sewing bobbins on the boat shuttle. Your scarf will transition from purple at one end to yellow-orange at the other.

FINISHING

(7) Cut the fabric from the loom, leaving enough unwoven warp at each end to twist a plied fringe of three working ends each. Before knotting the end of each fringe, thread a bead onto it.

Fuzzy Yarns

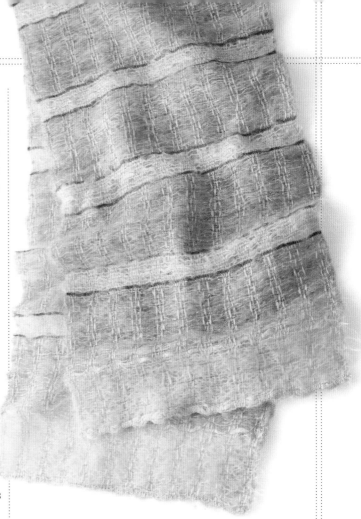

The knitting world has inspired yarn companies to create a wide variety of interesting, textured yarns, including sequined yarns, bouclé yarns, fuzzy halo yarns, and fringed eyelash yarns. These yarns are challenging to weave with, especially as warp.

» **THEY TEND TO BE WEAK.** A lot of their mass is in the decorative halo or fringe, so they're only as strong as the skinny binding cord holding them together.

» **THE VELCRO EFFECT.** The halo or fringe of a fuzzy yarn wants to tangle with its neighbors. When used as warp, creating the sheds can tangle the fluff of novelty yarns into an unweavable mess.

» **THEY'RE HARD TO SET PROPERLY.** A fuzzy yarn is visually big and fluffy, but a thin binder yarn is holding it together. If you choose a wide sett, based on appearances, the thin binder thread might shift, creating sleazy cloth. If you set for the binder thread, you can crush the fluffiness.

Given these challenges, how do you use fuzzy yarns in your rigid-heddle fabrics?

» **FUZZY YARNS AS WEFT.** When you use a fuzzy yarn as weft, you don't have to worry about abrasion or the Velcro effect. If you beat the weft in too densely, however, you may bury the fuzziness inside the fabric. In the scarf shown above, the silk warp threads are spaced by leaving empty holes and slots at consistent intervals across the warp. The stickiness of the mohair weft prevents the silk threads from "wandering.".

» **FUZZY YARNS AS SUPPLEMENTAL WARP.** Supplemental warps ride on top of a ground-cloth fabric, and the cloth's stability comes from the ground warp. If you space the supplemental warp threads far enough apart, you avoid the Velcro effect and show off your novelty yarn to its best effect.

» **OPEN-WEAVE STRUCTURES.** A fuzzy yarn is at its best when its fuzz has room to expand. Do this by setting the fabric for the fuzz, not the binder thread. This can work for sticky fuzzy yarns that will interlock to create stability. What works for a sticky mohair, however, won't work for a slippery rayon eyelash yarn.

Use slippery fuzzy yarn sparingly. For example, set a worsted-weight yarn at 8 epi and make every 16th thread a thin eyelash yarn. The densely set areas of worsted are accented with the skinny eyelash yarn, giving the fuzz room to bloom.

You can also use weave structures like leno to create openness in the fabric for your fuzzy yarns. Leno is stable even when open because of the extra twist in the warp yarns (see page 146). Warp or weft floats can also successfully show off fuzzy yarns.

DIAPHANOUS MOHAIR SHAWL

When you weave this project, leave a lot of room between weft picks. The fabric should look like little windowpanes of binder thread surrounding a window of fluff. The warp and weft fluff will interlock, especially after the project is washed, and create a gauzy but stable fabric.

LOOM AND HEDDLE

Rigid-heddle loom with a weaving width of at least 13"
One 8-dent heddle

WIDTH IN HEDDLE

13"

WARP YARN

Louet KidLin Lace, 49% linen/35% kid mohair/16% nylon (2,270 yards per pound; available in 50 g/250 yd skeins): 312 yards of Orange Berry

WEFT YARN

Warm Valley Orchard hand-dyed brushed kid mohair (2,000 yards per pound): 170 yards of Fuchsia. *Note:* I bought this yarn on a trip to Orcas Island, WA, but you can substitute Henry's Attic Kid Mohair III, 87% kid mohair/13% nylon (approximately 1,000 yards per 8-oz reeled skein) or any other kid mohair yarn of that approximate weight.

WEAVE STRUCTURE

Plain weave

EPI

8 ends per inch

PPI

6 picks per inch

MEASUREMENTS

PROJECT STAGE	WIDTH	LENGTH
Off the loom	12¾"	77½"
After wet-finishing	12"	70"
Shrinkage	6%	10%

WARPING

Wind a warp 3 yards long of 104 threads. Thread the heddle as described on pages 59–62.

WEAVING

Leaving 6" of warp unwoven for fringe, weave in plain weave until shawl measures 72". Remove the shawl from the loom. Make 4" twisted fringe, using 4 warp threads for each fringe.

FINISHING

Wash the shawl in warm water using a wool-safe soap or shampoo. Agitate slightly by hand for a few minutes, enough for the fuzz to mesh but not so much that the fabric felts. Rinse, gently squeeze to remove excess water, then remove more water by rolling the shawl in a towel and stepping on it with clean, bare feet. Hang to dry.

TIPS FOR SUCCESS:
Understand Your Materials

The first step to successfully weaving a mohair warp is to acknowledge that this is one project where little things can make the difference between happily weaving the impossible and . . . just plain impossible. Mohair is crimpy and has scales that act like little Velcro hooks, gluing it to the fuzz of its neighbors. Here are three key tips that should help:

▶ **RESPECT THE FUZZ.** Don't be fooled by the thin binder yarn; the halo of mohair really defines the yarn. Take a look at your yarn, roll it gently between your palms. When the fuzz is slightly compacted, what size is the yarn? The warp yarn in this project is 2,270 yards per pound, but I set it at 8 ends per inch. Any closer and I would have risked disaster.

▶ **TAKE CARE WHEN THREADING THE HOLES.** Usually I tell students that it doesn't matter which thread they pull out of the slot to put into the adjacent hole; any twists can be pushed to the back of the loom. In this project, however, it does matter. When you're threading the holes, look to the back of the loom and grab the thread that is on the same side of the hole so you don't inadvertently add any twists to the warp. This is one warp that won't let you push extra twist to the back of the loom.

▶ **USE FIRM TENSION.** Mohair will behave better as you weave if you keep it under firm tension.

Weaving with Wire

Wire is an interesting material to weave with. It doesn't have any stretch, and most wire can only be bent back and forth a given number of times before it breaks. That said, wire can be beautiful and add a structural element to your weaving. Its ductile nature makes it possible to mold the fabric once it's off the loom. You can even weave jewelry using precious-metal wire.

When I weave with wire, I set it much more loosely than I would a yarn of the same diameter. There are several reasons for this:

» Wire is rigid and maintains its shape, so some of the structure of metal fabric comes from the material itself.

» Wire is heavier than yarn, so setting it loosely reduces the weight of the finished piece.

» Wire is typically more expensive than yarn, and setting it loosely reduces the cost of the project.

» If you are also using wire as the weft, a loose sett makes it easier for the wire to bend over and under the warp threads.

LOOM AND HEDDLE
Rigid-heddle loom with a weaving width of at least 1"
10-dent heddle

WIDTH IN HEDDLE
1"

WARP YARN
Darice Craft Designer 26-gauge copper wire (369 yards per pound; available in 30-yard packs): 10 yards of Dark Green (#3950-70)

WEFT YARN
Darice Craft Designer 26-gauge brass wire (436 yards per pound; available in 30- yard packs): 10 yards of Gold (#3958-72)
Metallic ribbon

WEAVE STRUCTURE
Plain weave

EPI	PPI
10 ends per inch	10 picks per inch

OTHER SUPPLIES
Wire cutter
10"–12" long lengths of a strong yarn, such as 8/2 carpet warp, to lash the loop onto the front rod
Needle-nose pliers
Fire Mountain Gems five-strand slide clasp in gold-plated brass: 31 × 6mm (#H20-4216FY) for the wider bracelet and 21 × 6mm (#H20-4214 FY) for the narrower one

MEASUREMENTS
1" × 6"–10" long, depending on wrist circumference

WHY WEAVE WITH WIRE?
- Because it's beautiful, and it shines.
- Because, since it holds its shape, the finished fabric is easy to form into three-dimensional shapes, such as baskets and jewelry.
- Because it's strong.
- Because you have a roll of it in the garage and you're curious.

WIRE CUFF BRACELET

This is a quick weave and a fun way to get out of a weaving rut. After the bracelet is completed, you can leave it plain or mold it into a sculptural shape. The supplies listed here are enough to make three bracelets.

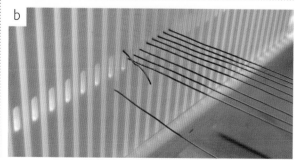

WARPING AND THREADING

Wind a warp 1 yard long and 10 wires wide. Warp the loom using the direct-peg method of warping beginning on page 51.

Wind onto the back beam using a warp separator.

Use a wire cutter to cut the loops at the front (a) and thread the holes as described on pages 59–62 (b).

Put the heddle in the up position. This step is necessary to produce the correct tension during weaving because wire does not stretch. A rigid-heddle loom makes an unbalanced shed; the hole threads rise and fall and thus travel farther than the slot threads. Most yarn can stretch to accommodate the small differences in length. Wire cannot.

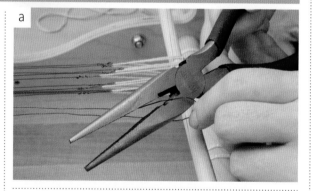

You cannot easily tie a knot in wire, so create a twisted loop in each strand, as shown below (a). Using a length of strong yarn, such as 8/2 carpet warp, lash each loop onto the front rod (b). (To make this step easier, it helps to loosen the tension a bit.)

Another way to do this, which I recommend, is to lash the loops continuously, with a single length of the strong yarn. Tie one end of it to the front rod, and then go up through a wire loop and back around the rod, up through a wire loop and back around the rod and so on across the warp. When you've lashed the last loop, tie the end of the yarn to the rod. A continous loop makes it easy to equalize the tension of the wires, as you can pull slack from one to the other until they are even.

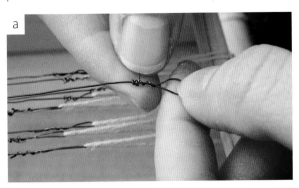

a

b

TO WEAVE THE ALL-METAL BRACELET. Loosely wind enough wire to weave the entire bracelet onto a stick shuttle, taking care not to crimp the wire. You can choose to pack the wire weft close together or space it widely, as shown on the previous page. Take care that the wire weft goes smoothly around the selvedge wires.

TO WEAVE THE WIRE AND RIBBON BRACELET. Wind the ribbon onto a stick shuttle and weave normally.

Weave until the bracelet is 6" to 10" long. You want the woven area to be 1" less than the desired circumference, to leave room for the clasp.

Cut the fabric from the loom with wire cutters, leaving at least 3" of loose wire at each end to attach the bracelet to the clasp. Using fine needle-nose pliers, twist two wires around each loop on the clasp. Wind the loose weft wires around the nearest loop, as shown.

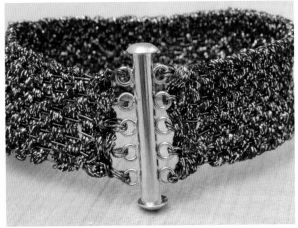

Going Further Outside the Yarn Box

It doesn't have to be yarn to weave with it. The first weaving was probably basketry — the weaving together of sticks to create shelter, traps, and containers. Similarly you can use your rigid-heddle loom to weave things other than traditional yarn. Take a moment to look around you, and as your eyes roam, ask yourself, "How would I weave that?" Even if you never plan on acting on them, having a few crazy project ideas is good for the brain. The simplest way to get started is to warp your loom with yarn and then weave in non-yarn wefts, such as branches, wheat, and dried flowers; clear acrylic rods; or the tape from old audio cassettes.

Conventional yarns like the rayon bouclé and silk on the tall cones can be combined with more surprising materials, such as (left to right) unfinished and dyed bamboo, natural sticks, printed cotton tape, leather thong, nylon cord, and assorted ribbons.

WARP SEPARATOR

Weave a beautiful and functional warp separator. This narrow warp separator is perfect for narrow projects. The 3-inch pieces of reed in this project come from a reed table runner that I cut down to exactly fit the back beam of my loom. With a rigid weft, some of the structure of the fabric comes from the fact that the weft can't flex and slip out of the warp. This is why we can space the warp threads out across the width of the fabric, saving yarn and letting the beauty of the reeds show through.

WARPING AND THREADING

Wind a warp 2½ yards long, with four loops (eight threads) of each color in a slot. Refer to the chart below for color order. Thread the heddle as described on pages 59-62 for one repeat of the colors and treating 4 threads of the 20/2 cotton together as one warp end. Leave 1" of the heddle unthreaded, then repeat the color order.

WARP SEPARATOR THREADING ORDER

8 Marine	8 Wine	8 Light Rust	8 Wine	8 Marine

WEAVING

Weave plain weave until warp separator measures about 74", centering the reeds between the two warp stripes.

FINISHING

Cut the woven mat from the loom. Tie the threads in each warp stripe together in a single square knot (two knots total). Add a drop of fabric glue to secure. When the glue has dried, trim the warp ends ½" from the knot.

LOOM AND HEDDLE

Rigid-heddle loom with a weaving width of at least 4"

10-dent heddle

WIDTH IN HEDDLE

3"

WARP

UKI 20/2 mercerized cotton (8,400 yards per pound, available on 5.5-ounce mini-cones): 80 yards each of Medium Blue (#033) and Wine (#017), and 40 yards of Light Rust (#108)

WEFT

3½" long pieces of 2 mm diameter reed cut off from the end of an IKEA table runner, (5 ounces). You could also substitute thin dowels from a hardware or hobby store.

WEAVE STRUCTURE

Plain weave

EPI

10 working ends per inch

PPI

8 picks per inch

OTHER SUPPLIES

Fray Check fabric glue

MEASUREMENTS

3" × 74"

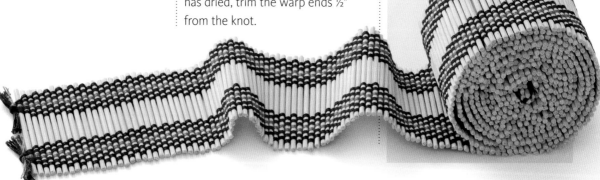

Creating E-Textiles

E-textiles are the love child of the fiber arts and electronics. In this emerging field of art and science, electronic circuitry is combined with traditional textile techniques such as weaving and sewing to produce fabrics that can glow, make noise, interact with their environment, and more. Over the past decade, developments such as conductive thread and microcontrollers (small computers) designed to be sewn onto fabric have made it possible for a growing number of artists to incorporate electronics into clothing and other textiles. E-textiles cover a wide range of projects: some are as simple as adding glowing lights to a garment; others are more interactive, such as a pillow that e-mails you a webcam picture when your cat lies down on it. You don't need a background in electronics to weave e-textiles; all you need is a basic understanding of how they work and a willingness to experiment. As with many of the techniques described in this book, handwoven e-textiles deserve a whole book of their own. I include only a small project here to give you a taste of how simple this area can be, in the hope that you will be tantalized to explore e-textiles further on your own.

LED BOOKMARK

How about a bookmark you can use to read in the dark? This project uses LED sequins and conductive thread to create a bookmark that lights up. You could use this same technique to weave a glowing bracelet to make you more visible on evening walks.

LOOM AND HEDDLE

Rigid-heddle loom with a weaving width of at least 2"

12-dent heddle

WIDTH IN HEDDLE

1½"

WARP YARN

Halcyon Yarns 3/2 100% pearl cotton (180-yard minicone): 18 yards of Magenta

WEFT YARN

Blue Moon Fiber Arts, Socks that Rock, 100% superwash Merino wool, lightweight (1,280 yards per pound): 5 yards of Cranberry Bogged

WEAVE STRUCTURE

Plain weave

EPI	PPI
12 ends per inch	10 picks per inch

E-TEXTILE SUPPLIES

One 3V coin battery (CR 2032)

Five white LED sequins (2V forward voltage, 20 milliamperes: mA)

Two yards Aniomagic conductive thread (8 ohms per foot)

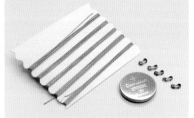

OTHER SUPPLIES

Tapestry needle

Sewing needle and thread to match wool weft

MEASUREMENTS

8½"–10" long × 1¼" wide

WARPING

Wind a warp 1 yard long and 18 ends wide out of the cotton yarn. Thread the loom as described on pages 59–62.

WEAVING

1. With the wool weft, leave an 8" tail at the beginning, and weave for 2". Hemstitch, using 2 threads per bundle, as explained on page 95.

2. Cut two 1-yard lengths of the conductive thread. Use a lark's head knot to attach one length to each side of an LED sequin. Both legs of the knot should be the same length. Tighten down the lark's head knot and tie a square knot over it to create a secure electrical connection.

3. Place the LED sequin, glass side up, into the shed. One hole of the LED sequin is brass (positive terminal), the other is silver (negative terminal). Put the brass side on the right. *Important:* Make sure each LED sequin is placed with the brass side on the right, or else your bookmark won't light up.

4. Weave 1" with the wool weft, running the conductive thread up along each selvedge; the conductive thread should follow the path of the first and last warp threads.

5. Place the next LED sequin into an open shed, with the brass side to the right. Bring the conductive thread in from the right, and tie it to the sequin with a square knot. Thread the conductive thread onto a needle, and pass it through the hole a few more times to create a tight electrical connection. Do the same on the left side.

→ *Repeat steps 4 and 5 to place the other three LEDs.*

6. Weave 3" with the wool weft, running the conductive thread along the selvedges.

7. Let the conductive thread fall to the sides, and weave 1" with only the wool weft.

8. Cut the fabric from the loom, and zigzag stitch or serge the raw edge to prevent it from unraveling.

(9) Fold the cut end under (away from the LEDs) for ½" and press. Sew a ¼" seam to tack the raw edge down.

(10) Fold under again for 1¼" and press. The place where the conductive thread stopped along the selvedge should be halfway up the pocket created by this second fold.

(11) Thread the conductive thread on the left side (silver side) onto a needle. Sew straight across to the center of the fabric behind the pocket, on the LED side of the fabric.

(12) With the conductive thread, sew a dense spiral in the center of the fabric. The spiral should be no more than ¼" across. This is the battery contact for your circuit, so the more stitching lines of thread in your spiral, the better. Work the tail end of the conductive thread back into the spiral.

(13) Flip the bookmark over and repeat steps 11 and 12 for the other (brass) conductive thread, this time working the spiral into the other side of the pocket. As you sew, make sure that the two spirals will overlap exactly when the sides of the pocket are sewn up.

(14) Sew up the sides of the pocket with a ⅛" seam. The battery should fit tightly in the pocket. This ensures good electrical contact with the spirals of conductive thread. If the pocket is not tight enough, sew a slightly wider seam.

(15) With the back side of the bookmark facing up, slide the battery into the pocket with the positive (+) side up. The LEDs on the other side of the fabric should light up. If they don't, check that:

- The pocket is tight enough for the spirals to make solid contact.

- The LEDs all have their brass holes on the right side.

- There are no loops or ends of conductive thread touching the other side of the circuit.

10

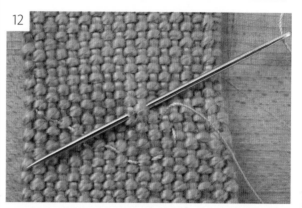

12

LED SEQUINS

These are tiny light-emitting diodes (LEDs) modified for sewing onto cloth. The ones shown here are surface-mount LEDs with crimp beads soldered onto the contacts. You can make your own LED sequins or purchase them online.

- The LEDs are tight and make solid contact with the conductive thread.

- The battery is positive side up.

- The battery is new and has charge.

To use the bookmark, slide the battery into the pocket, positive side up to light. To turn off, remove the battery, and store it separately.

Woven Shibori

Shibori is a traditional Japanese technique in which fabric is stitched, bound, or clamped before dyeing. When the mechanical resist is removed, the fabric opens up to reveal wonderfully organic patterns of dyed and un-dyed areas. Woven shibori is a variation where you weave in a supplemental weft while creating the fabric, which you then pull to create the resist. It's faster than hand-stitching threads in. Two pioneers in this area are Catherine Ellis and Kay Faulkner.

My explorations with woven shibori on a rigid-heddle loom began when a workshop student, Elizabeth Lee, brought me Catherine Ellis's book, *Woven Shibori,* and asked whether the technique could be modified to work on a rigid-heddle loom. After looking at the four-shaft drafts, and thinking about Betty Davenport's clever method of storing a pattern in a pickup stick behind the heddle (saving you from having to pick up a pattern with each row; see page 184), I realized that you could, indeed, create woven shibori efficiently on a rigid-heddle loom.

Yarns for Woven Shibori

WEFT FOR GROUND CLOTH. To create woven shibori, you use two wefts: one to weave the ground cloth (this remains in the fabric after the dyeing is complete) and a second supplemental weft that is woven in a pattern, pulled tight, and then removed from the fabric after dyeing. The ground weft is often the same yarn as the warp, and can be any fiber that you wish for your finished fabric. In the examples shown on the facing page, I used Koigu KPM, a fingering-weight Merino wool, for my ground warp and weft. The step-by-step instructions beginning on page 256 describe how to achieve a checkerboard pattern.

THE SUPPLEMENTAL WEFT needs to be strong enough to withstand the rigors of pulling and knotting without breaking, smooth enough to pull easily through the ground cloth, and small enough that it will not distort the ground cloth when it is removed from the fabric. It's also helpful if the fiber content of the waste yarn is different from the ground cloth so it doesn't take up the dye. It is much easier to locate and remove the waste yarn if it is a different color from the ground cloth.

In the examples shown, I used 10/2 pearl cotton as the waste weft. Since cotton reacts to a different dye chemistry mix than wool, it did not take up color in the dye bath. Being significantly smaller than the sock yarn of the ground fabric, it did not distort the finished fabric, and the smooth cotton yarn pulled easily through the wool fabric. Another good choice for supplemental weft is 100 percent nylon or polyester kite string.

OVERVIEW FOR WEAVING SHIBORI

① **WEAVE THE FABRIC** using a ground and supplemental weft. The ground weft weaves the fabric, usually in plain weave, while the supplemental weft weave floats in a pattern. The supplemental weft is not part of the finished fabric. (For information on weft floats, see page 144.)

② **PLEAT WITH THE SUPPLEMENTAL WEFT.** Pull tightly on the supplemental weft threads to pleat the fabric and knot them to hold the pleats in place.

③ **DYE THE FABRIC.** Dye the pleated fabric using a dye appropriate to the ground cloth, following the manufacturer's instructions.

④ **REMOVE THE SUPPLEMENTAL WEFT.** Carefully cut out the supplemental weft and pull it free from the fabric. As the pleats open, the shibori design is revealed.

LOOM AND HEDDLE
Rigid-heddle loom with a
weaving width of at least 11"
One 12-dent heddle

WIDTH IN HEDDLE
10⅘"

**WARP AND GROUND-CLOTH
WEFT YARNS**
Koigu KPM, 100% Merino
wool, fingering weight (50 gm/
175 yards): 3 skeins of white
(0000)

SUPPLEMENTAL WEFT YARN
10/2 pearl cotton: 100 yards

WEAVE STRUCTURE
Plain weave, with
supplemental weft

EPI
12 ends per inch

PPI
8 picks per inch

OTHER SUPPLIES
Country Classics dye or any
acid dye that acts on wool

FINISHED MEASUREMENTS
9⅓" × 67"

WOVEN SHIBORI SCARF

*The most fun part of weaving this scarf is the surprise
at the end when you remove the supplemental weft and
the organic shibori design is revealed.*

*The finished shibori scarves, ironed
to show off the pattern*

Wind a 2½ yard warp of 130 threads (65 loops) with the same yarn you are using for the ground-cloth weft. Wind the warp onto the back beam. Thread the heddle as described on pages 59–62.

PICKING UP THE CHECKERBOARD PATTERN

Put the heddle in the down position.

Using a pickup stick, and working only on the slot threads, pick up the following pattern all the way across: five up, five down. The final five threads should be up, completing the symmetry of the design.

WEAVING

① Weave 2"–3" of plain weave using the ground weft.

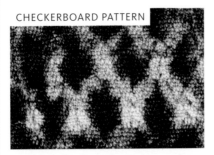

CHECKERBOARD PATTERN

WEAVING PATTERN A: FLOATS ON THE TOP

The shibori pattern shown here is a checkerboard. To weave the first part of it, you will create weft floats on top of the fabric in the waste yarn.

② Put the heddle in the neutral position.

③ Turn the pickup stick on edge to create a shed.

④ Weave with the supplemental weft.

Note: If you find that creating the pattern shed is difficult, or you are seeing multiple sheds, check that you haven't inadvertently picked up a hole thread.

After weaving step 4, you should see floats of the supplemental weft on top of the ground cloth. The areas where the supplemental weft weaves plain weave will create a

resist when the fabric is pleated. The areas where it floats will take up dye.

⑤ Weave two picks of plain weave with the ground weft.

⑥ Weave another pick with the supplemental weft as described above.

Continue weaving, alternating two picks of ground weft with one pick of supplemental weft, until the block is of the desired size. In the example shown, I wove two repeats (three supplemental wefts in all) of steps 5 and 6 before switching to block B. *Note:* The ground cloth should always weave plain weave. As you weave, look at the ground-cloth picks and verify that once the waste yarn is removed, what is left behind will be plain weave.

WEAVING PATTERN B: FLOATS ON THE BOTTOM

Weave the second half of the checkerboard. One way to accomplish this would be to remove the pickup stick and pick up the opposite blocks (all threads up in A would be down in B and vice versa). But this is not necessary: you can weave the opposite block without removing the pickup stick.

⑦ To switch to the second half of the checkerboard pattern, weave three picks of plain weave. *Note:* In general, I recommend two picks of plain weave between pattern picks, and three picks of plain weave between pattern blocks.

⑧ Put the heddle in the up position.

⑨ Slide the pickup stick forward. Note that you do not turn it on edge to create the shed; simply sliding it forward will bring the threads into position.

⑩ Weave with the supplemental weft. Now the floats appear on the bottom of the cloth. Notice also that the areas of plain weave and floats have shifted to create a checkerboard. *Note:* The fact that the floats are on the bottom of the cloth instead of the top will not affect the finished fabric and makes weaving the checkerboard on the rigid-heddle loom more efficient.

Continue weaving, alternating pattern A with pattern B every three supplemental-weft picks.

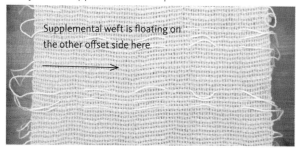

Supplemental weft is floating on the other offset side here

⑪ When you are nearing the end of your warp, weave another 2"–3" of plain weave.

⑫ Cut the fabric off the loom and secure the warp for dyeing. If you are planning a twisted fringe (page 92) you can tie a loose overhand knot in the warp threads to keep them from tangling in the dye pot. If you are weaving garment fabric, you can serge or zigzag-stitch the fabric edges to secure the warp.

PULLING THE THREADS

⑬ To create the resist, pull up two loops of the supplemental weft at a time. (Begin with the first end and a loop on the same side, then alternate sides as you tighten.) This pleats the fabric. Your goal is to pleat the fabric as tightly as you can without breaking the supplemental weft threads. The tighter the supplemental weft is pulled, the crisper the resist. I use a tool, such as a bobbin or stick, for tensioning so the threads don't cut into my hand.

13

⑭ Tie the two loops of supplemental weft together with a surgeon's knot (see page 45) to hold the tension in place.

Continue tying pairs of loops until all of the supplemental weft has been pulled tight.

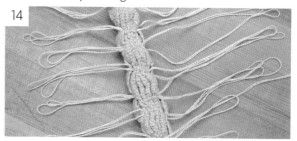

14

DYEING THE FABRIC

After all the supplemental weft threads have been pulled tight and knotted in place, the next step is to dye the fabric using a dye appropriate for your ground cloth. Follow the dye manufacturer's directions.

After all your hard work weaving, tying, and dyeing, it can be somewhat worrisome to pull out what looks like a completely black snake of fabric. Not to worry: if you pull apart the folds (and you pulled your supplemental weft tightly enough during knotting) you will see color peeking through.

THE DYED FABRIC

Allow your cloth to dry completely before you attempt to cut the supplemental weft threads out. If you try to cut them out while the cloth is still wet, you will stress, and possibly damage, the ground cloth.

I pull tightly on the knots to bring up a millimeter or so of the supplemental weft, and then carefully cut under the knot with sharp-pointed scissors. After the knot is cut off, it is easy to pull out the supplemental-weft threads and reveal the shibori patterning. *Note:* Be very careful not to inadvertently cut the ground cloth during this process.

FINISHING

Finish the warp ends as you normally would any textile — hem, twisted fringe, and so on (see pages 90–100) for options).

As for the shibori portion of the cloth, there is the question of whether or not to iron. If you don't iron the cloth, it retains the wonderfully rich, crinkled texture of the pleats (a). This is most durable in silk and wool fabrics. On the other hand, ironing reveals more of the color pattern (b). Whether you choose texture or pattern, is up to you. You could even combine the two options, to create a garment like a fisherman's scarf, where the back of the neck is pleated for warmth and the front is ironed flat to better tuck into the front of a jacket.

a

b

EXPLORING THE POSSIBILITIES OF SHIBORI

The checkerboard pattern creates a lovely design, but it is only the beginning of the possibilities for woven shibori on a rigid-heddle loom. Here are some ideas for additional designs and experimentation.

PLANNING A SYMMETRIC DESIGN
If you are going to create designs using a pickup stick, it helps to know a bit about designing with blocks. In this project, I wanted mirror symmetry, with the blocks on both outside edges weaving the same — that is, both up or both down. To achieve this, you need an odd number of blocks (1, 3, 5, and so on) because this allows for a central block, with equal numbers of blocks on either side. If your block size is 5 slot threads, you could make a symmetric design over 5, 15, 25, and so on slot threads.

Note: Remember that on a rigid-heddle loom, you pick up the pattern only over the slot threads. To plan your warp, you have to add in the hole threads, which doubles the count. The actual number of warp threads needed for symmetry is 10, 30, 50, and so on.

Once you have determined your block size, you can apply the following equation to figure out the number of warp threads you need for the project.

$$\text{(block size)} \times \text{(number of blocks)} \times 2$$
$$= \text{(number of warp threads)}$$

VARY SCALE

One of the easiest things to experiment with is varying the size of the blocks in the checkerboard pattern (a). For example, you could try larger 7-thread blocks, or smaller 3-thread blocks. You could even vary the size of the blocks within a row, having larger blocks in the center and smaller blocks along the selvedges (b). The shibori patterning will shift and change with the scale of the blocks: smaller blocks produce a more refined pattern; larger blocks, a bolder graphic.

STRIPES

To create vertical stripes (c) in the fabric, use the same technique as you used for the checkerboard, except do only pattern A and don't switch to pattern B at all.

Horizontal stripes are even easier; you don't even need a pickup stick. Simply alternate areas of plain-weave ground cloth with areas where the supplemental weft is woven in the same shed as the ground weft.

FREEFORM PICKUP

With freeform pickup, you lose the speed and efficiency of storing the pattern behind the heddle. What you gain in exchange is creative freedom (d). If you are willing to pick up the pattern blocks by hand, you can weave anything you can chart over your slot threads. For example, if your textile has 50 slot threads, you can create patterns with 50 blocks. You can also combine free-form areas of pickup with pickup stick areas.

When creating a free-form design, keep in mind that the resist is created in the areas where the supplemental weft weaves plain weave. The dye strikes in the areas with the supplemental weft floats. You can use this fact to create designs in the positive (undyed) or negative (dyed) space.

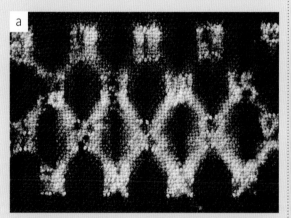

a

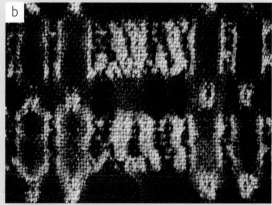

b

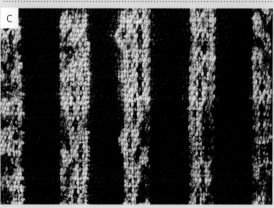

c

d

Shadow Weave

Shadow weave creates wonderfully complex-looking fabrics that often appear to be three-dimensional. Alternating light and dark threads in the warp and weft creates this effect. If you ignore color and just look at the interlacements of a shadow-weave fabric, you'll see a different structure than you might expect. A line of color that looks like a long float may in fact be weaving over and under several threads of the same color. This gives you the ability to design fabrics with bold geometrical designs that are structurally quite stable.

LOOM AND HEDDLE

Rigid-heddle loom with a weaving width of 10" or greater
Three 12-dent heddles

WIDTH IN HEDDLE

9⅗"

WARP AND WEFT YARN

Jamieson and Smith's 2-ply jumper-weight 100% Shetland wool (2,090 yards per pound; available in 25 g/115 yd skeins): 320 yards of Black

Kauni Effekt 100% wool (1,980 yards per pound; available in 150 g/660 yd balls): 320 yards of EQ (rainbow)

WEAVE STRUCTURE

Shadow weave

EPI

12 ends per inch, using three 12-dent heddles

PPI

8 picks per inch

MEASUREMENTS

PROJECT STAGE	WIDTH	LENGTH
Off the loom	9"	63"
After wet-finishing	7½"	56"
Shrinkage	17%	11%

SHADOW WEAVE SCARF

This project uses three 12-dent heddles to weave a 4-shaft shadow weave pattern. There are many ways to weave this threading, and each gives a different patterning. One lift-plan pattern is shown on the next page. For other options, see Marian Powell's 1000 (+) Patterns in 4, 6, and 8 Harness Shadow Weaves.

WARPING

① Wind a warp 2½ yards long of 116 ends, alternating the yarns.

② Thread the three heddles following the chart on the next page. *Note:* The diagram at the right illustrates how to thread the first eight threads. (See page 216 for information on threading three heddles.) Thread the 58-thread pattern twice across the warp.

WEAVING

Follow the weaving chart on page 262 to complete one repeat, then start at the beginning of the chart and weave the pattern 7 more times or until scarf is desired length. Alternate between dark and light shuttles as you weave, interlocking the wefts at the selvedge. Twist 3" fringes using four threads for each fringe: two black and two variegated for a barbershop effect.

FINISHING

Wash in hot water with Dawn dishwashing liquid or a similar detergent. To help hold the floats in place, agitate the scarf until it just starts to felt.

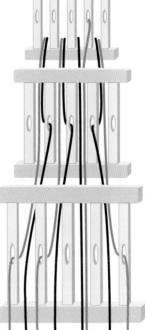

Moving right to left, this diagram shows the first eight threads of the shadow-weave pattern.

Shadow
Weave Scarf

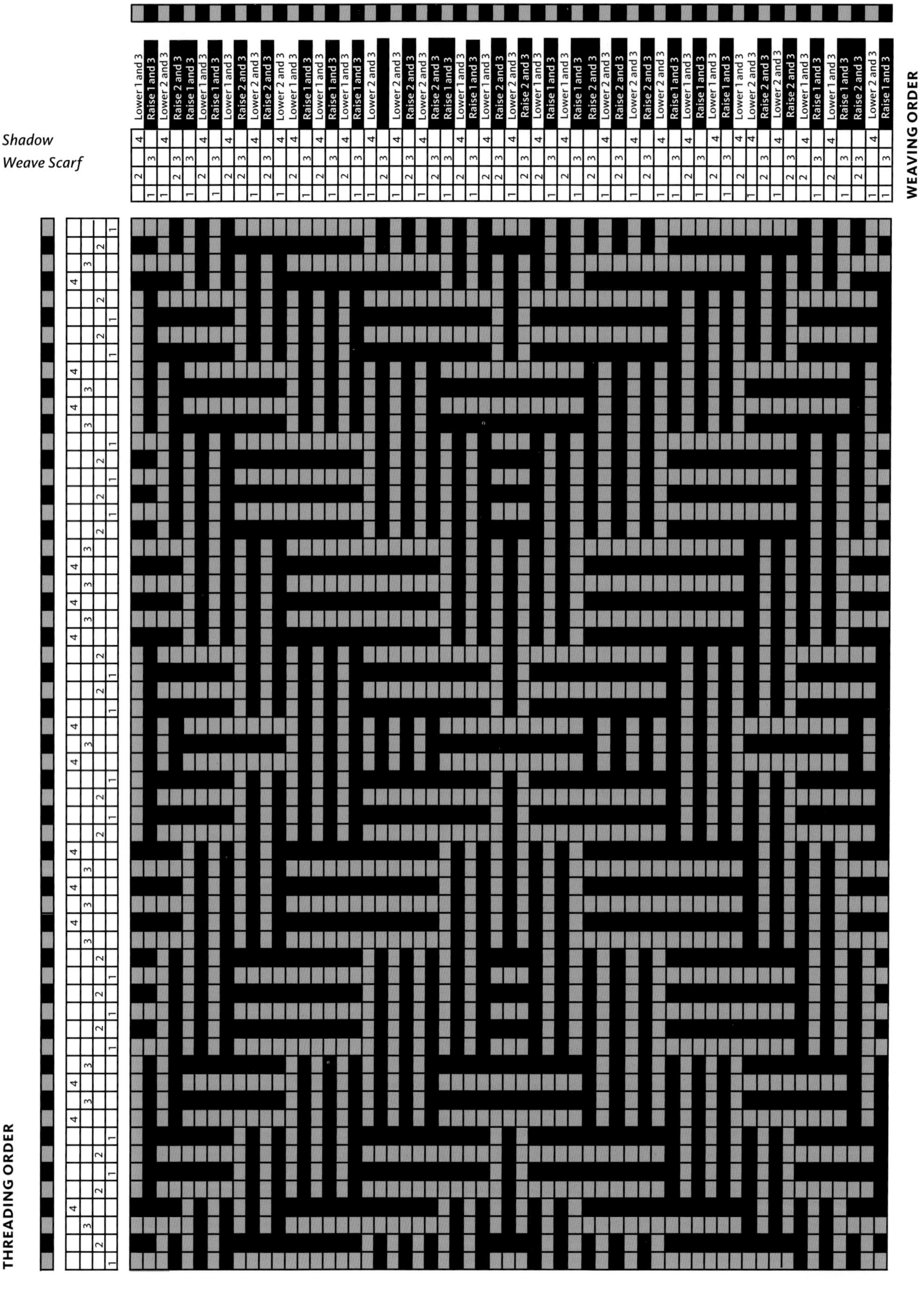

THREADING ORDER

WEAVING ORDER

Beads and Baubles

The simplest way to add beads to your fabric is to string beads onto the weft. As you weave, slip a bead down the weft to place it in the fabric. You can place beads in the fabric either randomly or in patterns. You can also use a commercial beaded yarn, especially if you just want a few beads on a background of fabric.

Because beads are hard and inflexible, as they wind onto the front beam they can create tension irregularities in the warp threads, distort the woven cloth, or become themselves damaged. To avoid this problem, wind on a towel between the layers of your beaded cloth.

Beaded cloth should be carefully hand-washed or dry-cleaned. (Check your beads for wash-fastness before you wash; some wooden or clay beads can't be immersed in water.)

Bead weaving takes the idea of beads on the weft yarn a step further, adding so many beads that the weft is completely covered. Done using very strong, fine yarns in the warp and weft, it is often associated with Native American artwork. While you can purchase specialty bead looms, your rigid-heddle loom is already a bead-weaving machine. Simply warp the loom with nylon bead-weaving thread, matching the bead size to the sett so the beads fit neatly between the warp threads.

The most common method of weaving beaded patterns is to use a long, thin beading needle on which you thread beads for each line of design. The beads themselves act as the shedding device. When you weave this way on your rigid-heddle loom, the heddle only spreads the warp; you don't use it to create

Randomly spaced beads give life to these handwovens.

a shed. This makes it (relatively) easy to create patterns in your weaving. The design always flows in one direction as you weave, and you only need to string enough beads for the current weft pick. You can use graph paper to design your own patterns, or make use of the wealth of pattern books written for bead weavers.

BEAD-WOVEN BRACELET

Bead weaving is one of my favorite kinds of weaving: the beads are so smooth and lovely to run through your fingers. And it's easy to create your own charted patterns or adapt them from cross-stitch patterns. The only downside is that it can be time-consuming. This small project will give you an introduction to bead weaving without a large investment of time. This project makes two or three bracelets, depending on the circumference of the wrists you intend to encircle.

LOOM
Rigid-heddle loom with a weaving width of at least 1"
Two 8-dent heddles

WIDTH IN HEDDLES
1"

WARP AND WEFT
Nymo Size D (beading thread), 100% nylon: 25 yards of Aubergine

EPI
16 ends per inch

PPI
13 picks per inch

OTHER SUPPLIES
Size 12 beading needle
Size 11/0 Delica beads in Frosted Aubergine, Metallic Teal, and Frosted, one 8-gram tube of each
Fabric glue, such as Fray Check
2 silver ribbon crimp ends (19 × 5 mm) to finish off the ends (for each bracelet)
1 silver 8mm lobster clasp (for each bracelet)
2 silver 6mm jump rings (for each bracelet)

BEAD-WOVEN BRACELET PATTERN

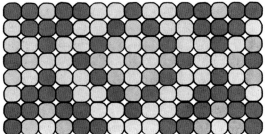

Row 1

WARPING

Wind a warp 1 yard long and 16 threads wide.

Thread the two heddles as described on pages 203–205.

WEAVING THE BRACELET

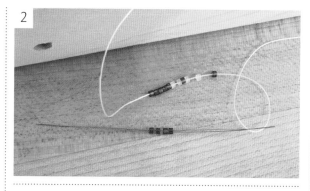

1. Do not wind the beading thread onto a shuttle. Instead cut a piece about 1 yard long and thread the weft onto a beading needle. Weave 10 rows of plain weave with the beading thread.

2. Pick up the 15 beads of the first pattern row in the chart on the facing page.

3. On a closed shed, run the beaded thread under the warp, pushing up on the beads so the 15 beads nestle between the 16 warp threads.

4. Pass the beading needle back through the beads. The needle should pass *over* the warp threads inside the beads.

→ *Repeat Steps 2 through 4 for each row of the pattern, then repeat the pattern until the bracelet is the desired length.*

Complete the bracelet by weaving another 10 rows of plain weave using the beading thread.

FINISHING

Cut the bracelet off the loom. Run a line of glue or Fray Check along the raw warp ends. When the glue is dry, trim the warp threads close. Fold over the header and close the ribbon crimp ends onto the plain-weave headers, completely encapsulating them. Attach the lobster clasp using the jump rings.

LOOM MAINTENANCE

WHEN YOU FIRST GET YOUR LOOM, whether it's new or used, it can seem mysterious and precious. This object, with all its gears and rods and that heddle thing, somehow produces cloth. The last thing you're probably thinking is, "Now where should I start drilling holes?" That's a good thing.

When you get a new-to-you loom, use it for a while as is. Once you've got a feel for how it works, think about how to make it better. Loom modifications and tinkering, while not necessary for weaving — most weavers never take power tools to their loom — are a worthwhile endeavor. There's nothing so freeing as looking at your loom as just another tool that you can bend to your will and weaving style. A great way to get started tweaking and improving looms is to purchase used looms. Often these come a bit damaged, and cheap enough that you don't mind risking some repairs-gone-awry while you learn the woodworking and loom-mechanical skills necessary to work on your loom.

In the pages that follow are suggestions for repairs and adaptations that can help you fix problems and/or add to the possibilities your rigid-heddle loom offers.

Unwanted Holiness

My favorite fix for holes that, um, didn't necessarily need to be drilled, is to find a dowel that's the size of the hole and cut off a length that's as deep as the hole. Then put a bit of wood glue on the dowel and pound it into place with a plastic or rubber mallet. (The plastic or rubber is so you don't mar the surrounding wood.) Ideally, the dowel should fit as snugly in the hole as possible. It's better to have to sand down a too-big dowel to fit than to try to add extra glue to a loose one.

Loom Assembled Incorrectly

With their simple construction, rigid-heddle looms are easy to assemble incorrectly. You can install brakes backward, attach heddle blocks in the wrong place, and even weave on them upside down without realizing it. If your rigid-heddle loom is giving you fits, the first thing to check is whether it's been put together correctly, and whether you have it in the correct orientation when you're weaving with it.

Modern rigid-heddle looms come largely assembled, with little to go wrong. Still, it's important to follow the instructions for the parts you do have to assemble. Older, used rigid-heddle looms are trickier to set up properly and may not have a manual to check the assembly against. In that case, it helps to have a weaver experienced with that model of loom take a look at it.

Loom Out of Square

In order to weave square fabric, the loom itself must be square. To check this, measure from the left back corner to the front right corner and then compare that measurement to the one you get between the right back corner and the front left corner. If they are the same, your loom is square. If they're not, you've got some fixing to do.

Older looms can have their frames warped by being stored in damp or unlevel conditions. Other looms, like the Beka, can become warped by the way they're tightened down. To check which situation you have, try the following:

» **WARPED FRAME PIECES.** Hold a ruler up to the various frame members. Are they straight? Are any curving inward or outward in the middle? If so, you can try misting the warped wood and clamping it to a board that's straight and letting it dry. Clamp it in many places with a soft-faced clamp, such as an Irwin Quick-Grip, that won't mar the wood. If that doesn't work and the warp is severe enough, you may need to replace the warped frame member.

» **TOO-TIGHT OR IMPROPER CONNECTIONS.** If the frame members are straight, and the loom is still warped, check that the loom hasn't been tightened too tightly. Loosen the bolts holding the loom together until you can start to wiggle the frame. Try to wiggle it into square, checking measurements as you did initially. If you get it square, tighten the bolts carefully and recheck for square.

» **BOLT HOLES IMPROPERLY POSITIONED.** If the frame members are straight, and loosening and wiggling can't get the loom square, look at where the holes are drilled on the loom. Does one of them seem higher or lower on the frame that the others? It may be a manufacturing mistake. One way to fix this is to redrill the hole. If the new hole overlaps or is too close to the old hole, you should patch the old hole first by cutting a piece of doweling that fits snugly in the hole and gluing it in place with wood glue, such as Gorilla Glue, before drilling the new hole. Make sure you allow the glue to dry thoroughly before you start drilling.

Split Wood

If you're buying a used rigid-heddle loom, before you purchase it, check all the frame members to make sure there aren't any cracks or splits. If there is just one crack or split, but the rest of the wood is sound, buy the loom, but use the crack as a negotiating point to get a better price. If the wood is fragile with many cracks, walk away: the loom is likely going to be more trouble to repair than it's worth.

I bought one of my looms at a discount because it had been previously damaged in shipping, and one side member had cracked. I repaired it with wood glue and have woven on it successfully for many years since at high tension with no problems.

OLYMPIC GOLD MEDAL GLUE

Modern wood glues, such as Gorilla Glue, make it possible to repair wood so that it's stronger than it was initially. When I was teaching high school physics, I juried a Physics Olympics event in which students built suspension bridges out of Popsicle sticks and wood glue. We loaded the bridges with weight until they broke. What we discovered was that the bridges always broke on the wood, not the glue.

How to Glue a Cracked or Broken Frame Member

1. Get the pieces to fit as tightly as possible. This may involve removing splinters and/or sanding to get a tight fit.

2. If you sanded the wood, vacuum or use tacky cloth to remove all the bits of sanding dust.

3. Use a high-quality wood glue and follow the manufacturer's instructions.

4. Clamp firmly with a wood clamp with rubber or felt grippers so it does not mar the wood.

5. Wipe off any excess glue and wait for it to dry before using.

Missing or Broken Brake

Fixing a missing or broken brake is trickier than repairing the wooden frame because few hardware stores sell gears (dogs and pawls). For this repair, I recommend contacting the loom manufacturer directly if they're still in business. In my experience, most loom manufacturers are willing to sell you spare parts to repair older looms.

If the manufacturer is no longer in business, you can see if the brake mechanism from a still-in-production loom might be retrofitted to your loom. The best way to do this is to go to a weaving shop or conference with your loom and compare what's on yours to others. Retrofitting a brake system may turn out to be a bit of an adventure, but since a non-working brake means a nonworking loom, what do you have to lose?

If you can't get a dog-and-pawl braking system for your loom, consider replacing it with a live-tension brake as explained in the following.

Live-Tension Brake

Do you hate the back-and-forth dance necessary to advance the warp on your rigid-heddle loom? The one where you unlock the front brake, then have to stretch back and unlock the back brake, then advance the warp the distance you want from the front of the loom, then have to tighten it at the back, and then the front, trying to match the warp tension you had last time so the cloth will weave the same, only to realize at the end that the fell line is too far forward now and you have to tweak it all over again?

Wouldn't it be great if there was a way to have to move only the front crank, and the tension would

How to Modify Your Loom

(1) Obtain two weights: a large weight of 2–3 pounds and a small weight of pound or less. I use hand weights for the large weight and a sack of pennies for the small weight.

(2) Tie one end of a 24" rope to the large weight and the other end to the small weight.

(3) Wrap the rope twice around the back beam, going in the opposite direction from the direction the warp winds on. The large weight should dangle behind the loom, pulling in a direction that adds tension to the warp.

Now, when you advance the warp using the front brake crank, the weights should shift around the warp beam so that tension is automatically applied to the warp. This system relies on friction between the rope and the back beam. If your back beam is square, you may need to round it out to get the live weight tensioning to work.

automatically reset itself to the exact same value each time? There is such a thing, and it's called a live-tension brake, usually available only on high-end dobby looms by manufacturers such as AVL. There's no reason, however, that you can't add this wonder of technology to your rigid-heddle loom.

The mechanics are simple: a friction brake (a cord wrapped several times around an axis) combines with a hanging weight to automatically roll the back beam up until the tension matches the resistance set by the weight. You control the tension on the warp beam by the amount of weight you hang as the live (free-hanging) weight, and once set, the tension remains constant throughout the weaving project. If you weave a project that requires more or less warp tension, you can use a heavier or lighter weight.

So why don't all rigid-heddle looms come with live-tension weights if they're so great? Because there are some disadvantages for a portable loom:

» The loom frame needs to be strong enough to handle a weight dangling from a corner without going out of square.

» You'll have a weight hanging off the back of your loom. If you're weaving without a stand, you may have to make sure the weight doesn't hit the table you're weaving against each time you start and stop. If you're using a stand, you may have to weight its base so it doesn't topple over.

» The weight makes the loom a bit heavier and more awkward to maneuver.

Removable Back Rods

It's handy to be able to slide your front and back rods out of the strings that attach them to your loom. Doing so gives you a way to quickly take projects off the loom and fix threading errors. Some rigid-heddle looms, such as the Schacht Flip and Cricket, come with this feature. Other looms, such as the Ashford Knitter's Loom, come with a back rod that is permanently fixed to the loom with plastic ties.

Changing a fixed-rod loom to a removable-rod loom is an easy fix. You need 2 yards of Texsolv, a nylon braid with a series of buttonholes along its length. It's available from most weaving suppliers.

Converting a Fixed-Rod Loom to a Removable-Rod Loom

(1) Cut the Texsolv into equal lengths, one for each tie you are going to replace.

(2) Remove the fixed ties.

Note: If you are working with an Ashford Knitter's Loom, you can either cut the plastic (if you're truly committed to change) or use a pair of needle-nose pliers to fold down the barb and remove the plastic tie for reuse later.

(3) Pass end A of the Texsolv through the hole in the warp beam.

(4) Split open the second-to-last buttonhole on end A and pass end B through the buttonhole. (You use the second-to-last buttonholes rather than the last buttonholes because sometimes the last buttonhole is too near the cut at the end and breaks.) This attaches the cord to the back beam.

(5) At end B, open up the second-to-last buttonhole and pass a pinch or fold of end B through it.

(6) Repeat for all the holes in the warp beam. Then slip the back rod through the loops you created in end B.

Note: To make threading easier and prevent the Texsolv from fraying, you may want to melt the ends of the cords. Be sure to take safety precautions. Working at a sink, briefly insert the end of the Texsolv into a candle flame, just until it begins to melt. Take care to keep your hair and loose fabrics away from the flame, and don't touch the melted end until you're sure it has cooled.

IT'S CLOTH . . . NOW WHAT?

THERE ARE FEW THINGS AS REWARDING as creating your own clothes and accessories, and there is nothing so personal and homey as a house well dressed in handwoven goods. Go to the house of any long-time weaver and you'll likely find handwoven towels, rugs, curtains, lamp shades, pillows, blankets, and more. Whether your interest is self-sufficiency, artistic expression, or simply the magic of transforming chaotic threads into a cohesive whole, a handwoven garment or pillow is a balm to the soul.

I'm going to confess here that I'm more of a weaver than a seamstress, so my handwoven projects tend toward the simple and easy to sew. I'm just giving you an overview of some of the techniques and equipment you'll need if you get excited about sewing handwoven fabric.

Weaving Fabric to Wear

Handwoven cloth has a bad rap as being difficult to sew with. You may even hear that you "can't sew with handwoven cloth." This is obviously wrong, otherwise there would have been a lot of cold Vikings back in the day. What is true is that handwoven cloth is different from commercial cloth, with properties that can be advantages or disadvantages when sewing. Here are some of the cons you'll hear about:

» Handwoven fabric drapes a bit like bias, but everywhere.

» It can be thick and hard to fit under a sewing-machine foot and also hard to keep the top and bottom layer moving together.

» It has a greater tendency to unravel than most commercial cloth.

There are reasons for these differences, and I'll tell you how to address them, but first let me tell you all the ways in which handwoven fabric is perfect for garments.

» **A NICE HAND.** Because handwoven fabric generally has a looser sett and is beaten more gently, it has more stretch and give than commercially woven cloth. In my experience, handwoven cloth on the grain tends to have as much stretch as commercial cloth on the bias, and handwoven cloth on the bias has as much stretch as commercial knit fabric.

» **A UNIQUE CLOTH.** Weaving your own cloth gives you access to unique fabrics you can't find in stores. When you design your cloth, literally thread by thread, it gives you that much more control over your finished product. You can add meaningful motifs to the fabric as you weave it, match colors, add textured floats, highlight amazing yarns, or add beads. Your loom is your own custom fabric store, able to be filled with amazing cloth that can't be found anywhere else in the world.

» **ABILITY TO MAKE MORE.** If you run out of cloth for a pattern, or decide you want pants to match the jacket, you can always weave more. With commercial fabrics, once it's sold out at the store, it's often gone for good.

» **SELVEDGES DON'T UNRAVEL.** If you are clever about how you place the seams in your garments, selvedges can save you time, be less bulky, and make a lovely finish on the inside of your garment. You do have to serge or zigzag along cut edges, however, to ensure that they don't unravel.

Tools for Sewing Handwovens

Only three things are required for sewing with handwoven cloth: scissors, needle, and thread. There are, however, other tools that will make the experience faster and/or more efficient, including, of course, a sewing machine. Here are just a few items you might want to have when you begin sewing with your handwoven yardage.

» **PRESSER FOOT FEATURES.** If you find yourself shopping for a new sewing machine, two features will make it easier to sew handwoven fabric. The first is a tip I learned from weaving instructor Robyn Spady. A walking presser foot moves the top layer of cloth along at the same rate as the feed dogs of the sewing machine move the bottom layer. This attachment is available on most modern sewing machines. Another thing to look for is how high the presser foot lifts. Because handwoven fabric is typically thicker than commercial fabric, the higher the pressure foot lifts, the better.

» **A SERGER.** This machine cuts and finishes edges in one pass. It's wonderful for securing the raw edges of fabric before you wash it, and it can be used for garment construction as well. It's not essential for sewing with handwoven fabric, but it does make the process easier.

» **A GOOD IRON AND IRONING BOARD.** One of the secrets to beautifully finished garments is pressing. A quality iron makes this easier and more fun.

» **OTHER SEWING TOOL ESSENTIALS** include needles and pins, a thimble that fits you, measuring tape, scissors, and a seam ripper.

» **USEFUL MATERIALS** that you may need, depending on what you're making, include at least 1 yard of prewashed commercial fabric in a coordinating color (for creating a lining and/or bias tape); cotton quilting fabric works well. In addition, purchase buttons, zippers, snaps, elastic and/or other closures that make you happy. It's also helpful to have extra weft and warp yarn from your handwoven fabric.

Working with Narrow-Width Fabric

It's a common misconception that you need a wide loom in order to weave cloth for clothing. It's easy to understand why you might think so: fabric stores carry fabric in 36" and 45" widths, and that's what clothing patterns list when indicating the needed yardage. However, weaving narrow yardage is common in cultures that hand-weave cloth for clothing. Think of the beautiful kente cloth from Ghana and the Ivory Coast, which is woven 4" to 6" wide, then pieced together to make wide sheets that are worn togalike, draped around the body. The weavers arrange the patterned strips to create dazzling quiltlike designs, effectively enabling them to do the work of a multishaft dobby loom (complicated block weaves on a simple loom). Another example is traditional Japanese kimono fabric, which is woven at widths 13" to 15" wide. If you measure less than 60" around the widest point of your body, you could make yourself a kimono with 15" wide yardage, with a seam up the back and two separate panels for the left and right front. If your measurement is larger than 60", simply add additional panels as needed. An excellent reference book for this approach is

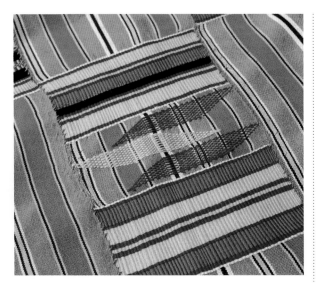

Detail of Kente cloth strips sewn together

Kente strips sewn together to make a large cloth

John Marshall's *Make Your Own Japanese Clothes* (Kodansha U.S.A., 2013).

If loom-shaped garments aren't your thing (and because of my curves, they're not mine), you can often adapt a commercial pattern to work with narrow yardage. Many sewing pattern pieces can easily fit on a fabric that's 15" to 20" wide, so place your pieces on the cloth and see if you get lucky. If not, here are some other techniques you can try:

» **FUDGE THE GRAIN LINE.** Although the grain line affects how a fabric stretches and getting this wrong can cause a garment to hang oddly, you can sometimes get away with tilting the pattern piece a bit to get it on without overly affecting the finished garment.

» **ADD SEAMS TO THE PATTERN.** This is as simple as cutting the pattern in half at a strategic place, such as the center back or along the inside line of a sleeve, then adding seam allowances to both sides of the cut.

» **SEAM THE CLOTH BEFORE CUTTING.** Use an invisible seam like mattress stitch to sew together fabric on the selvedges to create wider fabric before you cut out the pattern pieces. You could also choose to use a normal seam or a mock flat-fell seam, pressed flat before laying out the patterns pieces on it.

Assembling the Pieces

You can make almost invisible seams, or seams that are an obvious design element. You can piece together strips or use quilting techniques to bring together small irregular shapes. Here is one seaming technique I find useful for handwoven cloth. For more options, check online or in a sewing reference book.

How to Sew an Invisible Seam with Mattress Stitch

Weaving artist Bonnie Tarses taught me mattress stitch, a method of seaming that is nearly invisible. Another great tip from Bonnie is to use thread colors at the selvedges that don't match. If you join two different colors together, your eye won't expect regularity and will be more forgiving of the changes introduced by the join.

① Using a tapestry needle, thread a 1-yard length of warp. If this is not long enough to complete the seam, you can needleweave the end of the first length into the fabric. Start a second length of warp by needleweaving it into the cloth to secure it, and then continue the seam.

② Lay the two pieces of fabric that you are joining side by side, right side up, with the selvedges touching. Check whether the number of picks match exactly; if not, you'll have to fudge it a bit to make things come out even. If the seam is long, you may want to fasten safety pins or use fabric clips every 3" or so to keep the edges aligned properly.

③ Starting at the bottom of the fabric, come up from the back of the fabric into the first loop created at the selvedge where the weft came out and then turned to go back into the fabric.

④ Catch the corresponding loop on the other selvedge, coming up from the back of the fabric as you did in step 3. Snug up the slack in the yarn until the two fabrics exactly abut each other.

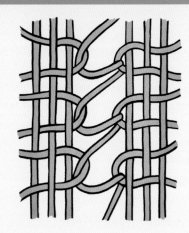

mattress stitch

→   Repeat steps 3 and 4 until the whole selvedge is sewn together. If one side has more picks than the other, you can occasionally skip over a weft turn on the side that has more picks to make up the difference. Be sure to spread the skipped turns out across the seam so they don't pile up in one area and become noticeable.

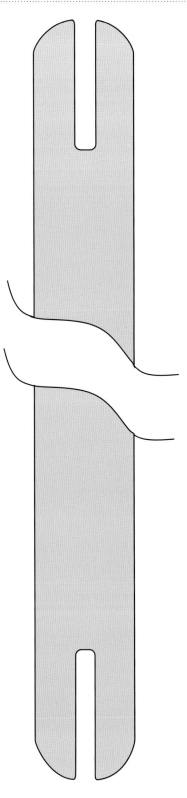

STICK SHUTTLE TEMPLATE
(see page 65)

Trace this pattern onto heavy cardboard,
adjusting the length as desired.

FELTED POT HOLDERS CUTTING PLAN (see page 132)

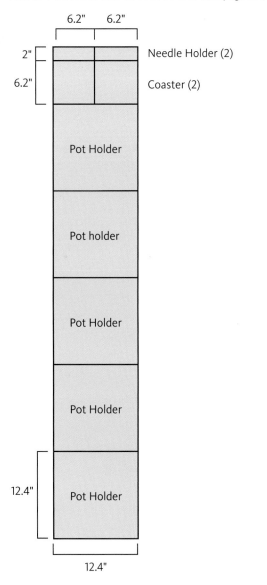

6.2"   6.2"

2"   Needle Holder (2)

6.2"   Coaster (2)

Pot Holder

Pot holder

Pot Holder

Pot Holder

12.4"   Pot Holder

12.4"

HANDLE TAB PATTERN FOR REWOVEN FABRIC BAG
(see pages 234–36)

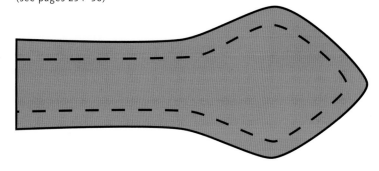

TAPESTRY COVER CARTOON (see pages 170–72)

TRANSPARENCY CARTOON (see pages 174–77)

WEAVE WITHIN YOUR BODY'S LIMITS

My grandmother used to encourage me to stand up tall, keeping my stomach muscles engaged for good posture. When I was nine, I thought she was plumb crazy. Turns out she was preparing me for weaving. When you weave, you should sit tall with your stomach muscles slightly engaged. Hunching is easy to fall into, especially when you reach forward to grab the heddle. But the heddle-grabbing motion should come from your hips. You lean forward to grab the heddle, and lean back to beat the weft into place. If you hunch, you build up tension in your shoulders and arms and make it harder to breathe, all of which will shorten the amount of time you can weave comfortably.

The other thing is to sit properly with your loom. If you don't have a stand, you should lock the loom into place by placing the feet or notch on the back of the loom against a table and then do something I call "bellying up to the bar": you brace the front of the rigid-heddle loom against your stomach. While you're weaving, the loom should be unable to shift around. Most rigid-heddle looms have a notch or feet to brace against a table, but some looms, like the Glimakra, do not have this feature and need to be clamped to a table or used with a stand instead.

If you are using a stand with your loom, make sure that you have a chair that is the proper height for the stand. You should be able to sit at the loom with your arms and legs at approximately 90-degree angles. Weaving should feel comfortable, and you should not have to strain to move the heddle.

Your most important weaving tool is your body, so take care of it. When you're weaving, especially when things are going well, it is easy to become focused and stay

Clasping your fingers, raise your arms over your head. Reclasp your fingers with opposite fingers on top and repeat.

With your arms raised, hold your left elbow with your right hand, at the same time stretching your left hand down your back. Repeat on the other side.

Clasping your fingers with your arms behind your back, lift your chest and stretch. Reclasp your fingers with opposite fingers on top and repeat the stretch.

at the loom until the entire warp is done. If you do this, especially if you're not used to weaving for long periods of time, you can end up with a stiff back, sore shoulders, a pulled neck, or all of the above. Take breaks; get up from the loom and do stretches, like those shown here. The weaving will be all the better for it, and your body will thank you, too.

In addition to stopping to take breaks, check your ergonomics at the loom. Not every loom fits every body. I've known weavers with short arms who found the Flip loom too deep for them to weave on comfortably, and weavers with long arms who had issues with the Ashford Knitter's Loom. Test-drive a loom with a warp or two, if you can, before you purchase it. Taking a class where you rent or borrow a loom is a great way to gain experience and see if the loom suits your body.

Just as the depth of a loom can be a problem, so can the width of the warp. As the warp gets wider, the amount of force your arms have to produce to raise and lower the heddle increases. There are rigid-heddle looms on the market that go as wide as 36". On a floor loom, a 36" wide warp isn't a problem, because you're opening the shed with your feet. On a rigid-heddle loom, all the force to open that shed comes from your shoulders and arms. This will either make you strong or make you hurt. In addition to the force required to open the shed, there's a physical price to pay for throwing a shuttle that wide: your arms have to continuously reach out to the side. I'm five foot six inches, and the widest I like to weave when I'm hand-throwing a shuttle is about 24".

GLOSSARY

Balanced weave. A weave structure in which the warp and weft appear equally on the face of the fabric. For example, plain weave is a balanced weave.

Beat. To press the weft into place. In rigid-heddle weaving, this is done by pulling the heddle forward.

Beater. The tool used to beat the weft into place. In rigid-heddle weaving, the heddle is used as the beater.

Counterbalance loom. A loom that creates a shed by raising some of the threads and lowering the rest. A rigid-heddle loom is not a counterbalance loom.

Crammed-and-spaced threading. A threading in which the sett varies, with some portions of the warp at a higher sett (crammed) than the others (spaced.)

Dog-and-pawl gear system. A gear system in which a lever catches in the teeth of a gear to lock it into place. Most modern rigid-heddle looms use dog-and-pawl gears to tension the warp.

Down shed. The shed created when the heddle is in the down position.

Ends per inch. The number of warp threads in an inch. *See also,* Sett.

Heddle. The part of the loom that controls which threads raise or lower. In a rigid-heddle loom, the heddle also serves as the beater.

Pick. A weft thread woven into the cloth.

Picks per inch. The number of weft threads in an inch of woven cloth.

Reed. The part of the loom that spreads the warp into the appropriate ends per inch. In a rigid-heddle loom, the heddle acts as the reed.

Sectional warping. A warping strategy in which portions of the warp are wound onto the back beam under tension, coming directly from the cone or ball of yarn. Each section is wound on individually. To warp by sections, you need a tensioning device such as a tension box or a warping wheel and a back beam that has short posts embedded in it to hold the sections separate.

Sett. The number of warp threads in an inch. *See also* Ends per inch.

Shed. The opening created in the warp when threads are raised or lowered by the heddle.

Singles. A yarn that is not plied. In other words, it is made up of a single thread, not several threads twisted together.

Sizing. A coating applied to yarn before weaving to make it easier to work with. A sizing might improve the strength or smoothness of the yarn. Sizing is washed out of the finished fabric.

Sley. To pull a warp thread through the heddle during the warping process.

Sley hook. The tool you use to pull a warp thread through the heddle.

Temple. A tool used to hold the warp out to full width during weaving and prevent it from drawing in.

Throw. To pass the shuttle through the warp shed from one side of the loom to the other.

Thrums. Unwoven warp threads after a project has been completed; loom waste.

Up shed. The shed created when the heddle is in the up position.

Warp separator. A material placed between layers of the warp as it is wound on. This prevents the upper warp layers from sinking down into the lower layers, which helps create even tension in the warp.

Warp-faced. A fabric in which the warp threads show more on the surface than the weft threads.

Warping board. A rectangular frame with pegs inserted into it at even intervals. You use it to wind a warp of a given length by selecting a path around the pegs. This warp then needs to be transferred to the loom.

Warping with flanges. A method of warping in which the warp is wound on to the back beam under tight tension without a warp separator. Flanges at either end of the beam hold the warp in place and prevent it from spreading across the back beam. This is common in industrial weaving, and works best with fine, closely sett threads.

Weft-faced. A fabric in which the weft threads show more on the surface than the warp threads.

Wet-finished. The process of using water to finish a fabric after it is off the loom. The type of wet finishing depends on the fabric, and may include hand-washing, machine-washing, and steaming with an iron.

FURTHER READING

Books

A wealth of weaving information has been published over the decades. The following books will help you explore the wide world of weaving. Some of these titles are hard to find or out of print, but I include them so you'll know what to look for in libraries and used bookstores.

Rigid-Heddle Weaving

These publications have techniques and projects written specifically for rigid-heddle looms.

Davenport, Betty Linn. *Hands On Rigid Heddle Weaving.* Interweave, 1987.

———. *Textures and Patterns for the Rigid Heddle Loom,* rev. ed. Davenport, 2008.

Gipson, Liz. *Weaving Made Easy: 17 Projects Using a Rigid-Heddle Loom,* rev. ed. Interweave, 2015.

Hart, Rowena. *The Ashford Book of Rigid Heddle Weaving,* rev. ed. Ashford Handicrafts, 2008.

———. *The Ashford Book of Weaving for Knitters.* Willson Scott Publishing, 2006.

Howard, Sarah, and Elisabeth Kendrick. *Creative Weaving: Beautiful Fabrics with a Simple Loom.* Lark Books, 2008.

McKinney, David B. *Weaving with Three Rigid Heddles: An Introduction to Multiple Rigid Heddle Weaving without Pick-up Sticks.* D.B. McKinney, 1985.

Patrick, Jane. *The Weaver's Idea Book: Creative Cloth on a Rigid Heddle Loom.* Interweave, 2010.

Searle, Karen. *Moorman Inlay Technique for Rigid Heddle Frame Looms,* rev. ed. Dos Tejedoras, 1983.

Xenakis, Athanasios David. *The Xenakis Technique: for the Construction of Four Harness Textiles.* Golden Fleece Publications, 1978.

Weaving Techniques and Patterns

These traditional weaving techniques can be adapted for the rigid heddle loom.

Battenfield, Jackie. *Ikat Technique*. Van Nostrand Reinhold, 1980.

Collingwood, Peter. *The Techniques of Rug Weaving*, rev. ed. Faber and Faber, 1993.

Davison, Marguerite Porter. *A Handweaver's Pattern Book*. Churchill & Dunn edition, 2014.

Ellis, Catharine. *Woven Shibori*. Interweave Press, 2005.

Glasbrook, Kirsten. *Tapestry Weaving*. Search Press, 2015.

Gray, Herbi. *On-Loom Cardweaving: A Modern Extension of an Ancient Craft*. Herbi Gray, 1982.

Harvey, Nancy. *Tapestry Weaving: A Comprehensive Study Guide*. Echo Point Books and Media, 2015.

Harvey, Virginia I., and Harriet Tidball. *Weft Twining*. Shuttle Craft Guild, 1969.

Keasbey, Doramay. *Sheer Delight: Handwoven Transparencies*. Stellar Publishing, 1990.

Lamb, Sara. *Woven Treasures: One-of-a-kind Bags with Folk Weaving Techniques*. Interweave Press, 2009.

Powell, Marian. *1000(+) Patterns in 4, 6, and 8 Harness Shadow Weaves*. Robin and Russ Handweavers, 1976.

Russell, Carol K. *Tapestry Handbook: The Next Generation*. Schiffer, 2007.

Swett, Sarah. *Kids Weaving: Projects for Kids of All Ages*. Stewart, Tabori & Chang, 2005.

Todd-Hooker, Kathe. *Tapestry 101*. Fine Fiber Press, 2007.

West, Virginia M. *Finishing Touches for the Handweaver*. Interweave, 1988.

Wilson, Jean Verseput. *The Pile Weaves: Twenty-six Techniques and How to do Them*, rev. ed. Scribner, 1979.

———. *Jean Wilson's Soumak Workbook*. Interweave, 1982.

Spinning

Learning to spin opens up new options for your weaving, such as collapse-weave fabrics. You'll also be able to create more types of yarn than are commercially available.

Amos, Alden. *The Alden Amos Big Book of Handspinning*. Interweave Press, 2001.

Field, Anne. *Learn to Spin with Anne Field: Spinning Basics*. Trafalgar Square, 2011.

McCuin, Judith MacKenzie. *The Intentional Spinner*. Interweave, 2009.

———. *Teach Yourself Visually: Handspinning*. Wiley Publishing, 2007.

Dyeing

Dyeing your own yarn makes it possible to create complex designs in simple weave structures. You'll also be able to work with a wider range of yarn colors than is commercially available.

Callahan, Gail. *Hand Dyeing Yarn and Fleece: Dip-Dyeing, Hand-Painting, Tie-Dyeing, and Other Creative Techniques*. Storey Publishing, 2010.

Dean, Jenny. *Wild Color*, rev. ed. Potter Craft, 2010.

Knutson, Linda. *Synthetic Dyes for Natural Fibers*, rev. ed. Interweave Press, 1986.

Lambert, Patricia, Barbara Staepelaere, and Mary G. Fry. *Color and Fiber*. Schiffer Publishing, 1986.

Menz, Deb. *Color in Spinning*. Interweave Press, 2005.

Van Stralen, Trudy. *Indigo, Madder, and Marigold*. Interweave Press, 1992.

Magazines

Complex Weavers Journal

Complex Weavers

www.complex-weavers.org

A subscription to this magazine, which is the journal of the Complex Weavers organization, is included with membership. It is targeted to weavers using 4- to 24-shaft looms, but can be an inspirational resource for any type of weaving.

Handwoven

Interweave Press

www.interweavestore.com/weaving/weaving-magazines

This magazine publishes weaving projects, mostly for weavers using looms with 2 to 8 shafts, but also includes rigid-heddle projects occasionally. Many of the 2- to 4-shaft projects can be converted for rigid-heddle weaving.

The Journal for Weavers, Spinners, and Dyers

The Association of Guilds of Weavers, Spinners, and Dyers

www.thejournalforwsd.org

Although this magazine is published by The Association of Guilds of Weavers, Spinners, and Dyers, you do not need to be a member to subscribe. Published in the United Kingdom, international subscriptions are available. This magazine features articles to interest many types of fiber artists, including artist interviews, discussions of fiber and textile history, and projects that use a wide range of techniques and tools.

Shuttle Spindle and Dyepot

Handweavers Guild of America

www.weavespindye.org

A subscription to this magazine, which is the journal of the Handweavers Guild of America, is included with membership. It features artist interviews, reviews of exhibitions, and weaving techniques. It can be a resource for inspiration and for following weaving trends in the United States.

Vävmagasinet

www.vävmagasinet.se

A Scandinavian magazine published in Sweden, it also offers English-edition subscriptions. The magazine publishes articles about the work of prominent weavers as well as instructional weaving projects.

Weaver's

Golden Fleece Publications

This out-of-print magazine is an excellent resource for in-depth coverage of weaving techniques. Each issue covers a specific weave structure. Though this magazine was targeted to weavers using 4- to 16-shaft looms, some techniques can also be applied to rigid-heddle weaving.

Weaver's Craft

Plain Tabby Press

www.weaverscraft.com

A small-press publication written and published by Jean Scorgie. Each issue focuses on a specific weave structure or technique. While not explicitly written for rigid-heddle looms, many of these techniques can be applied to rigid-heddle weaving.

ONLINE RESOURCES

Search social media websites like Facebook and Yahoo for "weaving" and "rigid heddle" to find special interest groups for handweavers. Search YouTube to find thousands of free videos demonstrating rigid-heddle weaving tips and techniques. Other online sources that are helpful include the following:

All Fiber Arts
www.allfiberarts.com
An online compendium of fiber arts information, it contains both articles written by the site owner, Päivi Suomi, as well as hand-selected links to fiber arts information on other websites.

Craftsy
www.craftsy.com
An education site offering online classes in a variety of crafts. It offers several classes on rigid-heddle weaving, including both basic and advanced techniques.

Habu Textiles
www.habutextiles.com
Features Japanese handwoven textile fabrics and ribbons from a wide variety of fibers, including extensive technical information.

Halcyon Yarn
https://halcyonyarn.com
Website provides useful information, such as sett and yarn weight.

Morse Code Translator
morsecode.scphillips.com/translator.html
Type in your message and receive a translation in Morse code

New York Guild of Handweavers
www.nyhandweavers.org
Furnishes inspiration, information, and mutual assistance to persons working in all aspects of handweaving.

Ravelry
www.ravelry.com
A social media site that is primarily for knitters and crocheters but also has dozens of special-interest groups for weaving.

The Scottish Registry of Tartans
www.tartanregister.gov.uk
A database of tartan designs, maintained by the National Records of Scotland.

WeaveCast
WeaveZine
www.weavezine.com/audio
An online talk-radio show for handweavers. Each episode contains my thoughts about weaving, as well as interviews from prominent weavers around the world. You can listen to episodes on the website, or find it as a podcast on iTunes.

WeaveZine Archives
www.weavezine.com
An archive of articles and patterns that I published in my online magazine, *WeaveZine*. Many of these feature rigid-heddle weaving.

Weaving Today

Interweave

www.weavingtoday.com

An online community for weavers, with forums, blogs, and free weaving patterns. The site is published by *Handwoven Magazine*. It has a rigid heddle forum as well as free rigid-heddle patterns.

Weavolution

http://weavolution.com

A social media site for hand weavers. It has an interest group for rigid heddle weavers as well online classes.

WEBS

www.yarn.com

Website provides useful information, such as sett and yarn weight.

Yarn Barn of Kansas

www.yarnbarn-ks.com

Website provides useful information, such as sett and yarn weight.

Metric Conversion Chart

TO CONVERT	TO	MULTIPLY
inches	millimeters	inches by 25.4
inches	centimeters	inches by 2.54
inches	meters	inches by 0.0254
feet	meters	feet by 0.3048
feet	kilometers	feet by 0.0003048
yards	centimeters	yards by 91.44
yards	meters	yards by 0.9144

US (inches)	METRIC (centimeters)
⅛	3.2 mm
¼	6.35 mm
⅜	9.5 mm
½	1.27
⅝	1.59
¾	1.91
⅞	2.22
1	2.54
1½	3.81
2	5.08
2½	6.35
3	7.62
3½	8.89
4	10.16
4½	11.43
5	12.70
5½	13.97
6	15.24
6½	16.51
7	17.78
7½	19.05
8	20.32
8½	21.59
9	22.86
9½	24.13
10	25.40
11	27.94
12	30.48
13	33.02
14	35.56
15	38.10

ACKNOWLEDGMENTS

Many thanks to Betty Davenport, whose book *Textures and Patterns for the Rigid Heddle Loom* first opened my eyes to the many possibilities of this little loom.

A book like this passes through many hands on the way to publication:

John Polak shot the many photographs in the book, including my favorites, the stacks of riotously colored and textured fabrics. Jessica Armstrong, art director, ensured the book had a clean and elegant look. Allegra Lockstadt created the illustrations and worked with Storey's illustration coordinator, Ilona Sherratt, who created the threading and weaving charts. Mary Lou Splain designed and wove the project At Home, page 175.

Elisabeth (Lisa) Hill wove sample fabrics, including the rya wall hanging on page 178 and the example of analytic weaving on page 22. She was the weaver present at the photoshoots and acted as technical advisor during the editing process.

A tremendous thank you to my editor, Gwen Steege, who never gave up on this project and shepherded it through its darkest hours. Without her tireless efforts and encouragement, this book would not exist.

And special thanks to Jane Patrick of Schacht Spindle Company. When I was a brand-new weaving teacher, she loaned me a set of looms so I'd be able to teach at my first conference. Once again, she's saved the day by lending a Flip and a Cricket rigid-heddle loom for photography and sample weaving during the making of this book.

INDEX

bold = chart

A

advancing the warp, 76
analytical weaving, 22-23
Andean weaving, 32
angling the weft, 75
Ashford Knitter's Loom, 18
    fixed back rod, 55, 81, 269-70
    multiple heddles, 206
At Home transparency, 174-77, 277

B

back beam
    correcting shed issues, 81
    correcting tension problems, 79
    how to wind onto, 57-58
    using a warp separator, 21
back rods, 16
    converting a fixed-rod loom to a
      removable-rod loom, 270
    removable back rods, 269-70
backstrap loom, 15, 145
Bag, Rewoven Fabric, 234-36, 275
balanced
    fabric, 32
    plain-weave structure, 38, 129, 280
    twist, 27
    yarn, 237, 238
bamboo yarns, 201, 249
beads
    as fringe ends, 242
    Bead-Woven Bracelet, 264-65
    LED sequins, 251-53
    threading beads onto weft yarn, 154
    weaving with, 263
    Wire Cuff Bracelet, 247-48
    with Brooks bouquet, 153

    with Spanish lace, 157
beater, 15-16, 66, 81, 168
Beka loom, 81, 267
bias strips or tape
    enclosing a hem, 98-99
    weaving with fabric strips, 232
blanket
    Blanket, Random-Striped, 124-25
    standard blanket sizes, **125**
    stitch (overcast hem), 97-98
boat shuttle, 63, 67
    how to use, 74
    how to wind the bobbin, 68
bracelets
    Bead-Woven Bracelet, 264-65
    Wire Cuff Bracelet, 247-48
brake, 16-17
    fixing a missing or broken brake, 268-69
broken warp threads, how to fix, 83-88
Brooks bouquet
    handwoven curtains, 200
    how to weave, 151-52
    threading beads onto weft yarn, 154
    variations, 153
bubbling the weft, 75, 79, 169

C

cartoons
    At Home transparency, 175-77, 277
    for tapestry weaving in general, 166
    Tapestry Cover, 169-71, 276
chaining the warp, 46-47
    alternatives to chaining, 48
cigar-shaped warps, 58
clasped weft
    how to weave, 162-63
    variations, 163

JUMP-START YOUR CREATIVITY
with More Books from Storey

by Gail Callahan

Satisfy all your color cravings, right in your own kitchen! Set yourself on the right color path with detailed advice on color theory and types of dyes, and learn how to dye your yarn using standard kitchen equipment.

by Beth Smith

This essential companion for spinners of all levels is a sheep-by-sheep guide to 21 breeds and the characteristics of their wool. Learn the best washing, prepping, and spinning methods for each kind of fleece.

by Sarah Anderson

Discover the fun and satisfaction of creating your own specialty yarns, from basic 2-ply to spirals, bouclés, crepes, and novelty styles. Step-by-step instructions and photographs feature 80 distinctive yarns.

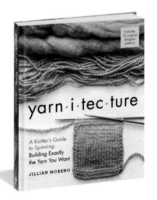

by Jillian Moreno

Walk through every phase of yarn construction with step-by-step photos showing how to select the fiber, establish a foundation, and achieve the desired structure, texture, and color patterning. In addition, 12 original knitting patterns showcase handspun yarn.